COMMANDO
to COLDITZ

DISPOSAL OF EFFECTS OF
PERSONNEL REPORTED MISSING
OR PRISONER OF WAR

-42

DATE

96A
91A.

No Further Minutes
To Be
Entered In This File

COMMANDO to COLDITZ

MICKY BURN'S JOURNEY TO THE FAR SIDE
OF TEARS—THE RAID ON ST NAZAIRE

Peter Stanley

PIER **9**

For Gordon Cruickshank, with thanks

FOREWORD

By Captain Micky Burn, MC

D uring the Second World War, on the night of 27–28 March 1942, a combined Royal Navy/Commando force of 611 sailors and soldiers destroyed the huge dry dock and ancillary installations of the port of St Nazaire, on the French Atlantic coast. Much has been written, much has been told on television, cinema and radio, about that Elizabethan-like uppercut to Nazi arrogance. The code name for the operation was 'Chariot'. In 1973, at peak hour for BBC television, John (Tony) Broughton directed a program for which I wrote and narrated the script, about the raid. About the same time I won an international prize for a poem (on a different theme) submitted under the pen name 'Chariot'.

I had been captain of Six Troop in No. 2 Commando and had taken 28 men with me, of whom fourteen, including both subalterns, had been killed. My archive relating to the raid has little about the fighting, but includes chiefly the correspondence between my parents and the parents of the dead; of those, myself included, who were captured and writing from prison camps; and those who, almost miraculously, got home by sea on the day following.

And now here is Peter Stanley's book, *Commando to Colditz*, whose subtitle includes a phrase from that code-named poem, and from Peter came the invitation that I should write this Foreword.

Commando to Colditz tells shining and tragic stories. One is to do with those who fought, another of civilians at home; one deals with those who were killed, another mainly with the remainder made prisoners.

On 2 April my parents received the official telegram that I was missing. They had twelve more days to wait before the anguish passed; for them, but not for many others. Then came, for them, the for-a-while all-healing telephone call from Brigadier Charles Haydon at Combined

Operations Headquarters. A photograph had arrived from a German propagandist newspaper, via our Embassy in neutral Sweden, showing two British soldiers being led into captivity, both apparently unwounded, one of whom looked rather like me. Would my father like to drive in to HQ to identify? My father would and did, and raced home to my mother (and was gonged en route for speeding). The photo showed Paddy Bushe, from Six Troop, and me with bayonets almost in our backs and hands up; my fingers looked as if I was making the V-for-Victory sign. That photograph became Peter's entry to my archive of hundreds of documents, compiled by my father and guarded by him for the three years until my liberation.

In a moment you can turn the page and get on with this story. Before that, I want to link St Nazaire, as I think of it, with Australia. First the Australian members of the St Nazaire Society, officers of the Royal Australian Naval Reserve, who served on the motor launches carrying my commando comrades.

Then, further back in time, the fighter pilot Richard Hillary, who wrote *The Last Enemy*, about his part in the Battle of Britain, was terribly burnt, was allowed to fly and died training on night fighters, aged 23. He was born in Sydney, but when he was three his parents had moved, first to the Sudan, then to London. His father had for a time been personal secretary to the rumbustious Prime Minister Billy Hughes. As a fighter pilot Richard had a love affair with my wife Mary before I knew her, about which I wrote a book, *Mary and Richard*.

Further back still, my father, of whom you'll be reading a good deal, fought on Gallipoli. He loved horses and started as a volunteer in the Sussex Yeomanry, then was moved, regretfully, to machine-guns. He was sent to the Western Front, probably after a row with a senior officer he thought overbearing, and was wounded in the leg in the last battle of the Marne in 1918. My mother told me that the only time he wept was when he found he could not get on his riding boots.

He was not a great reader, but in hospital another wounded officer recommended him a book, which he devoured himself, and passed on to my mother as good pasture for me as a growing boy. I read it and still have it. It and its author—a man who shall be nameless here for a few lines yet—are my last and most powerful link with Australia.

This briefly anonymous expatriate came of ancient Scottish stock. He arrived in Australia in 1853 and became very famous indeed there as a steeplechase rider—but slowly and lastingly, worldwide, as a poet. One four-line verse of his, used by the Queen in one of her Christmas addresses, is perfect for what I have been most desperate to find. It has become for me the password which, without forcing, links Peter's St Nazaire interpretation with the two-sided truth as his two groups had to and did face it: on one side, with their support for one another until the prisoners came home to them; and all who loved, and still yearn for those who did not come home.

Life is mostly froth and bubble,
Two things stand like stone,
Kindness in another's trouble,
Courage in your own.
    Adam Lindsay Gordon (1833–1870)

OF WAR
SAUCHIEHALL
GLASGOW
I think you would like to know that we have
an acknowledgment post-card from
that he had received a Red Cross Food Parcel
Glasgow Depot. The date on his postcard
OF WAR
from St. Nazaire.

CONTENTS

PROLOGUE

Wales, December 2004. I see the hills of Merioneth, literally slate grey, from the little Kia I had hired from Manchester airport that winter morning. They glower wetly as my car flies down the winding A470 south from Llandudno, along the Vale of Conwy and through the passes of Snowdonia. Past the desolate-looking quarries of Blaenau and down the broad Vale of Ffestiniog, the A487 takes me to the straggling village of Minffordd, where Michael Burn lives.

I had written to him months before, a letter out of the blue with an idea for a book telling his story. I had a hunch that his papers told more of the story than he used in his autobiography, *Turned Towards the Sun*. A fortunate commission to work on a television documentary on Gallipoli had taken me to its final location, at Bury in Lancashire, a few hours from North Wales. This was my chance to meet him: it was fate, surely.

I call for directions from the telephone box at the bottom of his lane. 'Hello!' he says, 'I'll come and guide you'. A minute later an old brown Peugeot appears. He waves to me to follow him up a rough farm track, the broad, steel-grey estuary of the Dwyryd on the left with the snow-clad mountains of Diffwys and Y Llethr on the horizon. I am about to meet one of the most extraordinary and engaging men I have ever known: I desperately wish I had met him sooner.

Micky, as he insists on being called, is still a striking man. White-haired but with a physique that is usually described as 'sprightly', he is somewhat shorter than the five foot nine of his army file—but that had been 60 years before. He retains the blue eyes, high cheekbones and fine features that made him so attractive to men and women. He speaks in what I suppose to be the drawl he learned at his prep school, but with a dry wit and a lively curiosity. He welcomes me warmly and, because I'm Australian, I suppose, he offers me a beer. I accept coffee and we talk.

We sit in the kitchen of a stone-built cottage, converted and extended from a barn some fifty years before, when he and his wife, Mary, first lived here. He shows me a memento of Bertrand Russell, once his neighbour (he does an amazingly lifelike imitation of Russell's piping voice). Interested in the world, he asks after politics in Australia—'John Howard, dreadful man!'—and denounces the folly of war in Iraq. 'How was Gallipoli?' he asks: his father had served there in the Great War. I had walked past the site of his dugout at Gully Ravine the week before.

Soon, our conversation turns to the Second World War and Micky's part in it. He is modest, but I have read his autobiography—that's what's drawn me here. Soon he is speaking of friends long dead and a story of devotion and love that begins, if anywhere, in Carrick Roads, off Falmouth, in the first warm days of spring in 1942. Micky's thoughts have often turned to that day, the day when his men wrote their last letters.

CARRICK ROADS, 24 MARCH 1942

In mid March of 1942 an odd assembly of vessels could be seen in Carrick Roads. A grey-painted cross-Channel ferry lay at anchor, its decks crowded with soldiers. Sixteen 'Fairmile' motor launches arrived in port. A powerful, dazzle-painted motor torpedo boat roared into the harbour, along with a more sedate motor gunboat. Soon, what keen students of *Jane's Fighting Ships* would recognise as a fair replica of a German Möwe class torpedo-boat destroyer glided into the roadstead. The word around Falmouth was that the launches were part of an anti-submarine flotilla soon to head south to search for U-boats preying on convoys making the dangerous passage across the Bay of Biscay towards Gibraltar.

From the ships, sailors and their passengers—not just soldiers but, it soon became clear, commandos—looked over the bright blue water towards the green hills of Cornwall, to Pendennis Castle on the headland to the west, and towards St Anthony Head and its lighthouse to the east. Looking towards the town of Falmouth they could make out the quays lining the harbour. Here the Post Office packet boats had long made their English landfalls and news of the victory of Trafalgar had first reached Britain. Falmouth, with its church steeple and neat houses seemed to one of the commandos' officers beautiful but unreal, like a backcloth to a drama.

That officer, Captain Micky Burn, was about to play a part in a drama that, as we shall see, would have profound effects on the commandos and their families. On a sunny Tuesday afternoon, aboard the Belgian ferry-turned-depot ship *Prinses Josephine Charlotte* his commandos sat and lay about the deck. Micky Burn had urged his commando troop to write what might be their last letters to their families before they embarked on the hazardous task about which he had just briefed them. Carrick Roads was the last sight of Britain for 169 of the 600 or so men who were to embark on Operation 'Chariot', the Combined Operations raid on the French port of St Nazaire.

As Micky glanced about the mess deck, he saw his men, stripped to their singlets, chatting, dozing, smoking and writing letters. One of Micky's men was Bill Gibson, a 22-year-old lance-sergeant, who was one of the liveliest men in his troop. As Micky's eyes fell on Bill, he suddenly felt what he described as 'a hideous shock'. He looked into Bill's face and 'knew that he knew that he would be killed'.

Bill Gibson sat down on deck to write to his father, Alex, a letter that would be posted only if Bill were to die. 'My dearest dad', he began; and perhaps then paused for a moment, before writing a line that must be as hard to write as it is to read. 'By the time you get this I shall be one of the many who have sacrificed their unimportant lives for what ideals we may have …'

From its awkward first words Bill Gibson's final letter expresses the ideas that this book explores. He was one of a small force of highly trained commandos, setting out on a daring and dangerous task. It was likely to end in death—like many commandos Bill seems to have known that he would not return. But if he was to die, he felt, it would be for a cause in which he believed; for 'ideals'. And he knew that those who loved him would have to be told of his death. Like many, Bill wanted to be the first to break that news to his loved ones.

Bill Gibson's last letter—of which we will hear more in this book—conveys the essence of the story of the St Nazaire commandos: comradeship and sacrifice; idealism and loss. It opens the story of the men of just one troop of one unit in one action, a tiny part of the world war in which they were caught up. If it is not also the story of all men and all families in war, it offers a microcosm of those who fought on the Allied side, on the side that consciously if imperfectly sought to fight for ideals that we still treasure.

Bill's—and Micky's—premonition on the deck in the warm spring sunshine that day would be fulfilled. Of Micky's 29-strong troop, only seven men would return to Britain a few days later. And yet theirs is a story of hope as well as anguish, of pride as well as grief, of humour as well as sadness.

The 'Chariot' force assembled in Carrick Roads, Falmouth, in the days before the raid on St Nazaire.

This last letter is now the only way we can hear Bill's voice. While he was to perish in the dark on a French estuary on a cold spring night in 1942, we can still reach him and the bonds he shared with his family and his fellow commandos. Through the letters written to and from bereaved families like Bill Gibson's we can comprehend the world of heartache and worry, but also dignity and comradeship, that suffused this network of British families, parents and sons, during the Second World War.

Bill's letter can touch us now because someone took the trouble to preserve it for over sixty years, until it became the prompt for this book. His letter is only one of scores sent or received by Clive and Phyllis Burn, Micky's parents. In the dark aftermath of the raid, when none of his men's families knew whether their sons were alive or dead, captive or free, the Burns began an extraordinary correspondence with them. Over the following three years of war they corresponded with families, with men in prison camps in Germany, with officials and soldiers, and with their own son. He kept these letters safe, and now they can tell the story of his comrades, including Bill Gibson.

The letters tell us more than just the story of these men at St Nazaire. They take us into commando billets, to prison camps, and even inside the most famous prisoner-of-war camp of all, Colditz. They lead us in time to cemeteries and memorials. Above all, they allow us to imagine scenes at firesides and kitchen tables, of families listening to the wireless or packing parcels for distant sons or waiting, half-hopeful, half-fearful, for the postman's arrival. They give us an understanding of what the commandos' sacrifice meant to those who loved them, and what it can mean to us still, so many years later. Micky's letters lead us from the terror of battle and the darkness of grief to understanding: a journey to what he—a poet as well as a soldier—was to call the 'far side of tears'.

This book concentrates on the war years, when love and respect for the men of his troop impelled Micky to urge his parents to make and maintain contact with the families of his men killed or captured in the raid on St Nazaire. That network of grief provided the impetus for this story, but it moves beyond parents' anxiety in wartime. It tells the story of who the commandos were and what allowed them to go willingly into one of the most hazardous actions of the war. It tells the story of the raid, a dramatic night of fire and death, and one that marked those who survived, forever. It tells the story of a captivity which is still obscured by popular myth. Above all, it shows how the Second World War became the central event of the lives of the generations which entered it, both those who fought and those who waited, worried and grieved: and perhaps also for us, who can listen, and remember, and understand.

COMMANDOS:
MICKY BURN AND
SIX TROOP

'WHAT LIFE IS REALLY LIKE': MICKY BURN'S 1930s

Six Troop's story must begin with its leader, Michael Burn, known to friends variously as Mick, Micky, Mickie or Mickey. Born in 1912 into the comfortable middle class of Edwardian England, the first child of a London lawyer, Clive Burn, Micky grew up in secure if relatively recent respectability. His paternal grandfather had made the transformation from North Country yeoman to London suburban solicitor in the last quarter of the nineteenth century and sent his son to Winchester. In the 1920s Clive had made a name as a solicitor, advising on the long-running (and lucrative) Labrador Boundary Dispute, a squabble between Quebec and Newfoundland going back to the eighteenth century that Clive helped to resolve in 1927. 'He never pretended to be a great lawyer', his patron Sir Walter Monckton wrote of him, 'but he had two qualities that matter more than learning: courage and wise judgment', not least, he thought, in refusing to simply settle the protracted Canadian case. A gambler, sometimes temporarily financially embarrassed, Clive rose in the esteem of wealthy and influential friends, whose largesse tided him over and garnered him a sinecure as the golfing manager of a French resort hotel. Coincidentally, Micky's mother's family had also invested in establishing Le Touquet as a golfing and gambling resort, so it was a familiar atmosphere. Much of Micky's boyhood was spent unconventionally in his father's hotel near Étaples, described in his novel *Childhood at Oriol*. Educated at prep and public schools, he wove an elaborate fantasy life, dramatising his perfectly respectable family's situation, scandalising masters, boys and his family with tales of illegitimacy and perverse crime. At his father's old school, Winchester, he learned to write good English by following Classical models and seemed destined for a scholarship at his father's university, Oxford.

In 1931, aged nineteen, Micky threw up this seemingly secure prospect. He abandoned a scholarship to ghost-write the autobiography of Sir Tim Birkin, the celebrated racing driver, and soon after *The Story of Brooklands*, a history of the famous motor racing circuit, with a foreword by the Prince of Wales. A handsome, hedonistic young man, Micky loafed his way around Europe, mixing with continental aristocracy and English society while coming to terms with his ambivalent sexuality. Living on the fringes of so-called 'Society', he made the most of his father's puzzled indulgence, repaying invitations to weekend parties by being agreeable and witty. In country houses and European resorts he picked up culture and social connections willy-nilly. In his novel *Yes, Farewell*, Micky summed up the life he had lived in the mid 1930s, before he began serious journalism: 'parties, week-ends, cars, admiration … I had only to lift a finger and it was all laid on'.

Attracted to men, he became the sometime lover of Cambridge communist Guy Burgess, though Burgess did not see Micky as a potential traitor: why not, he always wondered. Micky was rejected probably— ironically—because of his ambivalent sexuality. Perhaps Burgess also detected Micky's idealism and integrity concealed beneath the languid wit and the borrowed dinner jacket. Gradually he acknowledged his sexuality, though at a time when what he did with young men he met in the Charing Cross Road was—and would remain for another 30 years— illegal. His father, suspicious of the louche company he kept, asked him uncomfortably but directly whether he was homosexual. Uncertain himself, Micky equivocated and no more was said: a curtain of strained convention fell between them, to be ripped apart by the war.

Virtually self-educated after leaving Winchester, Micky picked up snippets of culture in conversation with hostesses, actors and Society figures out of the *Tatler*. Intelligent and sensitive, impressionable and pliant, he matured in taste, judgment and wisdom. In his candid memoir, *Turned Towards the Sun* he remembers being schooled by three older women of taste, elegance and theatrical and literary distinction: Syrie Maugham, Somerset Maugham's wife, who was a noted interior designer; writer and socialite Violet Trefusis; and especially actress Viola Tree. He lived a Bohemian life with zest and flamboyant drama, a contrast to the constrained respectability of his family.

Micky's father, Clive Burn, is central to this story because he largely created the archive of letters between prison camps and families on which it draws. Clive is a conundrum. A Gallipoli veteran and an industrious but not especially distinguished solicitor, his moving to France to manage a golfing hotel might hint at either failure or lack of ambition. In 1936, however, through his friendship with the Tory grandee Walter Monckton, he left behind the part-time sinecure, rising abruptly to become secretary to the Duchy of Cornwall. He arrived at the Duchy's offices (at Buckingham Gate, opposite the Palace) in time to see Edward VIII's abdication and to grow close to George VI's circle during the Second World War. In his autobiography Micky presents his father as a man so fearful of touch that he booked two tickets to the Wagner he loved, sitting in an aisle seat at Covent Garden and leaving his hat and coat between himself and his neighbour. His daughter Stella, whose mental illness shadowed the family during and after the war, saw her father as 'a woman-hater'. Indeed, Clive Burn lived by rigid rules. He believed that 'we do not show our emotions' and that 'the women don't count'. Uncomfortable with his children's individuality (both his daughter Stella and Michael were bisexual) he withdrew from them uncomprehendingly. As a family the Burns were seemingly warm but troubled. Micky and his brother, Alan, nine years his junior, had a difficult relationship. His sister Renée married a diplomat, Lees Mayall, and by the war's outbreak had moved out of the family circle, and was living in Switzerland. The Burns appear conventional, distant; affectionate on paper but undemonstrative in person. 'Sometimes my family scare me stiff', Stella wrote just before the war. 'I know they're really nice and well meaning but have got perverted into lost souls.'

But other sources give a quite different picture. Clive's letters and the recollections of his friends suggest an affable man, hearty, charming and clubbable. Canon Martin Andrews, who came to know Clive because he held a church living in Devon in the Duchy's gift, found Clive 'light-hearted and welcoming' with 'a magnetic personality'. Duchy tenants, he recalled, thought of him as 'a lovely man'. Even the Duchy's official correspondence confirms Andrews's affectionate memoir. Micky described him as an 'uncomplicated extrovert', devoted to risky sport, a man who 'rejoiced in the full stretching of the body'. But Clive's disinclination to express his feelings makes his wartime communication not just with his son but with his son's men's families all the more puzzling, and impressive. As Micky himself came to recognise, despite his seeming stiffness Clive became the caring centre of a network of anxious or grieving parents.

Micky's mother, Phyllis, described delicately by Canon Andrews as being 'of a retiring nature', remains overshadowed by her more assured husband. Micky recalled her children ridiculing her frustrated appeals to 'let me speak!'. She suffered from periodic depression—'glooms', as the family used to say. She secretly hoped that Micky would become a poet and helped to foster in him a sensitivity denied by the hearty Clive. Yet his mother too, painfully reserved, admonished the Burns: 'we do not show our emotions'. Phyllis Burn remains a less vigorous presence in the story of Six Troop's war, but she also formed warm bonds with other soldiers' parents. Clive and Phyllis's dedication and love—for other people's children as much as their own—became a force that allowed all their stories to be told.

Politically Micky spent the 1930s swinging between extremes. Applying his father's aphorism 'always go to the top', he sought a job on The Times. Obliged to first work an apprenticeship on a provincial paper, the Gloucester Citizen, for two years from the autumn of 1934, he witnessed and responded to the Great Depression dominating that decade. Uneasy with his family's unthinking Toryism, and temperamentally attuned to social justice (he remembered the caddies at his father's course huddling in a squalid hut on sodden links) he tried to establish a club for Gloucester's workless. Its secretary thanked him for understanding the burden of unemployment. Micky later saw that while seeking to learn, he had not let their plight interfere with his weekends and holidays away in the homes of wealthy friends or their Continental villas. His desire to 'do something' remained unfocused.

In the summer of 1935 he visited Germany, impressed in spite of himself (and to his later chagrin) with Hitler's having 'cured unemployment'. At Nuremberg, Unity Mitford (whom he knew from the smart set in London) introduced Micky to Hitler. These 'brief meetings with the Führer … for a time', he wrote, 'brought me

Micky Burn, aged 22, sitting beside Ella van Heemstra at a Nazi Party rally, Nuremberg 1935.

thoroughly under that extraordinary spell'. He sat behind the official party at several Nazi rallies, describing them to Clive as 'absolutely wonderful'. Hitler presented him with an inscribed copy of *Mein Kampf*, which he promptly lost through the floor of his ramshackle car. He spent a day visiting Dachau, the prototype concentration camp. There he met men behind bars on charges without counterpart in the democracies, serving sentences without end and enduring a casual brutality in what Micky came to see as 'a state of anxiety bordering on despair'. While he declined an invitation to publish pro-Nazi articles, he still failed to see the full truth about the monstrous regime Dachau enforced. Always honest with himself, he later expressed his disgust with his complacency and susceptibility to what he later called 'the propaganda drug'.

At a Nazi party rally at Nuremberg Micky met Baroness Ella van Heemstra. The daughter of a distinguished Dutch family, Ella had been divorced in the Dutch East Indies, where she had met and married

Joseph Ruston, a minor British consular official with an obscure not to say shady background. Ella and Joseph supported Sir Oswald Mosley's British Union of Fascists. Their daughter Andrey—later Audrey—had been born in Belgium, where her father worked as a banker. By this time Ella had separated from Joseph. Micky remembers 'an exhausting but on the whole laudatory week at Nuremberg' with Ella and a weekend in Brussels. They enjoyed a brief but passionate fling—Micky's first with a woman: an expression of his ambivalent sexuality.

Ella remained friendly with him though they never met again as lovers. 'I give you a holiday from yourself', Ella told him in 1939. 'We shall always love the feeling the other gives one', she predicted, 'a very delicate and tender filigree our emotions weave'. By the late 1930s, surer of his sexuality, he remained as fond of Ella as 'a very dear friend' but no longer saw her as a lover. Ella remained attracted to him. 'I never heard from Canada', she reproached him after his return from the 1938 royal tour of North America, which he was covering for *The Times*. 'Just let me know if we shall ever have a chance of seeing each other again.' Micky and Ella stayed in touch, with extraordinary consequences in wartime. In 1939 she told him that she still thought of him often. Remembering Nuremberg, she wrote, 'I do love to treasure the souvenirs of our weekend'. Within months, war would bring them into contact again, but in the meantime, it would part them. Micky's delusions about the Nazis took some months to fade. He read books by less credulous journalists (notably Edgar Mowrer's *Germany Puts the Clock Back*) and realised that 'what Hitler's Germany was offering me as soul-saving was shit'. Through this social, political and sexual odyssey, he began to grasp, as he recognised in his autobiography, 'what life is really like'.

The next summer, rather than return to the Riviera, Micky spent a week in the West Riding of Yorkshire under a Quaker scheme to show students and middle-class people the realities of life in depressed areas. He lodged for a week with the family of George Owen, an unemployed miner. The Owens' combined income, from the dole and a teenage son's job, was just over £2 a week. Micky helped the Owens by paying a small rental and working on their allotment. The experience —he later compared himself to 'some early explorer describing the discovery of an unknown tribe'—changed his life, more profoundly than all the flags and speeches at Nuremberg. He farewelled the Owens in tears, overwhelmed by the misery he had seen and by the dignified stoicism it aroused in Yorkshire's workless miners. Ever after he counted himself on the side of the powerless, a leftward leaning that would soon take him to the opposite extreme, to communism.

Having served his time on a provincial paper Micky joined *The Times*'s Imperial and Foreign Department. Life in London's smart set continued. He kissed girls at dances, but also fell for one or two young men, and was often rejected. He cruised dangerously in parks, slept again with Guy Burgess and learned the trade of a journalist. He watched Prime Minister Neville Chamberlain pronounce on 'peace in our time', feeling at the centre of the affairs of the Empire and the world through their most influential newspaper. Geoffrey Dawson, *The Times*'s authoritative but deluded editor, assured him that Munich and appeasement would ensure peace. But as a journalist Micky foresaw war, a war that would change him forever.

<hr />

'WIRE YOU WHEN WAR BREAKS OUT': MICKY AND *THE LABYRINTH OF EUROPE*

As the 1930s drew to a close, almost everyone in Europe expected that war would break out. Micky Burn was one of the few to write a book explaining why. In October 1938, Neville Chamberlain returned from meeting 'Herr Hitler' at Munich, bearing a piece of paper supposedly ensuring 'peace with honour'. Chamberlain had averted war with Nazi Germany at the cost of Germany's bloodless conquest of Czechoslovakia. Soon after, in the spring of 1939, Methuen published Micky's book *The Labyrinth of Europe*. Written hastily but clearly and with style and laconic wit, the book tried to make sense of Europe in the wake of the Munich Agreement. Based on his close reading of official pronouncements, League of Nations documents and above all, newspaper reports, it was a topical book. He began by observing that wherever he went he heard arguments about foreign affairs. 'This is the kind of book which might emerge from the arguments', he explained. His one-time lover Ella van Heemstra wrote from Holland to congratulate Micky (he sent her a copy as soon as it appeared). 'It is as anti-Nazi-ley as you could make it', she teased, 'and very Micky-ish'.

Surveying the 1920s and 1930s, he summed up the unhappy decades that were not quite yet 'between the wars', cataloguing:

> *the bombing of innocent folk, the murder of the old, the helpless, and the very young ... the desecration of desirable things ... the termination of liberty and of individual conscience, the breaking of promises, the repudiation of treaties, the growing dominion of force ... the persecution of defenceless minorities ... truth and justice outraged on all hands ...*

This, he got as far as thinking, made everyone feel that 'the world is not what it was meant to be'.

Micky identified German aggression as the single most immediate threat to Europe's fragile peace. He did not discount danger from the Soviet Union (and in fact devoted two long chapters to exposing the lies of Stalin's purges) and the possible shifts in the dictator's foreign policies. Like most of Europe, except for those blind to the Führer's megalomania, Micky could see now what was coming.

Engaged but non-partisan, *The Labyrinth of Europe* is neither of the right nor of the left. As a product of that polarised decade it reads as curiously detached. It resembles the writings of no one so much as George Orwell, with its refusal to think in conventional categories, resistance to dogma and willingness to embrace unfashionable positions. Micky combined mordantly witty shafts mixed with plain speaking. 'The best way of ensuring popular support is either to tell lies the whole time', he wrote, 'or to tell the truth the whole time, however unpleasant'. The Treaty of Versailles, he thought, 'showed an ironical logic to conclude a war waged to end war with a peace calculated to end peace'. Criticising the democracies for failing to realise and grasp their responsibilities in countering aggression, and wary of Stalin's ruthlessness, he still identified the single greatest danger as being Nazi

Germany 'pursuing her own aggrandizement, and not the well-being of the world'. Reading *Mein Kampf*, (presumably a different copy to the one that fell from his car) he concluded that 'Hitler left no doubt ... that absolute control is the real aim'. The contrast to his brief infatuation with Hitler's new order—now 'a trail of murder and untruth'—is striking. He acknowledged the phase in which people of goodwill blamed Hitler's rise on the excesses of Versailles. He knew the 'fashion to admire the constructive achievements of National Socialism', having suffered from it himself.

The Labyrinth of Europe was a prescient book. Micky predicted that the Nazis might use the Polish Corridor as a pretext for war, though going to war with a western alliance 'would be their ruin'. He anticipated the possibility of a German–Soviet non-aggression pact, and its repudiation. He foresaw 'appalling destruction from the air', a war that would continue for years, with victory in the end going to Britain with America the dominant partner, 'and to Russia'.

He enlarged upon the ideas he had been pondering from his first engagement with the unemployed of Gloucester. As well as closely analysing continental politics and explaining the choices Britain faced in confronting fascism in a coming war, he also wrote passionately about the need for a more positive 'vision' for Britain. It was not enough to merely resist aggression, he argued. He wanted to know what 'brave new world English people are to stand for ... a creed comprehensible to the common mind'. Though oppressed by Europe's and Britain's failure to avoid war he still looked to the world after war: he asked 'what lies beyond for us?'

Ella, living in the Netherlands a few kilometres from the German frontier, jokingly told him in May 1939 that she would 'wire you when war breaks out'. Through the summer of 1939 everyone sensed that a renewed European conflict could not be far off. Franco finally extinguished the last resistance of Republican Spain; the democracies re-armed at a frantic pace and Hitler pondered how he could best attain his goal of European domination. By this time, Micky and the men he would lead into the St Nazaire raid had become soldiers; the citizen volunteers of Britain's Territorial Army. He had joined in January 1938. As a middle-class professional gent, armed with a reference from the assistant editor of *The Times*, Robin Barrington Ward, he immediately gained a commission as an officer in the Queen's Westminsters. What was the character of the force that Micky joined by strolling a few hundred yards down Buckingham Gate to the local drill hall?

'TERRIERS': CITIZEN SOLDIERS

Britain had raised the Territorial Army just before the Great War as a home defence force. Micky's father served in a Territorial cavalry regiment, the Sussex Yeomanry, on Gallipoli and in Palestine. Tens of thousands of Territorials died on the Western Front, when wartime propaganda had fostered the nickname of 'Terriers', with its connotations of tenacity and energy. After 1918, the Territorials barely met their recruiting quotas, burdened by revulsion from the Great War and the pressures of economic depression. Re-armament in expectation of war demanded a larger army, especially gunners to serve the anti-aircraft batteries to prevent the bombers from getting through. The Terriers fitted the bill, attracting men wanting to defend their homeland (rather than police the Empire, like the regular army). Emerging from two decades of neglect, though, the Territorials were, by the late 1930s, Micky admitted in *The Labyrinth of Europe*, 'a tragical farce'.

Before the force's great expansion of the late 1930s the Territorials mainly drew their volunteers from the working class, men who liked the camaraderie and a paid holiday in the country or at the seaside in the annual camp. Their officers were the sons of county gentry or city professionals, both viewing the army as a hobby. With the growing awareness of impending war and appeals to increase the Territorial Army it gained funding, equipment and weapons, and attracted a new type of volunteer. Maurice Harrison (who would die at St Nazaire), an aspiring commercial artist from a comfortable commercial middle-class family in suburban Streatham, seems to have been representative. His sister Molly remembered how Maurice realised the threat Hitler posed to the peace of Europe and the security of Britain. He simply said, 'This man has got to be stopped', and joined the Terriers. Who were the other men who made the same decision?

The personnel files of all but five of the 28 soldiers Micky led into the raid have survived, in the Army Personnel Centre's warehouse. The files, some a few folios thick, others wads of tattered foolscap with letters interleaved, allow us to learn at least the outlines of their lives.

Of the 23 for which files survive, the eldest, Peter Harkness, had been born in 1915, the youngest, Maurice Harrison, in 1921. They were all children of the Great War; born during the war or after their fathers had been de-mobbed. Two had middle names reflecting their fathers' war service (Tom Ypres Roach and Robert Salonica Woodman, both born in 1917). They were almost all Londoners, by birth or residence. Most had been born in the city; others had shifted with fathers looking for work. Yet others arrived as young men; from Scotland, Ireland and Wales. (Tom Roach and Morgan Jenkins had grown up twelve miles apart in South Wales, but only met in the Territorials in London.) Some were practically neighbours.

They differed from the Territorial Army's traditional recruits. Only one, Paddy Bushe, was an unskilled labourer. (Despite his name and Irish background, he had been born in Lambeth, but after she had been widowed his mother had returned to Tipperary.) Some were semi-skilled—John Cudby a 'capstan operator'; Fred Penfold a butcher; George ('Lenny') Goss, Bill Spaul, Ronald ('Bobby') Burns and Bill Gibson mechanics or engineers. But the great majority were white-collar workers: Albert Lucy in a chemist in Regents Park; Tom Roach managing a shop; Stan Rodd a salesman; Maurice Harrison in 'advertising'. The largest single group—about half—had been clerks of some kind: Willie Bell a Civil Service clerk; Reg Tomsett a shipping clerk, others bank, or insurance clerks; Norman Fisher, George Hudson and Bill Watt simply 'clerks'. These men came from unlikely backgrounds: clerks who became commandos, unsung heroes of the Second World War. As war became expected and then imminent they became Riflemen, Fusiliers or Privates, depending on the units they joined. (In one of the British Army's many quirks, it called Privates in rifle regiments 'Riflemen' and those in fusilier regiments 'Fusiliers'.)

All but one of them had decided to join the Territorial Army. The exception was Bill Spaul, the tallest and heaviest of Micky's men. He had joined the regular army at the age of eighteen, perhaps modelling himself on his late father, a staff sergeant in the King's Royal Rifle Corps (or perhaps to escape his stepfather, whom his estranged wife, Bill's mother, Isabel Wyles, described as 'that dreadful person the Sergeant Major'). Bill joined the West Surreys, and rose swiftly to substantive sergeant within eighteen months before volunteering for 'Special Service'.

Others had joined the Terriers as Europe's crisis deepened. They were the products of a city that had weathered the depression and its privations. All were shorter and lighter than the strapping regular Bill Spaul. They averaged about five foot six inches and about 135 pounds, with Albert Lucy, the chemist's shop assistant, the shortest and lightest at five foot two inches and 107 pounds. As 'Saturday-night soldiers' they attended the weeknight and weekend parades and the annual training camps, passing from drill at the regimental drill hall to musketry instruction and more specialised training as machine-gunners or drivers (or, for Lenny Goss, as an army cook). Several (Bobby Burns and Maurice Harrison) served as 'Boys' and as they turned eighteen were classified as 'fit for General Service in Man class'. The opportunity for active service came soon enough.

As its name suggested, the Territorial Army was based on locally raised units. All joined units forming part of the 47th (London) Division. Paddy Bushe and Peter Westlake joined the London Irish Rifles, a battalion affiliated to the Royal Ulster Rifles. Inseparable friends, Peter Harkness and Bill Gibson joined the London Scottish (a Territorial battalion of the Gordon Highlanders). Six men joined Territorial battalions of one of London's own regiments, the Royal Fusiliers, and six joined Micky's regiment, the Queen's Westminsters. The Queen's Westminsters gives a good snapshot of the Territorials.

It had been created in 1921 by the amalgamation of the Queen's Westminsters and the incongruously named Civil Service Rifles. Recruiting in Mayfair and Westminster, it had managed, through astute use of Whitehall connections, to avoid becoming an anti-aircraft unit. The Westminsters were part of the King's Royal Rifle

Corps, one of the army's elite infantry regiments, with a history dating from the formation of the Royal Americans in the Seven Years War of the 1750s. The Westminsters' standing orders reflected its social tone. All of its members were obliged to be 'elected a member of The Queen's (Westminster and Civil Service) Association', for a fee, a relic from when a volunteer unit had resembled a gentlemen's club. But in the British Army social tone often sat happily beside military efficiency and the Queen's Westminsters seems to have been a smart and efficient battalion. The men Micky learned to lead as a Territorial officer were, he saw, 'keen and promising material, but they had enlisted in a mirage'. While they were ready to learn, starved of modern weapons and equipment, he wrote in *The Labyrinth of Europe*, 'there was nothing to learn on'.

As the German invasion of Poland on 1 September 1939 confronted Britain with the crisis, all Territorials (as they had expected since the Munich Agreement) received official letters. Territorial Army recruits had signed a form agreeing that 'in the event of a grave national Emergency' they would be 'embodied'—called up. All received light blue War Office notices headed 'Immediate and Important' instructing them to report to their regiments' depots. By the time Prime Minister Neville Chamberlain told the nation that '... consequently, this country is at war with Germany', on the morning of 3 September, they had arrived at their depots to be kitted out as soldiers for the duration.

Over the winter of 1939–40 their various battalions—the Queen's Westminsters, the London Irish and Scottish, and the Royal Fusiliers—trained as part of the 47th Division, mainly in Kent. They expected to join the British Expeditionary Force in France. In the meantime, other volunteers enlisted during what became known as the 'Phoney War'. They joined the Territorials voluntarily rather than await their call-up as conscripts, and conformed closely to the profile of the pre-war volunteers: they too were lower middle-class white-collar or commercial men: John ('Jimmy') Prescott, an insurance clerk; Peter Harkness, a Post Office mail sorter; Peter Westlake, a newspaper circulation clerk.

The Queen's Westminsters spent the war's first winter around Folkestone, in Kent. Ella's daughter Andrey was at a nearby school and she asked Micky to visit to check on her. He assured the baroness that her daughter was well. Soon after, Ella took the child back to Holland. They arrived in time to be trapped in Arnhem when the German Blitzkrieg erupted in the west. Ella and her children spent the war under German occupation and, in due course, under the great Allied airborne operation in 1944.

Meanwhile, Micky, like many young Territorials restless with conventional soldiering, volunteered for a special task. Bored with training intakes of conscripts and tired of some 'virulent anti-Semites' in the Westminsters' mess, he told Phyllis he had applied for 'a mysterious and highly secret course'. Charles Newman, a rotund 38-year-old major from the Essex Regiment whose blimpish and affable manner concealed a fighting man able to inspire respect and affection, raised 200 volunteers from the 47th Division to form an 'Independent Company'. Within days it embarked for active service in, of all places, Norway.

Sensing the German plan to invade Scandinavia—a plan implemented in April 1940—Britain and France formed an expeditionary force to forestall Germany seizing the coal and iron of northern Norway. The Germans got there first, better organised for a campaign fought across long stretches of rugged country in the snow-bound Norwegian spring.

Ten Territorial divisions had formed an independent company. Number 5 was formed from the 47th (London) Division. In this way, Micky and most of the men he would lead in war came together in April 1940, just in time to participate in one of the British Army's least impressive sideshows of the Second World War. The Norwegian Expeditionary Force included five independent companies. Newman's 5 Independent Company became part of 'Scissors Force' under Colin Gubbins, whom Micky recalled in *Yes, Farewell* as 'a brisk dapper general with a reputation for being energetic and unorthodox'. Gubbins did his best but the chronic disorganisation of the entire enterprise negated whatever contribution his independent force might have made.

Newman's independent company returned to Britain in June 1940, to be stationed around Glasgow. Its men generally were dissatisfied with the way they had been misused in what was seen as a debacle. The British Hollywood actor (and former regular officer) David Niven, who was to join the independent companies to escape stagnation in the

Rifle Brigade, described the 'remains' of the independent companies (which he thought had been 'defeated in Norway') as 'semi-mutinous'. Some men did return to their units but most remained with the independent companies, and the experiment survived. They were messed about for a while but were brought under the umbrella of what became 'Combined Operations'.

<hr>

'SPECIAL SERVICE': CHURCHILL'S COMMANDOS

Winston Churchill had founded Combined Operations in the dark days following Dunkirk as a gesture of defiance. He had appointed as its director the 70-year-old Admiral Roger Keyes, the hero of the raid on the U-boat base of Zeebrugge in 1918. Keyes began organising a force charged with taking the war to the Germans, by raiding the coast of occupied Europe. Its first raid had been improvised within days, but Keyes needed time to create and train a force that could launch damaging attacks on occupied Europe.

Combined Operations cultivated what Joan Bright (who worked in the Operations Directorate at the War Office) described as 'amusing and unconventional people'. Officers interviewed and selected volunteers for their own units. Some, like Charles Newman and Micky, brought men with them. Volunteers often dropped a rank to get into the force, though their calibre, and the need for leadership on operations, gave many the chance to regain their stripes. David Niven reflected on the varying motivations of those who, like him, volunteered for the new force. He saw 'the genuinely courageous who were itching to get at the throat of the enemy', but also the restless, men who would 'volunteer for anything ... to escape the boredom' of their situation. Niven placed himself among the restless, but he thought that most commando volunteers sought to get at their enemies' throats.

Finding a name for the new units took some time. The Norwegian fiasco tainted the idea of independent companies. Churchill spoke of 'Leopards', 'bands of brothers' and 'storm troops'. More prosaic minds coined 'Special Service' battalions, a name which, despite its unfortunate initials, proved durable. The originator of the idea of raiders, Colonel Dudley Clarke, was the antithesis of the conventional view of a War Office staff officer. 'Brilliantly clever and imaginative and always on the edge of laughter' according to his secretary's sister, Hermione Ranfurly, Clarke dreamt up some of the war's most daring intelligence spoofs. The Transvaal-born Clarke recommended 'Commandos', the name of the Boer guerrillas who had harassed the British Army in South Africa, and eventually the name took. Less imaginative officers opposed the idea of an irregular force, and in August 1940 Micky took the initiative to lobby Geoffrey Dawson, *The Times*'s editor, in favour of the Special Service force. Dawson happened to lunch that day with Churchill, who five days later reminded the War Office that 'we must develop the storm troop or Commando idea'. The units into which they were organised, however, chopped and changed for a year while the army worked out the best ways to use this new force. Micky and his men were first part of Charles Newman's small 'independent company', then merged into a large 'Special Service' battalion before becoming, in March 1941, 2 Commando.

An officer who faced a commando selection board just before the St Nazaire raid recalled what an ordeal it could be. Dressed faultlessly, he found four officers 'lolling languidly' in a drawing room in a mansion in Ayrshire. Saluting sharply, he nevertheless felt that 'like all selection boards they had a knack of making a man feel that he was something that had just crawled out from under a stone'. The questions fired at him were idiosyncratic, but they suggest how selection was as much a matter of intuition as of procedural criteria:

> '*What sports do you play?*'
> '*Do you drink beer?*'
> '*Can you swim?*'
> '*Do you play any musical instruments?*'
> '*Have you a sex life?*'
> '*Were you a boy scout?*'

Perhaps a yes to the last question necessarily implied a no to the one before, but the answers may not have been as important as the way men delivered them.

An American pamphlet on the commandos (produced in 1942 to help them understand their new allies) explained some of the unusual features of the unorthodox force. Commandos had all volunteered, and been selected, but still had to meet exacting standards. They not only had to be trained soldiers and physically tough; they were also expected to possess qualities the British Army did not usually value. American observers noted that selection panels looked for 'intelligence, self-reliance, and ... an independent frame of mind': a contrast to the British Army's traditional emphasis on discipline. As volunteers they could always ask to be 'Returned to Unit'—to go back to their original battalion, but to do so—and even more, to be sent back (RTU'd)—was seen as a disgrace. Each man wore the cap badge of his parent regiment, under the British system an incentive to competitive emulation, but by 1942 also a 'COMMANDO' shoulder flash. (Not until after the St Nazaire raid did commandos generally adopt the green beret that became their distinctive mark.)

Better-off commando officers found rooms at a succession of pricey hotels—the Redcliffe at Paignton, the Gloucester at Weymouth, the Argyll Arms in Inverary: 'broke as usual and as usual in the best hotel', as Micky told his father. Uniquely for fighting troops, their men lived not in barracks or camps but in billets. Men received six shillings and eight pence a day for subsistence (half the officers' rate). They were expected to travel to the seaside towns they were allotted, to find their own digs and meals and often to use their initiative to travel to training exercises. Commandos were required to keep civilian clothes (to use on exercises as well as on leave). The system saved on administrative overheads, but more importantly fostered a spirit of self-reliance. Commandos liked it: it cut down on 'bull' and routine obligations (such as camp fatigues or guard duty) and officers saw advantages in placing responsibility on their men—breaches of discipline could result in RTU. Billeted as they were in private homes, commandos became for a time a novel part of the British seaside landscape. Micky thought that billets made the troops soft. 'The men live all over the place and are grossly overfed

[and] spoilt' by their landladies, he wrote from Paignton to his mother. 'One has to knock at the door and ask if they are in', he complained, whimsically thinking of sending his men *cartes de visite*:

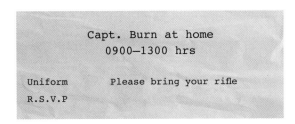

Capt. Burn at home
0900–1300 hrs

Uniform   Please bring your rifle
R.S.V.P

A man chipped for parading with a dirty weapon might reply, 'My landlady did it, sir'. The excuse did not always meet with an indulgent response: Albert Lucy forfeited a week's pay for 'appearing on parade with a rusty bayonet' at Paignton in January 1941. As time went by both landladies and commandos became more proficient. Living in seaside resorts and on Highland estates made many restive. Micky was conscious that his parents were in greater danger in London, but philosophically told Phyllis 'our time will come'.

Charles Newman, who had been frustrated by the failure to use his independent company in Norway, at last was able to run his own show. Promoted to lieutenant colonel (and universally known as Colonel Charles), he rid his unit of all but the most eager volunteers and subjected it to a relentless training regime. Newman, a portly, pipe-smoking middle-aged man, who looked very unlike the stereotypical commando, devised a list of precepts that exemplify the special qualities and calibre of his force. He expected his men to be proficient in a demanding range of skills, in mountain warfare, able to use a range of weapons (or fight without them) and to march, drive and swim. Highly trained and motivated, they all itched to use these skills. 'Everyone is speculating like mad', Micky wrote in May 1941, but it would be many months before the commandos were sent on the sort of operations they had trained for.

'POWERS OF LEADERSHIP': SIX TROOP'S OFFICERS

Six Troop had three officers: Micky, Tommy Peyton and Morgan Jenkins. They reflect the commandos' extraordinary social mixture, and point to why it was such an effective force. A force unusual, perhaps unprecedented in British military history, it judged its members on what they could do rather than who they had been. Six Troop's officers comprised two public school boys—Micky and Tommy—and Morgan, the son of a Welsh miner.

While still depending on his father ('Don't drop my allowance', Micky begged Clive soon after becoming a captain) Micky became an unorthodox but highly effective troop commander. Clive never ceased to urge him to 'put yourself on a sound financial basis', but military life—with material needs taken care of and unlimited supplies of pyrotechnics—took them all 'back to the state of mind of schoolboys', Micky admitted to his mother. In the ultimate prank he and his fellow subalterns blew out the windows of a hotel: someone miscalculated the size of the charge needed to blow up a tree as a joke. Arriving late, expecting to be court-martialled and lamely explaining to his brigadier, Charles Haydon, that he had tried to make amends by sending the owner a bouquet of lilies, Micky was relieved to detect Haydon trying not to laugh. This, Haydon knew, was the commando spirit.

While in Devon, Catholicism attracted him. Like the mother of his character Alan Maclaren in *Yes, Farewell*, he was perhaps attracted to 'the bells and images and incense', but more likely to Catholicism's 'misty enveloping assurances' and, as he made clear in his autobiography, the priests' capacity to accept his ambiguous sexuality. At Buckfast Abbey on 1 April 1941 he was received into the Catholic faith, reassuring his father that he had acted thoughtfully and not 'fallen into the hands of the priests'.

He also matured through his relationship with a woman who was to play a part in Six Troop's story, Dinah Jones. Tall, coltish, innocent, Dinah was painfully shy. She loved Micky without fully understanding how her intense affection could never be returned in full. Part of a well-off Norfolk landed family, she was as much an outsider in her world as Micky was in his. But she was warm and kind and Micky returned her shy, anxious love as a firm friend. His comrades assumed she was

Micky Burn and Dinah Jones at a 2 Commando sports day, Scotland, in the summer of 1941.

his girlfriend. It was, Dinah admitted after a visit to a 2 Commando sports day, 'a split second of Happiness'; all too brief. Dinah became both part of the consolation and the grieving that those around Micky would face.

Micky became a soldier but retained his distinctive, not to say idiosyncratic, personality. He was consciously un-military, 'a touch of the great English Eccentrics', as Arthur Young, who was to go into the raid with Micky, recalled. He read Stendhal ('so great a contrast to military life') and eighteenth-century literature. All he needed, he later told his parents, was 'Jane Austen and a little ammunition'. Micky displayed a vagueness towards the practical that exasperated some and charmed others. At Paignton a hired car he abandoned and forgot about provoked what he called a 'dreary correspondence' with an exasperated garage owner, sorted only after his father weighed in with some intimidating legalese about writs in the Devon County Court. Contrary to his superficially casual demeanour, though, he was, as Arthur recalled, 'tougher in mind than most of us, always leading by example'. Arthur remembered Micky's insouciance:

> *I can imagine no other officer who could take a parade with his belt at an angle of 45°, with various straps undone, and reprimand his men for their lack of smartness!*

Thomas Grenville Pitt Peyton, to give him his baptismal name, was the son of an upper middle-class family that had been providing officers for the British Army for generations. Like Micky's father Clive, Ivor Peyton had served on Gallipoli. Ivor had married late and died in the 1930s, when his sons were still in their teens. He had left a widow, Dorothy (herself an Elphinstone, one of the great families of Empire) to bring up her two surviving sons—the youngest had died of diphtheria. After Eton, Tommy entered the Royal Military College, Sandhurst. The entry form asked for 'Father's position in life': 'Gentleman', Tommy wrote. On the eve of war's outbreak Tommy joined the King's Royal Rifle Corps, one of the most prestigious regiments in the army. An adventurous spirit, he soon volunteered for an independent company and in due course found himself in Micky's commando troop. Not surprisingly, Tommy was six inches taller and ten pounds heavier than most of the men he was to lead. With his fresh complexion and hazel eyes, he took to the art of leadership effortlessly, with a grace that endeared him to all.

Dorothy Peyton, now a widow with her sons in the army, lived alone in her large house, Englemere Wood, near Ascot. While Tommy was at Sandhurst, John, the elder, had gained a commission in a hussar regiment after the Nazis annexed Czechoslovakia. The house was a royal residence: Field Marshal Sir Frederick Roberts—Kipling's

'Bobs'—had passed his declining years there before dying in the opening months of the Great War. Rather than give up her big house, Dorothy decided to share it, remarkably with 'evacuees' from the extremes of society. First, she offered rooms to the royal princesses Helena and Marie Louise, who prudently left their house in central London. Princess Marie Louise was an especially good friend of Dorothy's. A colourful minor royal, a granddaughter of Queen Victoria, she was childless after the annulment of her brief and unhappy marriage to the villainous and cruel Aribert of Anhalt. Plain, virtuous and good-hearted, for 40 years she had devoted herself to genteel pursuits and charitable works. The commandos acquired unlikely champions in the princesses. Through Dorothy and Tommy, Princess Marie Louise supported 2 Commando's Next of Kin Committee and especially Micky's Six Troop ('it's a matter of time before they're asked to shoot at Sandringham', he joked just before the St Nazaire raid). Though somewhat underemployed before March 1942, the committee was to assume heavier burdens as the war continued.

At the other end of the scale, Dorothy also welcomed the inmates of the Maurice Home, a girls' orphanage evacuated from Ealing. The girls, mostly illegitimate children given up as babies, answered to numbers rather than names. Educated in humility and destined for domestic service, they shared dormitories in what had been the games room and the ballroom. John Peyton recalled how his mother, helped by her aristocratic lodgers, presided at a slight distance over the couple of dozen girls, who were under the more direct charge of Matron Bailey. Sheila Stewart (number 21) wrote a fond memoir of her time at Englemere Wood, *A Home From Home*. She described how Dorothy's 'gracious presence' overwhelmed girls unused to elegance, recalling her as tall and dignified, 'the shining silver of her softly waved hair … emphasised by the formality of her long black evening dress'. Everyone called the girls, with cheerfully obtuse condescension, the 'Waifs and Strays', even the Rev. Herbert Walton at the Peytons' parish church, All Saints, when he included them in his prayers each week. The princesses, known to each other as Louie and 'Tora, presided at the girls' weekly knitting parties, while John and Tommy visited often on leave during the war's first winter. The girls, dumbfounded by handsome young 'Mr Tommy' and 'Mr John', stared at them from a distance and followed accounts of their doings at war through the servants' gossip.

Except that they had both lost their fathers, Morgan Jenkins's background could not have been more different to Tommy Peyton's. A bright boy, the son of a colliery man from Tynewydd in Glamorgan, Morgan had won a scholarship to Brecon County School, thirty-odd miles distant. Like so many ambitious provincial boys, he went to work in London. He too had enlisted in the Territorial Army, in the London Rifle Brigade. Morgan quickly became a sergeant, his gift for leadership obvious to his officer in 5 Independent Company, Bill Copland (who was to be Colonel Charles's second-in-command in the St Nazaire raid). Copland described him as 'an excellent soldier', conscientious but decisive, who 'possesses powers of leadership'. He recommended Morgan for a commission in April 1940. Morgan's army file shows that by November 1940 he had become a second lieutenant in the Welsh Regiment, seconded to 5 Independent Company. Colonel Charles seems to have contrived for Morgan to evade an officers' training course. In the meantime he had married Doris (known as Edna) in London. She remains a shadowy presence in Morgan's story, as we will see.

Full of Welsh charm and a good companion, Morgan also reminds us that commandos were men with feelings and fears. He attracted women, and inspired men to follow him. In spite of Colonel Charles's training precepts, Morgan feared the water and never learned to swim. He also feared heights (two conditions that must ostensibly have disqualified him for commando service). But late in 1941, when the troop did a mountaineering course in the Lake District, he overcame his terror. One night in the pub Micky missed him. He turned up just before closing time and murmured, 'I've done it'. By himself, in the dark, he had gone up a rock-face which the rest of the troop had climbed in daylight roped together. 'So contrary in background', Micky remembered, Tommy and Morgan made 'a perfect pair'.

'A STIR IN THE DOVECOTE': TRAINING 2 COMMANDO

For a year after it formed out of the Special Service battalion, 2 Commando's job was to train for the task ahead, whatever it might be. The commandos took war seriously, and their gloves-off attitude won them no friends, especially among regular soldiers. Micky had his troop parade as 'spies' and glean intelligence from the unsuspecting officials in the Scottish Lowlands. After learning that regular officers had described Arthur Young's ploy to trick stationmasters in Argyll into disclosing sensitive information as 'unfair', Micky remembered explaining that 'unfairness was the point' if the Nazis were to be beaten. His men prepared to fight anywhere—on beaches or mountains, in forests or towns—learning not only the skills of 'fieldcraft' and unconventional combat but also the attitudes of independent war waged with initiative. Micky took his men into what he called 'Unexpected Situations', giving them impromptu problems to solve and expecting followers to become leaders on the spot. Despite the occasional cigar Micky and his men became superlatively fit ('the other day', he told Phyllis, '50 of us demonstrated how you can get up 1200 feet in 45 minutes, why, I don't know, but everyone was impressed'). Other units, 2 Commando's adjutant, Captain Ronnie Mitchell, recorded, were 'somewhat angry' at what he described as 'our fifth column methods'. In an exercise in Dorset in 1941, as the unit's war diary noted, they 'went to enemy Div H.Q. and almost captured it. Caused quite a stir in the dovecote', the 2 Commando war diary recorded drily.

Much of the hardest training occurred in the bleak but beautiful west of Scotland at Inverailort on Loch Ailort in Argyll. Inverailort has been overshadowed by the celebrated training camp opened at Achnacarry, in Invernesshire in 1942, where most commandos were trained (and where the commando memorial would in time be built). Training at Inverailort was more amateurish but no less demanding. The commando training program aimed to equip men with a great range of skills. Finishing (or in some cases merely surviving) successive courses—in mountain-climbing, fieldcraft, unarmed combat, demolition and even train-driving—gave men a powerful sense of accomplishment. A Londoner told journalist Gordon Holman, who spent time with the commandos in 1942, that he had never gone to the public baths except in August but he had now swum in Scottish rivers in November. David Niven described the training at Inverailort as 'two months running up and down mountains … crawling up streams at night, and swimming in the loch with full equipment'. This left him 'unbearably fit'.

Late in 1941 Six Troop went to Rosthwaite in the Lake District for a mountaineering course ('don't tell me we are invading Switzerland', Clive quipped). They climbed peaks—they named pitches 'Harrison's Swing' and 'Fisher's Folly' where Maurice and Norman got into difficulties. In December 1941, while Six Troop climbed mountains in the Lake District an army cinematographer arrived to film them. The planned filming, on Micky's birthday, was rained out, though, 'being a Commando', Maurice Harrison wrote, 'we went for a trek' anyway. Their strenuous training—because until St Nazaire that was all they did—made the training the main point of the propaganda effort. 'Somewhere in the Highlands', a journalist reported, 'is a school for super-soldiers'. Civilians, the journalist wrote, looked at them with 'a kind of admiring nervousness'. Maurice Harrison admitted to his

For eighteen months before embarking on Operation 'Chariot', Special Service troops trained arduously in rugged Scottish country pictured here.

family that 'we are getting a lot of publicity just now' and that it was 'getting a bit exaggerated'.

Hilary St George Saunders, the official 'Recorder' at Combined Operations Headquarters at Richmond Terrace, did not fall into the trap of describing commando volunteers as supermen. He recalled them as 'a very ordinary individual, often indeed insignificant to look at'. 'Hard cases'—graduates of Borstal, weight-lifters or dirt-track riders—comprised a small minority. The commandos individually did not resemble the gangsters as the popular press portrayed them. Saunders thought it was generally agreed that the best volunteer was 'the full-blooded Cockney', like several of Six Troop: but this still sounds like flannel. As their files disclose, the men of Six Troop were a seemingly ordinary bunch.

Commandos carried rifles or Tommy guns (powerful enough to tear off rather than simply wound an arm but regarded by conventional soldiers as wasteful 'gangster guns'). Liberally supplied with grenades, they also carried the 'commando knife'. This weapon symbolised their role as stealthy raiders (it became the force's badge) but if found on prisoners it could get them executed: Six Troop's men did not carry them in the raid on St Nazaire. Less spectacularly, all commandos carried compasses and watches, a sign of the degree to which they were expected to rely on their own judgment and not simply obey an officer's or sergeant's instructions. Commandos also learned how to use a terrifyingly wide range of explosives. The most demanding aspect of their training, however, was the physical requirement to march or climb long distances and across rugged country in all weather and in one of the wettest climates in Britain. In 1941 Peter Westlake completed a course in which participants marched 67 miles in 24 hours: his family still cherish this army record. Though commando medical officers at Inverailort experimented with Benzedrine to combat fatigue, recording extraordinary effects on fatigued men, commandos were not usually given any artificial stimulants, and they completed these long marches under the impetus only of leadership and comradeship. Men were expected to remain alert, and were often asked to solve tactical problems at the end of exhausting cross-country treks. Micky and Maurice Roe passing a portable chess-board between them as they tramped across Highland moors exemplifies this determination.

Trainers accepted the possibility of casualties and insisted that any survivors should be proficient in survival methods. When learning to move stealthily across country, for example, men were at first shouted at when they broke cover. Later, instructors fired blanks at them. When they were expected to move without breaking cover they were fired at with live ammunition. 'This method produced excellent results', an American observer noted. Micky light-heartedly described several times when he was in more than what he reassuringly called 'a very hypothetical kind of danger'. Once when rock-climbing in the Lake District he tumbled twenty or thirty feet down a rock-face, belayed only by a more experienced climber next on the rope.

Commandos often trained with live ammunition, once near Moffat in Scotland in 1941 stopping just short of killing Sir Roger Keyes, the bullets halted only by Charles Haydon's murmured request, 'Can you stop them now?' A watching civilian (Jean Butler of the Star Hotel) innocently asked 'What was that whistling noise?' In February 1941 just how realistically they trained came home forcibly to Morgan Jenkins. One of Ronnie Mitchell's platoons staged an ambush, catching Morgan's platoon as it worked its way up a road past a disused brick kiln near Totnes. Mitchell's men fired several live rounds in the air, making it clear that Morgan's men had been successfully ambushed. One of Mitchell's men went to take Morgan prisoner. He refused and struggled with the man. Mitchell sent a man over to help. Thinking its safety catch was on, he cocked his Tommy gun and told Morgan to put up his hands. The soldier tucked his Tommy gun under his arm and reached for Morgan's revolver. Morgan then grabbed the barrel of the Tommy gun, resuming the struggle. The soldier, as Morgan's army file discloses, 'instinctively gripped the gun to pull it away from him, and the shot was fired'. A bullet passed through Morgan's thigh and he keeled over. 'The next thing I remember was that I was on the floor.' A court of inquiry—two of its three officers were to die at St Nazaire—found Morgan's wound to have been 'purely accidental': gunshot wounds were the price to be paid for the spirit Morgan had shown.

'HAPPY TO BE SERVING': SIX TROOP

Six Troop's men were truly among the British Army's best: Micky thought that about ten would have justified a commission. Fewer than a quarter of the men who served in the British Army during the Second World War chose to enlist. Not only had all of his men volunteered, most had volunteered before the war's outbreak. Historian David French found that in 1942 the army believed fewer than one man in twenty to be suited by disposition and personality to combat. By volunteering for a special force of aggressive raiders, all of Six Troop's men formed part of that élite number. Though at times uneasy about the 'SS' initials, many remained proud of their name, preferring it to 'commando'. They commissioned brown metal 'sweetheart brooches' for wives and girlfriends. Morgan Jenkins gave one to his wife, Edna.

Relations between officers and men in the commandos remained much more informal than in conventional units. In many units officers and men played sport together, and naturally developed a feeling of mutual regard and trust. But the intensity of this feeling in Six Troop seems unusual. Again and again Micky's men, as Bill Gibson's father wrote, 'always spoke of him in admiring terms'. Lewis Roach repeated 'what Tom used to say', that Micky had been a 'good friend and a Pal'. The clue to this esteem comes in a letter from Clive Burn to the father of a man killed in the St Nazaire raid: 'My boy was so very proud of them all and looked upon them as his personal friends'. This bond between leader and led was both different to the traditional relationship between officer and man in the British Army, and characteristic of the relationship in this war; a people's war.

As we have seen, Six Troop's men came from a range of backgrounds—mechanics, a butcher, shopkeepers and not least clerks—and they displayed a range of personalities and temperaments. Stan Rodd was a sharp, witty Londoner, his sleek black hair and Clark Gable moustache conveying a hint of that 1940s type, the spiv. Willie Bell, a working-class lad from Paisley, was, his father remembered, 'more of a quiet disposition'. Not so Willie's fellow Glaswegian, Bill Gibson, who with his mate Peter Harkness evaded a charge of being absent by the ingenuity of his explanation. When Micky and Tommy Peyton spotted him on a bus going into Glasgow, he blandly explained that, 'Och, sir, but it must have been my twin brother'. Another pair of contrasts were Lenny Goss, keen on little but motorcycles and girls, possibly in that order, and Jack Heery, a teacher in a poor school at Stockport who walked everywhere on principle and whose commitment to social justice was to Micky 'frightening in its purity'. Jack, Micky later told Heery's sister, 'shared with me the illusions of enthusiasm': the commandos were for him a living tutorial on the best and worst of British society. Attracting men of intelligence and initiative, the commandos were more likely to include men like Maurice Harrison, with his subtle wit and interest in the Victorian music hall, or Rifleman Maurice Roe, proficient in Swahili, than the thugs and he-men of the popular press.

From the beginning Micky encouraged his parents to take an interest in his men. In March 1941 he reminded Clive and Phyllis that they had agreed to contact their families when the unit went overseas. 'Otherwise', he wrote pointedly and presciently, 'their families will only know what [the] authorities choose to tell them'. Micky formed a realistically sceptical view of what families would or would not be told. While conscious of the need to preserve security, he proposed to Phyllis a simple code for signalling that operations were imminent.

Formed from the Special Service Battalion at Paignton, in Devon in February 1941, Newman's 2 Commando was ordered to shift to Weymouth. He declined transport but, loading kit bags onto lorries, marched his men the 120 miles, sleeping rough under hedges and marching up the main street of Weymouth four days later to take the salute of the mayor and town council. While at Weymouth Micky learned that his parents' house, and the offices of the Duchy, had been hit by a bomb on 10 May 1941. Clive and Phyllis were unhurt—one had been in the cellar and the other upstairs when the bomb hit, and they met dramatically on the staircase—but two young air raid wardens whom Clive had been speaking to a few minutes before died in the blast. The bomb tore down one side of the building, forcing Clive and Phyllis to live in a requisitioned house in Kingston-on-Thames, though Clive commuted to Buckingham Gate daily. The Duchy's council room lay ruined until 1950, the expertly repaired damage still visible once pointed out.

Six Troop, 2 Commando, photographed in the months before the raid on St Nazaire.

Some military historians argue that the British Army could not cultivate initiative in its junior leaders because independence was, as critics put it, 'contrary to the whole hierarchic and class system within the British army'. The commandos generally (and Six Troop in particular) refute this claim. The conduct of men in training and on operations demonstrates that men could exercise initiative given encouragement. They 'all liked their captain very much', Fred Penfold's mother told Clive, and were 'happy to be serving with him'. Micky characteristically later deprecated the praise, but the contemporary documents testify to its validity.

Six Troop's enthusiasm needs to be appreciated against the course of the war, which in 1941 seemed to be running heavily against Britain. While the Royal Air Force had defeated the *Luftwaffe's* preparation for an invasion of Britain, the war everywhere else was going badly. Britain and its Empire stood alone, supported morally and materially by a sympathetic United States. But Hitler had occupied Western Europe and early in 1941 conquered Yugoslavia. In the

Mediterranean, a Nazi invasion of Greece and then Crete left thousands of prisoners in Axis hands (including many of the first Special Service battalions posted overseas). In North Africa, seemingly easy victories over the Italians were followed by the intervention of Rommel's *Afrika Korps*, and for most of 1941 British Empire forces battled to hold or relieve the fortress of Tobruk. In the Atlantic, Germany's U-boats seemed to be winning the war against the convoys supplying Britain. The Nazi invasion of Russia opening in June, though it would in time destroy Hitler's chances for victory, brought Germany staggering and seemingly unstoppable success. In Asia, it was obvious that sooner or later Imperial Japan would enter the war, a further blow against the overstretched democracies. In late 1941 it was an optimistic mind that looked beyond the dark present to a post-war future.

'I HOPE WHEN THIS IS OVER': MICKY'S 'EDUCATIONAL PROGRAMME'

Living intimately among the men of his troop, Micky learned more about them and their lives, hopes and plans. Building upon his exposure to the working people of Gloucester during the 1930s, he pondered what the war would do for the men of his troop. Even before the army began to organise formal 'current affairs' sessions in units, he became curious about his men's wider outlook. He gave them a talk, 'Rulers I have known', describing his encounters with Hitler, Roosevelt and the King, in which, he told his mother, 'they took a vast interest'. Extraordinarily (given both how badly the war was going and how precarious a commando's chances of survival might be) Micky became increasingly concerned that his men should finish the war with better prospects than they had in 1939. 'I hope when this is over they get the good jobs they deserve', he told Phyllis.

In November 1941 he finally put onto paper a scheme he had been mulling over. Maurice Harrison was so impressed that he opened the diary that he kept until his death at St Nazaire. 'It is as though a new phase has begun in our Army life', Maurice wrote. Micky gave his troop a lecture, telling his men that their military training had reached a state where they needed only four or five days a week to maintain their form. That left a day free to institute 'a scheme for furthering our general education'. Arguing that the army could 'train men for the peace as well as for the war', Micky proposed 'courses in civic education', encompassing not just lectures and discussions but practical experience in fulfilling the potential of the intelligent but not always educated men he led. This, Maurice noted, was 'an idea of great imagination in which there is surely great promise'. A few days later Micky put his scheme (known to the troop as the E.P.—the Educational Programme) to his military superiors. While Newman defended Micky, higher commanders did indeed regard his plan, as he had foreseen, as 'unorthodox, irregular, unmilitary, and therefore to be condemned'. In the meantime Micky adopted it in Six Troop.

He circulated a questionnaire asking his men to say what careers they wanted to investigate. Their aspirations are touching. 'Is it possible to obtain a direct entry ... into the higher positions of the Police Force?' Reg Tomsett asked. 'My trade in civilian life was furniture making', Bob Woodman explained, 'would it be possible to study this line of trade?' 'Would it be possible for me to attend a local engineering firm?' Bill Spaul asked. 'Is it thought likely that after the war', another asked, 'the closed professions like, diplomacy, law, etc. are likely to open to the common people?' Having established the men's interests, Micky wrote to organisations and businesses for advice on qualifications and opportunities: to the Colonial Office, the London School of Economics (LSE), Miss (later Dame) Margery Perham (Reader in Colonial Administration at Oxford) and Cammell Laird shipyard. Miss Perham warned that jobs in African colonies had little future. She encouraged Micky to think about 'reorganising Britain herself in order to give more equal opportunities'. He urged them to read (the LSE suggested W.A. Lewis's *Economic Problems of Today*): 'we had sent him all sorts of educational books', Clive later told John Cudby's father. Inspired by the BBC wireless program, Micky formed a 'Brains Trust'—the War Office's Army Bureau of Current Affairs greatly approved. Even Clive was impressed and positive. 'Don't omit

Britain and Ireland, showing places associated with Six Troop.

the political side', he urged, on the day Japan entered the war. 'I think a great deal can be done by advocating modified socialism', he advised.

Micky's scheme must be seen against the background of the extraordinary phenomenon of citizenship education in what had become a people's war. Army education grew during the war from a small scattering of army schoolmasters teaching men to read into a huge organisation stimulating men to think about the 'British Way and Purpose' and their future in a post-war world. At the urging of visionary officers and under a sympathetic Adjutant-General, Sir Ronald Adam, the Army Bureau of Current Affairs made the discussion of 'current affairs' a part of military training. One of the triumphs of the British scheme was that it was rarely simply a propaganda arm. Its discussion groups were led not by commissars, but by officers and sergeants inviting men to talk about what it was they were fighting for. Army Education sessions asked exactly the sorts of questions Micky had put in *The Labyrinth of Europe*. These discussions did not just span why Britain was, say, allied to the Soviet Union or what the Nazi creed meant, they dealt with the sort of Britain the war would create.

Even in the middle of a mountaineering course the troop devoted half a day to 'the E.P.'. Daytime sessions formalised the arguments between officers and men in billets, pubs, canteens, in lorries or on ships all the time. Virtually on the eve of 2 Commando's departure for the St Nazaire raid, Morgan Jenkins, Tommy Peyton, Peter Harkness and Maurice Harrison 'had a terrific discussion on post-war policies', as Maurice's diary recorded. The ideal, they agreed, was 'equality of opportunity'. It seems churlish to point out that despite his advocacy Micky inevitably enjoyed an entrée to circles of decision denied to, say, Morgan Jenkins. Clive Burn lunched with Charles Haydon at Boodles and Micky himself wrote directly to his brigadier, and sensibly used his contacts when late in 1941 the commandos seemed to have turned out to be a dead end.

From mid 1941 until they headed to St Nazaire Scotland became 2 Commando's base. For a time Newman's unit wore Scottish bonnets, a sign of their affection for the country they trained in. They moved between Dumfries, Inverailort, Perth (where brawling with Polish troops led to a hasty shift) and lastly, in Ayrshire in south-west Scotland.

The people of Dumfries and Ayrshire especially welcomed the commandos and they remembered the place most fondly. While the officers lived in the Victorian splendour of the Station Hotel (disturbed by trains running directly beneath their windows) their men again lodged in billets. The headquarters of 2 Commando was in Wellington Square, a handsome Georgian precinct facing the Sheriff Court and the Edwardian folly of the Park Theatre. The *memento mori* of Ayr's sombre Great War memorial stood in the centre of the square, where the unit paraded before going off on exercises and training courses.

From the summer of 1941 Six Troop lived in billets around Moffat in Dumfriesshire for long stretches. People in Moffat today recall having commandos among them. Micky, Morgan and Tommy as usual found rooms at the town's handsome but eccentric hotel, the Star, famous as Britain's narrowest hotel. Their men lived with families in the area, arriving and departing mysteriously and at short notice. On the assumption that they would not be returning on their first departure, some men behaved badly in unspecified ways (but including making 'their girls ... all kinds of promises')—so much so that Micky reported that when they returned several men slept in shelters in the park rather 'than face the indignation of their landladies'. The Star Hotel's proprietors, the Butlers, became the troop's special friends—'Moffat will always mean the Butlers, the best friends ever', Maurice Harrison recorded in his diary. Both men and officers kept in touch with the Butlers, returning there from their billets in nearby Ayr for weekend leave.

Moffat—'a lovely place, very prosperous and very Scottish'—welcomed Six Troop. No other troops lived nearby, and the rest of 2 Commando was at Ayr. Despite rationing, food was abundant, on the same scale as in peacetime (except for an inexplicable shortage of onions). 'The troops live like officers and the officers like kings.' Micky was invited to shoot grouse, but he decided that he should take up arms only against Germans 'in the public interest'. So warm did relations become that Micky told his mother how his men had 'made this place their home'.

Meanwhile, life continued irrespective of their military tasks. So few sources remain from this period that it is hard to reconstruct it in detail. But from the sources to hand—such as Maurice Harrison's diary and Micky's letters—it is clear that these high-spirited, intelligent young men continued to respond to the stimulus of lives lived to their fullest. In a pub in the Lake District after a day's mountaineering, Maurice invited a 'lonely-looking' girl, Dorothy, to join a group of commandos. 'She did and I liked her immediately … very headstrong but very charming.' Maurice was 'very excited' to meet her again a few days later. Nothing came of this brief attraction—within a few weeks he was sent away to Edinburgh, back to Ayr, on an exercise in the western isles of Scotland and down to Kent before leaving for his final operation. His diary brims with possibilities: potential never to be realised.

'COMBINED OPERATIONS': MOUNTBATTEN TAKES OVER

By the time the commandos had been formed for a year a staleness became obvious. Charles Haydon acknowledged that the enthusiasm of 1940 had declined. In September 1941 Field Marshal Alanbrooke, Chief of the Imperial General Staff, visited Scotland for three days to inspect the commandos' training. Squired by Roger Keyes and Charles Haydon, Alanbrooke watched commandos training to make amphibious landings. He was unimpressed. Taken to a beach at Troon, near Ayr, he observed commandos landing from open boats: 'much too noisy' he noted in his diary. Commando training, he thought, had become 'far too stereotyped'. Haydon acknowledged that for those remaining in Britain repeated postponements of operations and frequent moves left 'a growing irritation … a sense of frustration'. (As readers of Evelyn Waugh's *Sword of Honour* trilogy know, commandos had gone off to Crete and North Africa in 1941.) Haydon urged the commandos' officers to vary and intensify their training. But Alanbrooke's critique bit deeper. He thought that Britain was 'still thinking much too small' in envisaging raids on occupied Europe.

In the fifteen months of his command Keyes had created a force of commandos and specialised vessels but had actually done little more than mount a few pinprick raids. This occurred in the face of suspicion and dislike of the chiefs of staff of the army and navy especially. The commander-in-chief of Home Forces (under whose control they fell) thought commandos 'largely a waste of effort'. The feud owed as much to Keyes's petulance and attempts to trade on his supposed special relationship with Churchill as to the services' understandable antipathy to a new competitor. But Keyes's command, a staff officer later remembered, had been 'almost entirely administrative': by late 1941 Combined Operations had not fulfilled its promise. A long hiatus followed a couple of premature and farcical raids in mid 1940. Except for an isolated raid on the remote Lofoten Islands in northern Norway, Combined Operations failed to live up to Churchill's hopes. In September 1941 Churchill demoted an indignant Keyes from Director of to merely 'Advisor' on Combined Operations, and in October sacked him. Despite his Great War reputation for daring, Keyes had not delivered the results Combined Operations had seemed to offer. Alanbrooke's bolder vision, frustrated by Keyes, would bear fruit in 1942 under a more dynamic commander.

Newman's men returned to training as energetically as ever, hoping to be sent on the raids they were ready for: 'I never felt better but do wish they would make some use of us soon', Micky wrote to his mother. Through 1941 even a hard training regime could not prevent men from becoming stale, a feeling reflected in small-scale indiscipline. Willie Bell, the Glasgow-born Civil Service clerk, found himself on three charges of 'failing to comply with an order' and 'absence from parade'. Tom Roach, the Welsh-born shop manager, went absent in December 1941 and faced three weeks in Glasgow's notorious Riddrie Detention Barracks, a punishment somehow commuted to three days. He might have served more but for Micky's intervention. When Peter Westlake received three 'entries' in his conduct sheet in Scotland in the summer of 1941—a bad sign—Micky forestalled what could have become an excuse for Westlake to be RTU'd. He had been 'crimed' for being out of billets after 11 pm (for which he received fourteen days confined to barracks; or billets, perhaps). A week later he was up again for 'slackness on parade', a charge Micky dismissed. While awaiting that charge to be heard Westlake was found in the canteen, and failed to leave when ordered. Micky gave him another week's confinement, but he kept him in the unit. They felt a loyalty to each other rather than to the letter of the *King's Regulations*.

Charles Haydon, the commander of the 1st Special Service Brigade, was to become closely involved in Micky's story. A regular soldier, an Irish Guardsman, Haydon resembled a conventional soldier only in his soldierly bearing and solid military and social connections. He remained mentally flexible, striving to understand and get the best from his high-spirited but unconventional units. The commandos' reputation for unorthodoxy contaminated their name as soldiers. Micky, defending Haydon from criticism in 1946, reminded his readers that in 1941, before the force had justified its existence, 'the lurid Press were describing the Commandos as thugs and cat-burglars'. Though a Guardsman, he recalled, Haydon had 'insisted that their discipline should be as strict in essential respects as that of the Regular Army'. The commandos did not always meet this standard. After arriving at Dumfries the unit war diary acknowledged encountering 'some trouble' from 'irresponsible members … losing their self control in town at night'.

While Micky and his men had trained in Scotland and waited impatiently for action, Churchill made changes in the command of Combined Operations. In October 1941 Captain Lord Louis Mountbatten, the King's cousin, replaced Sir Roger Keyes. Mountbatten, a youthful 41, dashing, imaginative and supremely well connected, had lost his destroyer, HMS *Kelly*, off Crete earlier in the year. (He became the inspiration for Noel Coward's coolly courageous Captain Kinross in his film *In Which We Serve*.) Losing a ship is not usually a springboard to advancement, but Mountbatten was soon a vice-admiral with a seat on the Chiefs of Staff Committee, surely the most rapid elevation in recent military history. He set out to reinvigorate Combined Operations. Though like Keyes he was believed to give friends, members of his smart set, jobs on his staff, unlike Keyes he gave his command a renewed sense of purpose. Where Keyes had antagonised the three service chiefs and competed with them, Mountbatten adopted a more constructive approach. Within weeks of his arrival Alanbrooke recorded in his diary that they had 'arrived at a successful solution to the handling of commandos'. Under Mountbatten commandos would mount raids on a larger scale and with a greater range, and they would be made to assist the other services. Indeed, the St Nazaire raid grew out of a need to help the navy fight the battle of the Atlantic.

Other commando units were being given operations. At Christmas 1941, 3 Commando raided the island of Vaagso in northern Norway. Charles Newman had planned to go along with the Vaagso raiders, since he had lent two sections of his commando to make up the numbers. He didn't make it, as he was plucked from HMS *Kenya* at Scapa Flow and ordered to report to London. Newman spent a long, cold, weary journey to London—Christmas dinner was a cold meat pie and a bottle of whiskey in a transit mess in Glasgow—and when he reached Richmond Terrace he learned that he wasn't needed after all. But Newman secured a promise from the chief of staff at Combined Operations that 2 Commando would be given the next big job.

'CHARIOT':
SIX TROOP IN THE RAID
ON ST NAZAIRE

'SOMETHING IN THE WIND': THE MONTHS BEFORE
THE RAID

Newman's men had begun to wonder whether their turn
would ever come. Soon after Christmas 1941 Micky and
Maurice spent an evening with fellow 2 Commando captain
David Birney and his wife, Cécilie ('very gay and understanding ...
an ideal S.S. wife in fact', Maurice thought). Eventually talk turned
to their frustration at their inaction, 'both of us wondering why
Six Troop didn't do Commando raid' on Vaagso. In the meantime,
they continued to train, spending February 1942 in the Hebrides,
practising amphibious landings in what Bill Copland (Newman's
deputy) recalled as 'lovely, calm, warm weather'. Rumours—too
fantastic to be hopeful—spread. When David Paton arrived in
2 Commando early in 1942 as medical officer he was told that the
dawn landings they had rehearsed in the Hebrides were intended to
prepare for an operation in which 'when Hitler went to Norway we
would sail across and nick him'. In the meantime, Colonel Charles's
unit ran the risk of becoming stale. 'The only thing they could get to
fight', Paton recalled, 'was the Polish army'.

Even Micky's enthusiasm waned. His papers from this time are full
of letters inquiring about jobs elsewhere: in the forestry departments
of colonies or the East African police. It looks like daydreaming.
But he applied and was accepted for Special Operations Executive
(SOE), run by Colin Gubbins, the unorthodox general who had
commanded Scissors Force in Norway. On 11 January 1942, Micky
told his troop that he would be leaving.

That evening Micky and Maurice Harrison, a captain and a sergeant, went out to the pictures. Usually so lively, they remained wistful and spoke little, 'both wrapped up in the past'. Micky's relationship with Maurice was uneven: not in taste, education or wit, but in emotional intensity. Maurice regarded Micky, his troop commander, as a special friend. Micky, as he was later to acknowledge, loved Maurice. Their relationship remained platonic, though no less profound a friendship for that. Maurice's pleasure in Micky's company was unfeigned but also unmarked by any homoerotic feeling. On 19 February 1942, Maurice recorded in his diary how he had returned to his billet in Ayr without his key and too late to disturb his landlady, Mrs Collinson. He walked to the Station Hotel 'so finally slept on the couch in Micky's room'. It is one prosaic sentence in his diary, a testament to friendship but nothing more. For Micky, the incident remained one of the emotional climaxes of his friendship with Maurice. In a poem published a decade after, Micky remembered the night:

> *You returned to my room after nightfall*
> *With a story of losing your key,*
> *And I said in casual tones,*
> *Speaking against my heart,*
> *You could sleep in my bed if you chose …*

Micky's departure had Six Troop feeling, as Willie Bell's father later confided to Phyllis, 'very despondent', so much so that Willie planned to seek a transfer to the Royal Air Force. Willie later changed his mind and stayed. Peter Harkness too returned to Six Troop. He had been posted to the Special Training Centre at Inverailort in January, but seems to have wangled a posting back to 2 Commando, as a lance-sergeant (acting unpaid) in time to join those selected for the raid leaving Ayr. Others stayed when they might have missed out. Tommy Peyton almost missed the raid. He had fractured his leg training in rough country at Achnacarry in December 1941: had the accident occurred any later he might still have been convalescing. He too insisted on staying with the troop.

Maurice Harrison likewise almost did not go to St Nazaire. On 'a momentous day', 24 February 1942, just over a month before the raid, Maurice was offered the chance to leave the troop and join a commando-training mission to go to the Middle East, India or perhaps Australia. He had four hours to decide. Maurice recognised that this was a day on which 'I literally hold my life in my hands ... '. He decided against leaving the troop, partly because an overseas posting would separate him from his family in Streatham. 'What would have happened if I'd made different decisions?', he wondered, sure that he was right, but realising that 'I shall probably never know'.

At last, later in February, Haydon again summoned Colonel Charles Newman to Richmond Terrace. This time it was on, though only Newman knew the objective of their first operation. Haydon advised Newman to have his unit train in street-fighting by night and laid down a policy of 'No Questions and No Answers'; still, all 2 Commando's officers sniffed 'something in the wind', Bill Copland remembered. Micky, disappointed in the desk job he had found at SOE in London, learned that Colonel Charles would have him back with 2 Commando. The morning after he slept with Dinah Jones for the first and only time, he bumped into Newman in the Mall. 'This is it!' Newman said. Micky returned, to the great joy of his troop.

Early in 1942, Allied fortunes reached their lowest ebb. Japan's entry into the war brought swift and shocking defeats in South-East Asia, culminating in the fall of Singapore in mid February. With disasters in Russia—the Germans got almost to Moscow before winter stopped them—this was among the war's blackest times. Maurice Harrison confessed to his family how depressing he found the war news. 'We do seem bad at this sort of thing', he admitted, 'it'll be a long time before we win', though he never lost his faith in ultimate victory. Maurice was not alone. 'The prevailing mood', the Ministry of Information reported to Cabinet, 'has been one of frustration and loss of interest in the war and war news'. Reports from regions across Britain detected a mood of 'fatalism', and the 'desire for successful *British* military action': Britain's alliance with the United States, only three months old, was already generating resentment that the new, more powerful ally was making the news. A commando raid would meet the desire for Britain to strike a blow at what seemed like the war's darkest moment.

By then 2 Commando was as ready as it could be. Already many men had become restive at their prolonged training and inaction and like Micky tried to get away. They had finally finished with the increasingly embarrassing 'SS' badges. In early February, just before they were informed about the St Nazaire raid, 2 Commando's men had put up shoulder flashes reading 'COMMANDO' in white on a black cloth background. 'We have come into the open', Maurice Harrison told his parents. Ironically, as soon as they were ordered to prepare for the operation they were told to discard the flashes on the grounds of security.

'HIGH STRATEGY': THE ORIGINS OF 'CHARIOT'

The Atlantic remained Britain's most crucial theatre of war. Britain faced its longest and most critical battle against the U-boats. The submarine peril, Churchill famously admitted, was 'the only thing that ever really frightened me'. Almost every day reports reached the Cabinet War Rooms of a convoy attacked or a merchant ship sunk. By early 1942, the initiative had fallen again to the Germans. Though it would ultimately cost it the war, Germany's declaration of war against the United States allowed its submarines to prey upon shipping along America's eastern seaboard, and the U-boats' 'happy time' continued for another six months. In European waters it seemed that Germany would be able to add powerful surface warships to join its undersea fleet. In January the battleship *Tirpitz* (the *Bismarck*'s sister ship) moved to Foettenfjord in Norway, posing a potential threat to the Arctic convoys supplying the Soviet Union. The following month the battle-cruisers *Scharnhorst* and *Gneisenau*, as the Admiralty had predicted, humiliatingly evaded British attempts to stop them making for Germany. Fearing another irruption by German battleships into the Atlantic (in May 1941 the *Bismarck* had been sunk while attempting to run for St Nazaire), Admiralty planning staff pondered how they could disable the one port on the French coast capable of accommodating the *Tirpitz*. To do so would remove the threat of German surface ships to the convoys and would free British battleships for other theatres. The answer, a raid on St Nazaire, arose as a pre-emptive blow in the battle of the Atlantic.

An unknown naval staff officer first put the idea for an attack on St Nazaire in July 1941. Motor torpedo boats and 'a small landing party' could, he suggested, attack St Nazaire's huge dry dock. Admiralty staff officers batted the idea around for several weeks and in August the Commander-in-Chief Plymouth, in whose operational area St Nazaire fell, took on the task of developing a plan. At the outset, they accepted that the attack would be costly. Whatever warships they used they thought—and they canvassed submarines, destroyers, torpedo boats and fast minelayers—'we must accept the very possible if not probable loss of the landing party'. Planning lapsed during the final months of Roger Keyes's tenure at Combined Operations, but in early February 1942 Mountbatten revived the idea, and took it to the War Cabinet. Churchill and the chiefs of staff approved what Churchill later described (both in his memoirs and in his history, *The Hinge of Fate*) as 'a deed of glory intimately involved in high strategy'. Mountbatten accepted that his plan would be 'somewhat hazardous'. Taking an understandably pragmatic view, he thought the stakes—a couple of hundred soldiers and a few hundred sailors— 'not high', but 'the prize was considerable'. Churchill said that he 'fully approved' the idea. If an attack on St Nazaire's dry dock needed soldiers, that meant commandos.

The commandos had trained for just such a daring plan. Until now they had been used in a series of pinprick raids of limited value, and often worth as much in propaganda as strategy. This raid offered a chance to employ the tactics they had learned so well over so many frustrating months. Under Mountbatten's direction, they had already begun to raid with renewed vigour. The commandos followed their attack on Vaagso with a daring swoop on a German radar station at Bruneval, near Le Havre, exactly a month before St Nazaire. But both the objective, and the raiding force, would be on a grander scale than these operations.

St Nazaire's massive dry dock, the 'Forme Ecluse', had been built in the late 1920s. It had witnessed the creation of the *Normandie*, the world's largest ship to have been built up to that time, an ocean liner symbolising France's greatness. The attackers called it the Normandie Dock. As its French name suggested, the Forme Ecluse was able to exclude water, sucked out by three massive engines located in pumphouses ranged alongside the dock. Ships entered the dock by the great lock gates, technically known as caissons, as big as the side of a block of flats and nearly 100 feet thick. It was the outer caisson that the *Campbeltown* was to crash through at the climax of the attack.

The commando force comprised two parts: thirteen demolition parties drawn from six other commando units, and a protection force made up of most of Charles Newman's 2 Commando. The demolition parties, each comprising an officer and several men, sharpened their training in demolition at Burntisland, a port on the north shore of the Firth of Forth, at Barry Docks, Cardiff and at the King George V graving dock at Southampton. (The machinery at Southampton was almost identical to that at St Nazaire, and the attackers learned to find their way about it practically blindfolded.) Then they were sent to Falmouth, the attacking force's base, to join 2 Commando and billeted in the Belgian *Prinses Josephine Charlotte*, a Channel ferry, regarded as the first true car ferry, requisitioned as a now overcrowded depot ship. While most now suspected that a long-awaited operation might be afoot, none besides Newman and his naval counterpart knew that it was to be St Nazaire.

'A GREAT LOT OF LADS': SIX TROOP PREPARES

Operation 'Chariot', as it was called, came together rapidly. Because St Nazaire lay on an estuary entered by a narrow channel covered by heavy guns, the raid had to be mounted on a high spring tide.

This would give just enough water over the shoals to allow a surprise attack. The only possible date was late in March. The Chiefs of Staff Committee approved the outline plan on 25 February, just a month before the force sailed.

Meanwhile, Newman went to London and then Falmouth and worked with the naval force commander Robert Ryder, a bearded veteran of both polar exploration and the battle of the Atlantic. They refined the plan passed on from headquarters at Plymouth. After much thought and argument, the plan for attack at last resolved into a relatively simple but very risky and probably costly scheme. An old ship—described in the planning documents as 'the expendable destroyer'—was to ram the dock gates. Commando demolition teams would pour out, then the destroyer, with a delayed-action charge of 4.5 tons of high explosives, would blow apart the dock gates. Meanwhile a force of commandos, carried in motor launches, would land to protect the demolition parties from the inevitable German reaction. A raid by 60 bombers would, they hoped, distract the defenders and the launches would carry the raiders home after what was expected to be two hours' ashore.

While Mountbatten's appointment signalled the beginning of a more co-operative relationship between the three services, the Royal Navy's support for Chariot remained niggardly. The planners had hoped for two old destroyers, but the Admiralty had allotted only one, HMS *Campbeltown*, under Lieutenant Commander Sam Beattie (a tall, handsome officer sporting an Elizabethan beard). HMS *Campbeltown*, one of the 50 old American destroyers obtained in exchange for bases in the Caribbean, was stripped of its usual armaments and lightened to pass over the shallow approaches to the port, and converted to resemble a German warship.

The attacking force comprised a fast motor torpedo boat (MTB 74), a motor gun boat (MGB 314) carrying the headquarters party, and twelve, later sixteen Fairmile B motor launches, each carrying about fifteen soldiers. The launches, 112 feet long and of mahogany plywood, formed the mainstay of the Royal Navy's Coastal Forces flotillas. With the more powerful and celebrated motor torpedo boats, they warred with the *Kriegsmarine*'s E-boats for the control of the English Channel and the North Sea. Powered by two

Europe, showing St Nazaire and the prisoner-of-war camps in which Six Troop men were held.

petrol engines, they could run at about 16 knots, with a range of about 1500 miles. Still, this would not get them to and from St Nazaire, so deck tanks were hastily fitted. Two officers and fourteen sailors crewed each motor launch, though few had any idea of the task until they sailed and none was given the chance to volunteer for it.

Lieutenant Commander Billie Stephens commanded ML 192, the launch on which most of Six Troop were to enter action in the raid. Stephens's men had been expecting to hand over their launches to Free French crews early in March, but instead were ordered to join a force assembling at Falmouth. As a cover story, the launches were referred to as an anti-submarine flotilla, and tropical stores arrived to spread the idea that they were heading for Gibraltar and parts south. At St Nazaire, each launch's commander had an exact point to steer for. Six Troop's were to land around the Old Entrance and make for the far end of the dock to destroy German gun positions and hold the perimeter while the demolition parties re-embarked on launches.

The attacking force included two journalists, Gordon Holman from the *Daily Telegraph* and Ted Gilling from the *Exchange Telegraph*. Holman, a bespectacled 38-year-old, was, as a colleague admitted, 'not the Commando type', but he had gone on the Lofoten raid and had now boarded the *Campbeltown* for Operation Chariot. Ted Gilling was to play a part in Micky's family's ordeal. Officials in the Ministry of Information, whose job was to support and secure the war effort rather than inform the public, had worried for months before the raid that the publicity the commandos had attracted had 'not been on quite the right lines'. Newspapermen had chided War Office staff officers that the sorts of stories they had instigated or allowed had been 'very feeble stuff'. (This was the judgment of Walter Monckton, Clive's patron and now Director General of the Ministry of Information.) Stories about Combined Operations, Monckton had complained three weeks before the raid, '[make] us all look silly and amateurish'. The amateurism grew out of the Combined Operations staff not trusting Ministry of Information officials and especially journalists with advance notice of operational plans. In return, Ministry of Information officials patronised Mountbatten for his naïve ideas about when communiqués could be released. Brendan Bracken, the

Minister for Information, explained that a press release intended for the nine o'clock news needed to be distributed somewhat earlier than 8.30 in the evening. Still, in a war dominated by propaganda, everyone understood the need for trained journalists to report actions.

Here a mystery needs to be sorted out. Micky's troop was almost at full strength—over fifty men. The Chariot plan called for only a couple of hundred men in the assault and protection parties. Micky and the other troop commanders had to select who would go and who would stay—all had volunteered. But Bill Copland passed on the order to select the most suitable and only about half the troop was picked. Even in the memories of those who survived, those who did not go seem to fade from the St Nazaire story. They remained in Ayr, 'left-out-of-battle', as the army said, to rebuild the unit if things went wrong. As a result, Micky's troop, in its memory and in this story, numbers him, his two officers (Tommy Peyton and Morgan Jenkins) and 26 men. Early in March Bill Copland took those selected aboard the *Prinses Josephine Charlotte* from the Clyde to Falmouth—no one knew their eventual destination.

The raid had to be kept secret, not only from the Germans, but also from the people of Falmouth, and even from commandos and sailors until the last possible moment. Senior officers became preoccupied with secrecy, and later investigated startling but unjustified claims that breaches had compromised the raid's security. Another officer who would figure in Six Troop's story, Stuart Chant, suspiciously reported seeing a merchant seaman (one of the *Prinses Josephine Charlotte*'s stewards) looking at a map. All the same, the commandos' presence became an open secret in Falmouth. The commandos, supposedly confined aboard the *Prinses Josephine Charlotte*, were plainly visible from shore. In any case, men slipped ashore on one pretext or another, the merchant seamen, it seems, unsupervised (though in fact they learned of the force's destination just twenty minutes before it sailed). The very concentration of vessels in the harbour, including the largest force of motor launches yet assembled, aroused speculation. Some actions seemed almost calculated to fuel curiosity. On 20 March the commandos even made a route march through the Cornish countryside. As they returned through Falmouth civilians came out into the streets, cheering. Though they had taken down their 'COMMANDO' shoulder flashes the profusion of regimental badges and the unusual rucksacks gave the game away. 'Everybody seemed to know we were not ordinary troops', a man in a 12 Commando demolition party recorded in his diary. These and other breaches led a commando officer to describe it as 'the worst bit of security I have seen'. Propaganda and security policies worked at cross-purposes.

In beautiful spring weather sailors and commandos readied their vessels and kit. Gradually the raiders were briefed on their part in the attack, officers first, on 17 March. Micky recalled that Tommy Peyton gasped at the plan's audacity. In a gesture typical of his own insouciance, he recalls sending an ironic note up the table to Colonel Charles, 'Please may I go back to my unit?' Newman read it out; everyone laughed, and the tension relaxed. Micky the poet sensed the inevitable underlying anxiety. In verses written 'Just before the Briefing for St Nazaire' he saw how

> *Laughter and jokes hide*
> *the inner mind,*
> *as now we await*
> *brief knowledge of our fate.*

He foresaw 'for all but few ... something new ... the sight of dead'. And he examined his own feelings:

> *Though trained for long*
> *and hard affrays.*
> *Body perfect, mind alert;*
> *what use in these*
> *if courage flees?*

The commandos' easy camaraderie between officers and men persisted. While officers were briefed separately to their men, in the evenings they sat together, a very different atmosphere to the formality usual in British units. Corporal Wright described his mess aboard the *Prinses Josephine Charlotte* one evening, in which a lieutenant sat playing draughts with one of his men on one side of him while another sat beside him drinking tea.

The next day Colonel Charles introduced his men to the task that would cost so many their lives. He gravely told them that success would depend on surprise, not strength. 'How everyone laughed', Maurice Harrison recorded in his diary that evening, 'I wonder why, because it's really rather serious'. But the laughter, he wrote, was not nervous, 'but the laugh of a challenge accepted'. Later, troop officers briefed their men in detail, though they still did not disclose the port's name. Micky described his men as listening quietly and asking few questions. Outwardly calm, they were excited by the prospect of imminent action. They were to put into practice all that they had learned and trained for. 'Everyone is happy', Corporal Wright noted, 'this is Commando stuff'. Maurice Harrison described how that evening he and Peter Harkness had strolled about the deck of the *Prinses Josephine Charlotte* talking over the job ahead. He felt apprehensive, worried that 'I might be afraid at the wrong moment'. But all of them, he wrote, were optimistic at the chances of such an 'audacious enterprise'. 'What a wonderful story it will make', he wrote, reflecting that all of them were 'extremely proud to be a part of it'.

With the launches carrying only about fifteen commandos each and many men having particular tasks, Micky had to distribute his two officers and 26 men into several launches. His pencil jottings, 'Order of landing', are still among his papers. Crossings-out suggest that he thought hard about who would go in which launch. Micky went in Billie Stephens's ML 192. Its job was to land near the port's Old Mole—a breakwater constructed a century before. With him were Tommy Peyton, Maurice Harrison, Bill Spaul, Fred Penfold, Lenny Goss, Norman Fisher, Willie Bell, Stan Rodd, Albert Lucy, Reg Tomsett, Peter Westlake, Arthur Young, and Bob Woodman. Micky changed several men's places on the launch—Fisher and Goss and Woodman and Tomsett changing. Not that it mattered: all of the men he moved were to die. Morgan Jenkins led the Six Troop men in ML 268. With him went George Hudson, Bobby Burns and inseparable friends Bill Gibson and Peter Harkness, their job to protect a demolition party. Micky allotted Dawson, Fursse, Lloyd, Prescott, Tucker and Watt to

ML 156, Bushe, Cudby and Roach to ML 177, and Jack Heery to ML 443. Each had a particular task, but all besides ML 443 were to land at the Old Entrance and move into the docks to protect the raiders.

Preparations for the voyage included taking the commandos on a run to the Scilly Isles, in rough spring seas. Despite being trained in small boat work, many soldiers fell miserably seasick as the launches wallowed in huge Atlantic rollers. On the night of 22 March, the flotilla made a mock attack on Plymouth, Exercise 'Vivid'. Taking on a port defended by Home Guard units intimidated by having to face commandos, the attackers were unduly complacent. Searchlights blinded launch crews and as the commandos stepped ashore, they were collared by jubilant Home Guard troops, who none-too-gently threw some into the harbour. The exercise degenerated into what a sailor called a 'farcical shambles'. At least it gave the naval officers an idea of how disorienting searchlights could be, and there was much comforting reference to theatrical adages about lousy dress rehearsals. Perhaps it would be all right on the night.

'IF IT COMES TO THE WORST': SIX TROOP'S LAST LETTERS

Micky soberly advised Six Troop's men to make out their wills—'it seems so silly', Bill Gibson thought—and to write letters that would be delivered to their families if they were posted missing. 'Micky had a talk with us all', Bill Gibson told his father, 'he is a really good man and has promised all of us that you will be notified if the worst has happened'.

In the meantime young men were asked to write 'almost like condemned criminals', as Bill Gibson put it, the bleak prospect of death breaking into the holiday mood the troop had enjoyed. 'It seems ever so peculiar to be writing this letter', Bill confessed. 'We've just finished our tea and God's lovely sunshine is streaming in through the portholes.' Most men had been on deck sunbathing all day—Bill and his great friend Peter Harkness had become very red.

The pleasure of a relaxing day in the spring sunshine 'and everything looking so beautiful' seemed 'so far removed from the job ahead of us' that to have to write what could be a last letter seemed surreal. In justifying the raid to his family Bill Gibson's explanation drew in its youngest members, his nephews in Glasgow. Having been told in the briefing that destroying the Normandie Dock would help to save the merchant ships bringing food to Britain, he told them that if they succeeded, his five- and eight-year-old nephews 'wee Jimmy and Ali will be getting food that might otherwise be denied them'.

Did the commandos discuss what they might write in their final letters? Though reflecting their individual personalities they also express a common pride. Mrs Janet Burns, Bobby Burns's mother, passed on the gist of the letter she received from her son three months before. She, like many bereaved parents, copied or transcribed letters from their sons for the Burns. 'He said how proud he was to have been chosen to go on that trip as it was one that really mattered.' (Fifty years later a friend disclosed that Bobby had recently been hurt when his girlfriend jilted him to become engaged to another man.) Curiously, while Micky urged his men to write to their families just in case, his own letters to his mother in the week before the raid are evasive and general ('Have you seen *Citizen Kane* … ? … I'm awfully sorry to write such a dull letter … ').

Maurice Harrison 'tried hard to say what I felt' but, he wrote in his diary that evening, 'being so full of life it was difficult to think of what I would write if I were dead'. Unlike Bill Gibson, he remained convinced that 'I shall be O.K.'. But Maurice was a man whose faith in his God and love for his family had already led him to consider his future. Two months earlier he had told his mother how 'you and Dad and the family will always mean everything in the world to me'. Though he was far away he felt that the war had 'brought us much "nearer" each other'. Thinking of how he would feel if anything happened to his family, Maurice gave them a veiled lesson in how they might respond to his loss: 'I shouldn't know how to carry on', he thought, but then realised that 'I must carry on and … together we should have to pick up the threads'. It was counsel that the Harrisons of Streatham would need to heed before long.

Lieutenant Tommy Peyton, sitting on the deck of HMS *Prinses Josephine Charlotte*, writing his last letters to his mother, Dorothy, March 1942.

Tom Roach's last letter, to his father, himself a Great War veteran who understood a man's feelings on the eve of battle, was cheerful. 'Keep your chin up Dad', he wrote, 'I am going into the biggest raid of all times'. He knew the risk, but 'if it comes to the worst' his father 'could always say ... he died for the best country in the whole world'. 'I thought it was brave of him to speak that way', Lewis Roach told Clive. 'I should have done the same thing.'

Tommy Peyton sent two letters. In one he wrote of the ideals he believed in and fought for. In the other, he tried to express his feelings for his mother. The first suggested how powerfully Tommy, the privileged Etonian, had responded to Micky's scheme for civic education. He wrote of how he and his men were 'fighting for something concrete'. He refuted the idea that, as in the Great War, 'this is just another war', victory in which would 'only re-establish prewar conditions'. He deplored the possibility that 'if they survive and the war is won' his men would 'stand a very good chance of being unemployed ... as the forgotten heroes'. Instead, Tommy hoped that 'this war will achieve a better place and system ... some new British Order'. It was long on abstraction, awkwardly couched in a pessimism that threw his idealism into relief ('if they are killed their widows and children will ... [get] a miserly pension ... '). 'Forgive this outburst', he wrote. It was less a fond farewell than a political homily.

Clearly unhappy at such a final letter to his mother, Tommy wrote a second, about two hours before the force left Falmouth, 'trusting to God that the time will never come for you to read it'. If she did, Tommy encouraged her to believe 'that there is every chance that I will be at large in France'. But if the worst happened, he wrote, 'no sacrifice however great it may be is too much as long as it is helping to defeat the enemy'. Tommy felt himself to be 'amongst my greatest friends'. Perhaps his greatest sadness was his inability to convey to his mother his love. 'I have always wished that I could in some way show my affection for you and I would like you to think that we have gone into this fighting on your behalf.' He ended, 'A bientôt and God bless'. Tommy's letters suggest how cruelly war robbed the world of a man growing intellectually and emotionally.

As the men sat and smoked and sucked their pencils thinking of the right words the *Campbeltown* steamed into Falmouth harbour, completing Chariot's little flotilla. Micky caught a glimpse of Bill Gibson's expression and with a sudden intuition realised that he knew he would die. 'The reason I'm writing this at all Dad', Bill had written, 'is just the thought that it might be a little bit better for you to get rather than the dreaded plain telegram'.

'CARRY OUT CHARIOT': THE RAIDERS SET OFF

Soldiers often recall that they anticipated wounds or death but never capture: the St Nazaire commandos were formally prepared for it. Their final briefings covered how to evade capture and 'behaviour if captured'. Charles Newman and Squadron Leader Arthur Evans (who had escaped from German camps in the Great War and written an exciting memoir, *The Escaping Club*) left the commandos in no doubt that they were to 'avoid capture'. Though conceding that 'luck may be against you' he showed them likely routes out of St Nazaire, advised them to find poor rather than wealthy French people and to obey implicitly instructions given by the Resistance. Realistically, though, commandos were also told how to behave if they were captured. This was straightforward. They were to give only number, rank and name ('NOTHING ELSE'), not to tell lies ('the interrogating officer is an expert ... and will not be fooled') and were advised not to try to bluff. As a final tip, men were warned not to look their interrogator in the eye, but to focus on a spot just above his head. This practical advice presented its own security problem: in his memoir *St Nazaire Commando*, Stuart Chant recalled the RAF officer lecturing his men over the *Prinses Josephine Charlotte*'s public address system, with the sound carrying to shore.

The commandos scrubbed and blancoed their webbing belts and anklets. The white belts would be a recognition sign in the darkness. They loaded and checked again weapons, ammunition and kit. Finally, soldiers and sailors loaded the necessary equipment and stores—demolition charges and gear, ladders, weapons and ammunition: not much in the way of rations. At lunchtime on 26 March the Commander-in-Chief Plymouth sent Ryder the signal, 'Carry out Chariot' and that afternoon the vessels of his force slipped out of Carrick Roads. One by one they assembled in a loose armada steaming to the south-west. Fighters accompanied the force, just before dusk a lone aircraft circling low over the water as the British coast disappeared in the haze on the horizon.

The evening was clear with odd patches of mist rising off the Atlantic, the sea calm. Ralph Batteson, a sailor in ML 306, recalled that 'everyone was unusually quiet and watchful, waiting for something to happen'. Even the ebullient commandos, at last embarked on the operation for which they had waited for so long, remained quiet. The journalist Gordon Holman noticed their preoccupation: 'We did not know which of us would be the lucky ones to see those shores again', he remembered. Later that evening they broke the ice and became themselves again. Survivors found it hard to recollect how they felt during the long day's voyage towards the night at St Nazaire. Some, like Stuart Chant, felt 'curiously relaxed, light-hearted even', relieved to see the back of the bustle of preparation and briefing. Some slept in the spring sunshine, feeling, as an anonymous commando officer later wrote, 'more like trippers than anything else'.

The morning of March 27 dawned clear and cloudless. The force had a brush with a German submarine (which fortunately reported it, as hoped, as an anti-submarine force heading south) and with a fleet of French fishing boats. On the *Campbeltown*, realising that the ship was on a one-way voyage, men broke open the remaining canteen stores and feasted and played practical jokes. Robert Burtinshaw, one of Stuart Chant's fellow officers in 5 Commando, led a mad fancy dress party in which he purloined Sam Beattie's cap and parodied the navy to everyone's delight. In the launches commandos were allowed on deck only if dressed in naval jumpers and duffel coats, to reinforce the impression that the force was an anti-submarine flotilla rather than a raiding force. By late afternoon the sky had clouded over again. At dusk the flotilla passed through a vast school of jellyfish. Ralph

Batteson would never forget their phosphorescent glow casting an eerie light on the craft moving through the sea like a ghostly fleet.

By midnight, under clouds and a thin drizzle, the flotilla was passing over the shoals at the mouth of the Loire, *Campbeltown's* stern twice dragging on mud-banks despite having been lightened of every inessential item. Though a German submarine and French fishing boats had seen the force, it entered the estuary untroubled. Everyone went to the positions they had been allocated. On the launches the Lewis and Oerlikon gunners stood behind their guns in their exposed 'bandstands' above deck, while commandos crouched, some lying between the deck-mounted fuel tanks, now drained of petrol and full of seawater. As they approached they could smell the countryside as the shores closed, and even make out clumps of trees on each darkened bank. A few noticed that they passed the rusting upper works of the British liner *Lancastria*, dive-bombed in the Loire estuary in June 1940 resulting in the loss of over 3000 soldiers or refugees.

Above the roar of their launches' engines they could make out the bombers flying to and fro above the clouds and the crump of German anti-aircraft fire: but not the explosions of bombs. While Whitleys and Wellingtons of Bomber Command had taken off to attack St Nazaire their pilots found bad weather over the target—one pilot reported thick clouds below him at 1500 feet. Only three aircraft actually dropped bombs, and they were unsure of the aiming point. Cautiously trying to avoid civilian casualties, bomber crews stooged about above the clouds, dropping few bombs but alerting the garrison.

One aircraft was lost in the sea and three others crashed on landing. A report from Bomber Command to Sir Charles Portal, the Chief of the Air Staff, condemned the diversion as 'very heavy losses of aircraft to no purpose'. Mountbatten was furious at the RAF's delinquency, but he needed its co-operation in future, so cannily sent his deputy to meet Bomber Command's staff officers, and 'talked them over'. Mountbatten's Military Assistant thought that the bombers 'could have done little but put everyone on the alert and … arouse the strongest suspicions that something else was likely to develop'. The policy of attempting to bomb French targets without risking civilian casualties, he thought, 'lamentable'.

HMS *Campbeltown* lying in the dock gates at St Nazaire on the morning of 28 March 1942, shortly before the charges within the bow exploded, destroying the Normandie Dock and killing hundreds of Germans.

It later emerged that while the Germans had radar able to pick up warships approaching the port it could also be used to assist flak guns to fire at bombers—but not both. So the apparently abortive raid in fact blinded the coast gunners from about 12.30 am: exactly when the raiding force entered the estuary. No one knew that the bombers had helped to divert German radar until years later: when David Paton's party of survivors arrived back in Falmouth at dawn on 29 March, his men booed the RAF men they saw on the wharf; unfairly, we now realise.

German actions had also alerted St Nazaire's defenders to a possible attack. The port was an important potential target anyway, strongly defended by batteries of heavy and light guns, searchlights and a naval force. Just four days earlier Hitler had distributed a Directive warning that 'the coastline of Europe will ... be exposed to the danger of an enemy landing in force'. He warned the commanders of 'important military and industrial establishments' to expect 'surprise attacks of a local nature' and issued detailed instructions to meet the threat.

Hitler had become so alarmed at the possibility of an invasion that he ordered a Panzer division to shift into Brittany. Coincidentally, no sooner had this order arrived than just such a threat arose.

As the launches manoeuvred into two columns, on ML 192 Micky went around his vessel shaking hands with his men and wishing them luck before lying down on the deck as the launches ran up the Loire. Most of his men were crouching aft of the bridge, ready to spring ashore as the launch drew alongside the Old Mole. Micky stationed himself closer to Stephens on the bridge, with Maurice Harrison and Willie Bell. As it entered the estuary, the force came within range of the searchlights and coastal batteries. At 1 am German coastal searchlights first picked out the force and some guns opened fire. Stephens recalled how a 40mm gun fired a burst of tracer at the launches. He (and others) watched fascinated as the beautiful bright red tracer rounds curved lazily towards them. 'I couldn't imagine that if it hit us it was going to harm us', he remembered thinking. *Campbeltown* was flying a *Kriegsmarine* ensign and a signaller trained in German codes demanded that the fire cease, buying the raiders precious minutes.

Six minutes away from *Campbeltown* striking the dock the lights picked the leading ships out again in a dazzling white glare across the dark water. This time, German ensigns and confusing signals could not save them. Suddenly, the guns covering the port's approaches opened fire, a tornado of noise and sensation. Strings of tracer arced towards them, and they felt the blast of heavier guns. It was astonishing that they had got so far unscathed.

Blinded by searchlights, with shells striking his bridge and his men falling wounded, Sam Beattie still managed to steer *Campbeltown* straight into the dock gates. It made what Gordon Holman reported as 'a devil of a clout'. At 1.34 am—just four minutes behind schedule—the raid had succeeded. *Campbeltown* had literally hit its objective. As has been told many times, the commandos' demolition parties swarmed down from the destroyer's deck and made for the pumphouses. Working in the dark, commandos, some wounded, swiftly placed charges exactly as they had been trained, and soon destroyed the dry dock's machinery. The force's sixteen motor launches surged along behind the *Campbeltown* in two parallel columns, their skippers peering ahead trying to discern their allotted landing places.

'THEN OUR LUCK TURNED':
THE MASSACRE OF THE MOTOR LAUNCHES

Whether the men of Six Troop lived or died depended above all on the blind fate that had placed them in one launch or another. The troop's 29 men were distributed among five launches, though mainly in MLs 192 and 268, the first and the fourth of the starboard column. After the war—when the survivors had returned—Admiralty staff officers meticulously plotted the tracks of the launches as they weaved drunkenly through the shot-blasted, searchlight-blinded darkness. One by one, the track plots show boats slewing off course, chugging in circles while on fire or simply blowing up. Of the six launches in the starboard column only two were able to land their parties as planned; of the port column only one.

Most of Six Troop, including Micky, were in Billie Stephens's ML 192. It became the first launch to be seriously hit. Just after 1.30 (though no one can be precise about times) two heavy shells, probably from the battery at Le Pointeau, on the Loire's eastern shore, hit the starboard side of Stephens's craft. He recalled the blow as a shell tore through the hull and into the engine-room as 'sudden and disastrous'. The hundreds of gallons of petrol in the launch's tanks exploded. The shells knocked out its steering gear and Stephens could not stop the boat careering out of line and cutting through the port column, heading towards the Old Mole. Telegraphist George Davidson, stationed right-forrard firing a Lewis machine-gun, described the launch striking the Mole on its starboard bow and scraping along, stopping beside the concrete blockhouse about halfway along the breakwater. As his launch grazed the Mole, Billie Stephens shouted to Micky to 'Jump!' Micky shouted to his men, 'Follow me when I

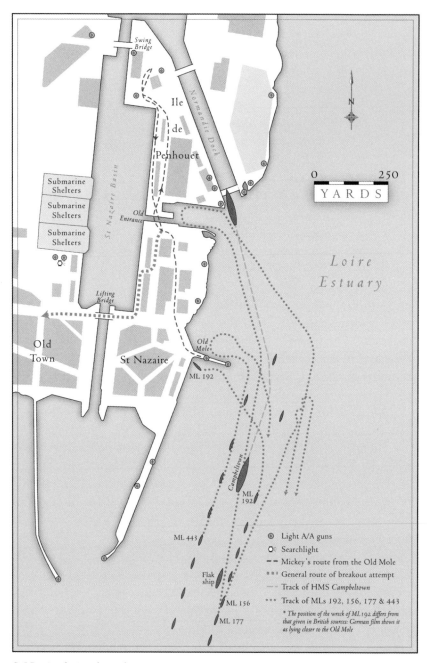

St Nazaire during the raid.

jump!' He and several others—Arthur Young and several sailors—threw themselves overboard. All the while 20mm cannon fire from the gun on the Mole raked the launch.

Arthur Young somehow reached the steps on the Mole and, though wounded in the foot, reached down and grabbed Micky as he struggled in the water. Micky scrambled up the steps. They saw a body—Tommy Peyton's—sweep past in the current out of reach. 'What do we do?' Young asked. 'We must leave him', Micky answered, 'we must get on'. He climbed onto the Mole. There he met a German, possibly already dead, and bashed at his head with the butt of his revolver. In the frenzy of battle, Micky became, as he remembered, 'someone I had not met before and never wish to meet again'.

Meanwhile, the gap between launch and Mole widened. As the burning ML 192 drifted away it broke in two. The living all abandoned ship. 'Our boat blew up ten yards from shore', Micky wrote to his parents, 'we all had to jump ... I somehow got past the flames'. They struggled to swim towards the dock, while the current pushed them down river. Stephens thought it took him seven or eight minutes of near-panic-stricken swimming to reach the wall, when someone hauled him onto the Mole. Richard Collinson, one of ML 192's officers, dressed Arthur Young's wounded foot. Bill Spaul also reached the Old Mole, where a shell struck him in the head, killing him instantly.

In its first analysis of the raid (compiled within weeks and without any evidence from most of those aboard the launches) an Admiralty staff officer concluded that ML 192 had been 'burnt out before reaching objective' and that it beached at the end of the Old Mole. He saw 'no reason why the crew could not have swum ashore as they were only ten yards from it'. Micky could. In his first letter home after the raid he described what had happened to ML 192: 'hit by a shell in the petrol tank just as we were landing'. It seems certain that either shells or flame killed four of the launch's crew and about twelve commandos immediately or soon after the explosion or by drowning as they struggled in the water, booted, fully dressed and laden with kit.

Fourth in the starboard column was Lieutenant Bill Tillie's ML 268, carrying Morgan Jenkins's assault party, their task being to protect a demolition party. It included George Hudson and Bobby Burns, and the two inseparable friends Bill Gibson and Peter Harkness. It turned towards its objective, the Old Entrance, but as it neared the dock wall a shell hit it. The launch blew up about a hundred yards directly behind the *Campbeltown*, wedged in the dock gates. The explosion killed seven of the crew and all five of Six Troop's men, seemingly instantly.

Lieutenant Mark Rodier's ML 177 was the last launch in the starboard column. It carried fourteen commandos, including three men of Six Troop. It was one of only two launches to land as planned, at the Old Entrance. Tom Roach, John Cudby and Paddy Bushe got ashore. After the commandos disembarked Rodier's launch was hit and he and four of his crew died.

None of the Six Troop in the three launches that were destroyed returned after the raid. Among the three launches' crews the proportions were quite different: 31 of the 48 sailors survived, all captured. Commandos were twice as likely to be killed as their naval comrades. Why was this, since they all shared the same small vessels? The answer seems to be that the commandos were weighed down with kit and ammunition; they wore unwieldy boots and had less practice in getting off a sinking ship. Crucially, most commandos crouched on the open decks practically over their vessels' engine-rooms and the petrol tanks.

Many of the sailors who reached home rightly received bravery awards. The Admiralty tactfully admitted, 'those who have not returned are those who are most likely to be deserving recognition'. That qualification should take nothing away from the awards made to those whose bravery was recorded. But it should remind us that too often we laud not all heroes but the heroes whose deeds are recorded. Nine of the sixteen motor launches sank during the raid. Another four, too badly damaged to make the return journey, were scuttled on the way back. (The Germans recovered one boat and used it, until Allied aircraft sank it off Normandy in 1944. Another survived St Nazaire but hit a mine off Italy.) In fact, the few frenzied hours of Operation Chariot caused the loss of exactly one-third of the 39 Fairmile launches the Royal Navy lost in action during the entire war against Germany.

'PROCEEDED ALONE TO HIS OBJECTIVE': MICKY'S MISSION

Panting, lying wet, cold and wounded on the stone of the seawall, Micky acted in accordance with his commando training and with the notes he had made in Falmouth harbour. Though far from the planned landing point, the Old Entrance, he was ashore. His 'Order of landing' notes include the line 'Reconnaissance by me'. He thought that his men were behind him. If they reached the shore able to follow they would: if not, he still had a job to do. He had memorised the layout of the docks and knew that he was hundreds of yards from where he ought to be. Armed only with a revolver and some grenades, he set out alone to make his way across the battlefield to fulfil his troop's mission. In hindsight, this was a Quixotic gesture. The tragic vulnerability of the protection parties' motor launches had destroyed any hope the attackers had of holding a defensive perimeter around the port. Imbued with the commando ethos, though, Micky set off alone.

Naval officers later traced his route in detail for the official Admiralty report published in 1948. A plan shows how Micky made it alone about a thousand yards from the Old Mole to the northern end of the Normandie Dock and back. The remarkable thing is that he managed to find his way in the dark and confusion, with so much firing. At the gun positions he found that their crews were gone, presumably caught up in the chaos of the fight. While waiting in vain for Morgan Jenkins (both Morgan and the demolition party he was detailed to protect had been killed in ML 268) he met Bill Copland and made his way back towards the rest of Newman's party, sheltering among railway wagons on the eastern side of the basin. He later deprecated his part in the fight: 'I had led no one, destroyed nothing, protected no one ...' Higher authorities would disagree.

The demolition parties from the *Campbeltown*, their tasks spectacularly complete, and the few commandos landed from launches gathered in the shadow of railway goods wagons in the dockyard. Small groups and individuals ran crouching towards them while rifle and machine-gun fire echoed about the dockside battlefield. Corran Purdon, the young Regular Rifle lieutenant of 12 Commando, whose demolition party had destroyed the winding house, recalled the white light of the searchlights, criss-crossed by coloured tracer, punctuated by heavy pillars of smoke and orange explosions as more launches blew up. 'There were indeed no ships to take us home', he remembered.

Burning ships and explosions illuminated a nightmarish scene, while the bangs of bullets, grenades and the hammering of anti-aircraft guns continued. The attackers remained outwardly cheerful, though they soon noticed the burning hulks of the launches in the harbour. Charles Newman, who arrived with his second-in-command Bill Copland, said, quite calmly, Stuart Chant remembered, 'Good heavens, Bill, surely those are ours'. Copland, who had retained 'visions of fourteen beautifully empty MLs waiting at the Old Mole', looked out on 'a scene from "The Inferno"' with burnt-out hulls glowing, surrounded by patches of still-burning oil. It dawned upon the raiders that they were not going home as planned.

About this time Stuart Chant was surprised to see Micky walk in, alone. He had in fact almost been shot out of hand. On the way back towards the raiders' perimeter, three German soldiers accosted him. '*Sollen Wir ihm töten?*' one asked his comrades—'Shall we kill him?' Micky, shocked but keeping his wits, replied in German, arguing that it would be a mistake to kill such an important prisoner and giving them his watch and compass. Commandos arrived, the Germans ran off, and Micky reached the relative safety of Newman's lines. He reported that he had got ashore but that his men had not, and asked after Morgan Jenkins and his party aboard ML 268. Copland could tell him nothing. Copland remembered Micky saying quietly, 'I'll wait a little longer for them'.

Newman and Copland conferred. Newman decided that the only course open to the stranded raiders was to fight their way out through the town and make for open country. Later it became apparent that over half had been wounded, some badly, but Newman led them in a break-out through the old town. Acting on their training, the commandos, members of half a dozen different units, shook into groups of about twenty to make their way along narrow streets and past dark warehouses, certain to run into the parties of German troops and sailors who were all around. Led by the assault and protection parties, they ran on, moving and firing in 'bounds' as they had been trained. In small groups, dashing from cover to cover, risking German machine-gun fire and hurling grenades they ran out of the dock area and into the maze of streets of the old town. Few commandos would get beyond the town. Holing up in houses, sheds and gardens as daylight strengthened, the stragglers were eventually flushed out and rounded up by the Germans. An armoured car captured Fusilier John Cudby, one of Six Troop's three men aboard ML 177, after he became separated from Bill Copland's party. It was time to give in.

<hr />

'COMMANDO SURRENDER!': CAPTURE

Billie Stephens had marshalled the surviving commandos and sailors from ML 192 on the dockside. They moved off (ludicrously, he later realised, 'almost marching in threes') but without a clear idea where they were going. Soon a party of German soldiers appeared and rounded them up. *'Raus! Raus! Hände hoch! Raus!'*—'Move! Hands up!' they shouted, pushing the sailors and commandos along a few streets towards the yard of the big parish church in the old town. Here they doffed their steel helmets and cork life jackets and were made to line up along a wall. Billie Stephens felt 'very frightened', fearing that they would be shot, but a German officer appeared and sent them on through the town at the double, most bootless, with their hands held above their heads. Telegraphist George Davidson had managed to slip away in the confusion and hid in some rolls of wire netting. He watched the Motor Torpedo Boat 314 set off back to sea ('like the last bus leaving') and later ran into a German patrol and gave himself up.

St Nazaire's German defenders—soldiers and sailors—had reacted swiftly to the attack and fought back fiercely. They collected their prisoners at the concrete submarine pens on the inner harbour, searching—and looting—as they brought parties in. Watches, cigarette cases, letters and photographs went into a sack, never to be seen again. There the prisoners stayed while the battle raged around them, cold and wet, many wounded, occasionally jeered at by German soldiers curious to see their defeated enemies.

Through the small hours Newman's commandos made their way through the warren of the old town, over the Lifting Bridge and across streets laced with machine-gun fire, making for the town's outskirts, carrying or helping their wounded. Men fell dead or wounded, those hit often telling the others to leave them. Stuart Chant went down with a bullet in his knee, watching the rest run over the bridge, bullets striking sparks off the metal. Alone, he lay against a wall in the shadow of a warehouse for more than an hour before being joined by a young soldier he knew to be of 2 Commando. He did not recognise him and never knew his name, but the two teamed up, though Chant could barely move. He had the commando scout about for a boat in which they might hide, but there was none, so together they waited for the dawn. No one will ever know who this young man was. Perhaps he was a Six Troop man who made it to shore but died before dawn.

As the sky brightened and they lay there unarmed and in silence three German soldiers came upon them. The Germans seemed as startled as Chant and his companion. They were 'jumpy', Chant recalled, shouting and pointing their machine-pistols as they stopped a yard or so away. Chant froze and whispered to the soldier not to move. They shouted '*Hände hoch!*'—'Hands up!' The wounded commando perhaps misunderstood their shouts and stood up. They shot him. They shouted at Chant to surrender but, shocked and stiff from his wounds, he could not move. Shouting into his face they did not shoot, but picked him up under the arms and half-dragged, half-carried him along the dockside to a café full of wounded German soldiers and commandos. The young commando who died so needlessly might stand for those men of Six Troop whose actual fate we will never know.

Meanwhile, Micky met only two men of his troop, Paddy Bushe and Tom Roach, who had landed at the Old Entrance from ML 177. He told them to dump their telltale steel helmets and led them back towards the swing bridge at the northern end of the basin—attempting to get out of the town, as they had been briefed. Tom somehow became separated in the chaos and he was later found dead. How did he die? Was he the man with Chant?

By now the sky had brightened, and Micky and Paddy sheltered in the engine-room of a merchant ship moored in the basin. Soon German troops began systematically searching the ships. As they entered the engine-room, Micky stood in front of Paddy and offered their surrender, in German. Bayonets at their backs, they were taken along the dockside, past warehouses, hands upraised. Micky held his fingers in a subtle but recognisable V-for-Victory sign, though characteristically he later doubted the accuracy of his memory. French civilians watching from their doorways made surreptitious friendly gestures at them. German propaganda teams were already at work photographing and filming the aftermath of the raid.

At mid morning on 28 March (hours later than planned, and with curious German soldiers and sailors swarming over it), the *Campbeltown* exploded, totally destroying the dock gates. A French witness described the dockside as littered with the dismembered bodies of perhaps three hundred Germans. Two days later delayed-action torpedoes fired by Micky Wynn from his motor torpedo boat (MTB 74) went up, wrecking the lock gates at the Old Entrance and making the submarine pens tidal. The Germans remained jumpy and clashes continued for several days. French patriots (especially among workers in the dockyard, many of whom had been pressed into working for the Germans) continued to fight, while the Germans fired recklessly. The continuing resistance, a French patriot wrote, showed 'the French were ready to join their liberators the day the Continent is invaded. St Nazaire has proved it.'

Meanwhile the surviving motor launches had collected sailors from *Campbeltown* and many wounded and made for the open sea. Two launches carrying men of Six Troop were among the seven that managed to get away more or less intact. Jack Heery was the sole member of Six Troop in Lieutenant Leslie Horlock's ML 443, the fifth launch in the port column. Its task was to land fifteen commandos, ordered to destroy the power station and boiler house near the South Entrance. Horlock lost his way and 'was unable to get alongside' and Jack Heery survived. Six other Six Troop men were in Lieutenant Leslie Fenton's ML 156. Shell-fire hit and disabled it in the run up the Loire. Its men abandoned the launch and transferred to a destroyer in the Bay of Biscay. None of these seven survivors of Six Troop landed at St Nazaire: indeed, 60 per cent of the commandos did not get ashore.

'A VERY GOOD JOB OF WORK': VERDICT ON THE RAID
In the small hours, the remaining motor launches roared away from the blazing wrecks and headed down the river for the open sea. One ran into a force of German torpedo boats and was sunk after a bloody fight, in which a commando, Sergeant Tom Durrant, manned his gun to the death, an act recognised by the award of a Victoria Cross; until 1945 the only VC awarded to a soldier in the raid. Four launches, too badly damaged, had to be scuttled. Only four launches reached Falmouth at dawn the next morning: the destroyers made for Plymouth. For a short time, survivors could hope that absent comrades might be at the other port.

Despite the losses, the raid had succeeded. *Campbeltown's* explosion had torn apart both the ship's bows and the caisson on which it rested, ripping the dock gate from its hinges and making the Normandie Dock unusable by the *Tirpitz* or any other ship until well after the war. German claims that an invasion had been foiled seem to have persuaded some, but aerial reconnaissance settled the matter. Some historians have questioned the raid's necessity. In a study of the strategy of British special operations, Colin Gray has described Chariot as 'a heroic example of doing the wrong thing well for the right reason'. We now know that, short of oil fuel and reluctant to risk its last battleship, the *Kriegsmarine* had decided not to send capital ships into the Atlantic. Chariot was arguably a blow against a strategy the Germans had abandoned. The only response (besides pointing out that no one knew that the German strategy had altered) is to observe that the destruction of the Normandie Dock meant that the Germans could never change their minds.

Micky Burn and Paddy Bushe walk into captivity. Micky is making the 'V' sign with his fingers.

The raid succeeded because Sam Beattie placed *Campbeltown* so it drove into the caisson, exactly where the charge could do the most damage, and because the demolition parties were able to get ashore and place their explosives in the machinery. Everything else was secondary, but almost everything else went wrong.

The motor launches' part in the plan failed tragically. The Admiralty's planners had sacrificed sailors and commandos' lives to avoid risking a second destroyer. The storm of heavy and light flak that burst from the German gun positions on the estuary's banks tore into the launches' flimsy wooden hulls. They had no chance against such heavy and sustained fire. Most commandos and many sailors died without even setting foot upon land. Many survivors believed that the Admiralty's decision not to use another destroyer committed soldiers and sailors to captivity and cost the lives of the crews and commandos in the launches. The Commander-in-Chief later admitted 'the unsuitability of the motor launches'.

Still, the attackers missed some opportunities, with costs they would continue to pay. So effective had the Combined Operations security been that the Political Warfare Executive, Britain's propaganda arm, only heard about the raid on the wireless like everyone else. The Germans had a twelve-hour lead on British broadcasters and made the most of it. German wireless bulletins issued on the day of the raid talked about the 'smashing' of an attempted landing, described the ineffective diversionary air raid and the prisoners, and gave reasonably accurate figures for the number of British vessels lost. They lied, saying that *Campbeltown* had blown up before reaching its target and (of course) denied that the Normandie Dock had been destroyed. They insinuated that the raid had been intended to foreshadow the hoped-for invasion and had been defeated.

Indeed, because many French civilians had died in the raid—a fact attributed by the Germans to British neglect or malice—it became possible for the Germans to use the raid to undermine British goodwill in occupied France. British prestige had become a perishable commodity in the wake of Dunkirk, the destruction of the French fleet at Mers-el-Kebir and the Allied bombing of French industrial targets like St Nazaire. With German cinematographers at work on the morning of 28 March filming wet, wounded and bemused commandos being rounded up, it became easy for the Germans to assert that the raid had been decisively repelled. The cinematographers and sound recordists' work was to have significant effects for Six Troop and their families.

In Britain, news of the raid boosted people's spirits. The Ministry of Information's 'reports on the state of home morale' for April included the first positive references for months. People expressed satisfaction at the increasing weight of bombing raids on Germany, the daring American air raid on Tokyo, and on 'the new austerity' (a sign that in clothes rationing at least everyone would share the war's burdens more evenly). Not least, though, 'the growing number of combined operations' helped to make for 'a steady improvement in spirits'. The week after the raid, Ministry of Information investigators—people labelled them 'snoopers'—detected 'a slight though definite rise in confidence and public spirits'. In four regions officials found that St Nazaire was praised as 'a very good job of work' that had 'captured the public's imagination'.

The raid had cost the lives of between 120 and 400 Germans (no one seems sure), many killed when the *Campbeltown* exploded, some shot by their own in the confusion after the delayed detonations. Hundreds of French civilians, many workers but others women and children from the town, had also died, some on the night of the raid; many more in the dockyard, shot by panicky Germans. The numbers for British losses vary between sources, but taking the Commonwealth War Graves Commission's lists as definitive, among the raiders the Royal Navy lost 103 and the commandos 66. These, the British official historian Stephen Roskill thought, were 'astonishingly small casualties' for such an achievement.

A death toll of just under a quarter of the attackers, though heavy, seems a fair price for the certainty that the *Tirpitz* could not use St Nazaire and therefore could not disrupt the all-important Atlantic convoys. As Mountbatten had foreseen, at the level of grand strategy 169 British dead was indeed a price worth paying. On the other hand, the losses fell unevenly on those called upon to risk their lives. Six Troop suffered particularly badly, more than any of the commando sub-units. Newman's 2 Commando lost 42. None of its other five troops lost more than seven men. But of Six Troop's 29 men fourteen did not survive. It alone accounted for almost one in ten of the raid's dead. In the meantime, all of Six Troop had become 'casualties': dead and missing; wounded and captured.

CASUALTIES:
DEAD AND MISSING;
WOUNDED AND
CAPTURED

'A GREAT NUMBER HAVE BEEN WOUNDED':
LA BAULE

Around midday on 28 March, eleven hours after the raid began, most unwounded commandos and sailors had been pushed onto lorries and taken to Rennes, the capital of Brittany. They were in good spirits. Photographs taken by the Germans show them smiling broadly—Peter Westlake beams in a group in a dockside café—relieved to be alive, of course, but also exhilarated that their raid had succeeded. On the way some saw heartening signs of French support. Commando Ronnie Swayne recalled how they passed a brothel, whose 'fairly low class French prostitutes … blew us kisses and shouted "vive l'Angleterre!"' until German troops 'hit the girls about' and stopped them. At the other end of the spectrum, Philip Dark, first lieutenant of an ML, saw a priest surreptitiously give the commandos the V-for-Victory sign. While many were shocked and disoriented, gestures like these helped sustain their morale. They had heard the explosions signalling the success of the attack, and they had survived. The many wounded were taken to the nearby holiday resort of La Baule.

Arthur Young and the rest of the wounded attackers were brought to the improvised hospital at La Baule—curiously, very much like the hotel Micky's father had managed at Le Touquet. Micky hoped that his missing men were among the wounded if they had not evaded capture.

The hospital, in fact the ballroom of the resort Hotel l'Hermitage that had closed for the duration of the war, was the scene of one of the grimmest episodes of the St Nazaire story. Some lightly wounded went with the main body of the captured, including Micky, though he had bullet wounds in an arm and a thigh and a shard of shrapnel in his back. (Virtually untreated, his wounds healed rapidly and cleanly, a result he attributed to his fitness.) Most wounded, however, were taken on the backs of lorries to the hotel a few miles west of St Nazaire. When Philip Dark limped through the entrance of the hotel, he found several dozen sailors and commandos sitting and lying about a large reception room. Most had not slept since the first night of the voyage from Falmouth, and they had spent the night running, climbing and fighting, drawing on reserves that now needed replenishment. They lay exhausted on mattresses, still in their uniforms and boots, watched over by armed German soldiers and attended by some French nurses and German medical orderlies, who gave them water and—memorably for some—lemonade. Germans with Red Cross armbands moved among them, Stuart Chant recalled in his memoir,

Micky Burn, photographed by a German photographer within minutes of becoming a prisoner of war, on the dockside at St Nazaire, 28 March 1942.

asking questions. 'They got little response', he remembered, 'name, rank and number', though, as we will see, the contemporary record reveals otherwise. The German wounded—perhaps two hundred of them—seem to have been treated first (a breach of custom if not of the Geneva Convention).

German doctors appeared, clad in long white coats and white rubber boots, all bloodstained. They at last took the most severely wounded of the British commandos and sailors into the operating theatres towards lunchtime. They carried them into what had been a dining room or ballroom, set stretchers upon three or four tables and began the grisly task of cutting and stitching. To those lying on the stretchers awaiting their turn, the scene was nightmarish. The doctors donned long red rubber aprons, by now also smeared with blood. Several men were treated at once, some seriously wounded, and for some men (Stuart Chant among them) the ether failed to work. Arthur Young later candidly described the situation to his parents: 'some had amputations, and some lost eyes'. He went on, 'several died since capture'.

'We all felt pretty dizzy from fatigue', Philip Dark wrote, but when they slept 'our dreams were violent and nightmarish'. As they woke towards evening and were given a bowl of soup and hospital nightshirts, many looked about, trying to find comrades and friends. For many, such as Corran Purdon of 12 Commando, this became 'the most depressing time of my life', as they realised how many of their comrades were missing. Among the men on the mattresses was Arthur Young, his foot still wrapped in the now dirty and wet dressing Richard Collinson had applied on the Old Mole. Two other men of Six Troop lay in the improvised hospital at La Baule. Albert Lucy died of his wounds on the twenty-eighth. Stan Rodd later told Micky that Lucy 'fell into a pool of fire'. Also probably badly burned was Norman Fisher, who also reached shore from ML 192. Norman hung on for a month before he died on 25 April. Had he been badly burned, or did he succumb to infection? No one now knows.

'OK ARTHUR':
THE GERMAN PROPAGANDA BROADCAST

As the wounded lay in the hotel ballroom, Philip Dark looked warily at the German Red Cross officials. He recalled them as 'two rather loathsome looking types' who 'hovered around' behaving 'ingratiatingly and yet in a supercilious manner'. Dark 'had a feeling that there was a catch in it', and indeed, the officials were bogus. 'They managed to persuade one or two of our chaps to speak into the radio', Dark later wrote. But many more than 'one or two' were duped into taking part in a propaganda broadcast. A transcript records how they were fooled.

It seems to depict German sailors and soldiers rounding up shocked and disoriented commandos on the morning of the raid. The German reporter describes the scene before him. 'And here we have a poor chap', he says, 'he can hardly walk', helped along by 'a young German soldier'. The reporter says, 'I'll have a talk with one of the prisoners', a man who has apparently just been helped ashore. 'Did you jump into the water when you were hit?' he asks. The commando describes how he was aboard a launch sunk while escaping down the estuary and pulled from the water, wounded in the arm. 'You must feel quite cold and shivery', the reporter says sympathetically. The exchange, between a solicitous commentator and a shocked captive, sets the tone for an opportunist and clever piece of radio propaganda.

The reporter seems to gather a few men around him, but actually at La Baule, not on the dockside at St Nazaire, as the listener imagines. He sounds sympathetic. 'Well, it doesn't feel too good, does it?' he asks, explaining for his listeners how 'some of the boys are making angry faces at me'. But he manages to establish a rapport of sorts, and soon gets the commandos to begin giving their names and even some cheerio messages. One by one, they state their names and give brief messages. 'I should like my people to know that I am fit even though I am not at home', says one. 'Hullo to Mother, Father and brother Fred. Am quite well and safe', says another. 'It's Arthur speaking', says a third, picking up the thread, 'I'm quite well and safe'. The fourteenth prisoner sends a cheerio to 'Mrs Young, 14 Brendan

Avenue, OK Arthur'. This was Arthur Young, with his wounded foot. We imagine him shivering in his wet battledress after floundering onto the dockside with Micky in tow, but of course he is actually in the improvised hospital at La Baule. The reporter then seems to turn to another prisoner, this time an officer.

'What do you say?' the officer asks dully, though a dozen men have preceded him. 'Say your name and your home town and then all my love to so and so', the reporter coaches him. Wounded and confused, the officer is slow on the uptake and he asks several more questions. 'My name or my father's name?' he asks. 'Your name', the reporter replies, 'who you are'. 'Stuart Chant', the officer at last says, giving his parents' address, 'Am well'. By the end of the sequence, 24 commandos or sailors have given their names and addresses and many have sent messages home. None observed the strict instructions they had received on the *Prinses Josephine Charlotte* three days before. All sound as if they are dispirited, tired and disoriented, and wounded. Having got the raiders talking, the reporter is able to observe (probably later, in a commentary added in a studio) how 'this miniature invasion' was 'doomed to failure from the beginning … a suicide attempt'. The commandos, he says, 'hadn't the slightest idea what they were to do'. As radio propaganda it works very well indeed, a classic product of Goebbels's Ministry of Propaganda. Clive Burn told Charles Haydon that he had heard of this broadcast on 2 April, five days after the raid. Stuart Chant would eventually be called to account for this conversation.

<hr />

'FULL MILITARY HONOURS':
THE FUNERAL AT ESCOUBLAC

On 1 April, four days after the raid, the Germans buried the dead of both attackers and defenders in the growing cemetery at nearby Escoublac, on a hillside overlooking the sea. The Germans allowed some of the wounded prisoners who were able to walk to attend.

After shaving with razors kept by enterprising commandos and swapping the most presentable of their crumpled and bloodstained uniforms, about twenty boarded an old American bus for the short journey out of La Baule. They formed up beside the bus and, filmed

Commandos march past their dead at Escoublac. At right, Sergeant Stan Rodd of Six Troop marches stiffly at attention

and photographed the whole way, marched as best they could up the lane towards a field now scored with deep pits. The Germans presented the prisoners with a wreath and handed over a list of those to be interred.

Arthur Young told his father how the Germans buried dead raiders 'with full military honours'. Corran Purdon, wounded in the leg and shoulder in the break-out before being captured holing up in a cellar, had been well enough to be taken to view the open coffins in which the dead lay. He was able to identify some. Now he returned to take part in the funeral. One coffin was draped in the White Ensign. Some fifty others lay in a double row in a long common grave. Another trench contained the coffins of the raid's German victims. Two German padres conducted a funeral service, in German, while the prisoners stood by. A small crowd of French civilians stood by the fence in a gesture of solidarity.

The ceremony proceeded in silence, Philip Dark remembered, a hush broken only by the clicking of camera shutters. A German photographer captured the British pall-bearers marching past the flag-draped coffin, giving the 'eyes right'. One of them was Sergeant Stan Rodd of Six Troop, his back straight, head up, conscious that he represented the dignity of the attackers, honouring those who had not survived. Then Purdon and several others lowered the coffin into the grave. Still weak from his wounds, he remembered the trial of holding the rope, wet and slimy with mud, as he helped to lower the coffin and the relief as the task ended. A lieutenant cast the wreath into the pit. Eight of Six Troop's dead lay in the grave pit: one more would follow before the month was out.

The Germans behaved correctly, clearly wishing to honour the attackers, and later allowed French civilians to cover the graves with flowers and wreaths. The prisoners, Philip Dark wrote, felt 'twisted and unintelligible emotions'. Still shaky and feeling the effects of their wounds, the prisoners jumped when a German firing party loosed off a volley, and could not help starting as further volleys rang out.

'MOANS AND SUDDEN CRIES':
TRAUMA AND BEREAVEMENT

The wounded commandos' reaction to the volleys fired over their dead comrades' grave reminds us how they continued to suffer from the effects of their brief but intense exposure to the sights, sounds and sensations of battle. Those in captivity had to cope with a sudden change in their situation, from skilful fighters, sustained by comradeship, to powerless captives. Besides the physical change from plentiful tea, meat and vegetables to bitter ersatz coffee and weak soup, they had to cope with a more profound emotional shift. They felt as bereaved as did the parents of those who had died in the raid. Some concealed their grief beneath a rough pragmatism—signified by the casual finality of wartime phrases such as 'bought it', 'gone for a Burton' or 'got the chop'. Many of the newly captured men felt severely traumatised. Alan Maclaren, the protagonist of Micky's Colditz novel, *Yes, Farewell*, described the disturbed nights common in a prison camp hut: 'often, at other camps, Alan had heard moans and sudden cries, as prisoners struggled with themselves'.

For months after the raid Micky recalled it as a blurred, silent film. Like the anxious families, he was buoyed by hope. As news reached him of the death of one friend after another, though, it became increasingly untenable to believe that some were in hiding, or had been captured and were held elsewhere. There came a time, in the summer of 1942, when the dawning realisation of the truth—that half of his men were dead—brought on memories 'on full blast'. He saw vividly the guns, the explosions, 'the cries from the boats, the river, the burning oil, and the hideous nature of their deaths'. In his dreams he saw the river and the sky turn grey, saw the shore of the Loire 'strewn with bodies of dead men and burned out ships, and I knew that all those I had waited for had been killed'. 'They had been my life', he recalled. 'Now they were dead.' He turned to poetry to express his loss, writing 'To the Commando': 'And now the worst is fulfilled', he wrote, 'the intrepid are killed'.

Arthur Young represents a different response. He tackled his feelings of loss by writing about them as clearly as he could, by describing exactly how his friends had died. The wound in his ankle had separated him from the other members of his troop, and he must not have known for days or weeks who had or had not survived. Eventually he caught up with the others at Rennes and like them began to piece together what had happened to his mates. After musing on his loss for several months Arthur wrote a long letter to his parents describing in greater detail what he had seen at the instant ML 192 had blown up. He thought especially about Maurice Harrison.

A German photograph of dead commandos lying on the dockside at St Nazaire.

'He was a damned good chap', Arthur wrote, and proceeded to describe those few moments in the estuary, ostensibly for Maurice's family, but as much for himself:

> *While we were in the water after abandoning the ship there*
> *was a good bit of machine-gun fire going on. Harry and [Fred*
> *Penfold] were clinging to the boat's 'Carley Float'. Penfold was*
> *towing the float and when he looked round a second time*
> *Sgt. Harrison had vanished. It appears that Harry must either*
> *have been hit by the M.G. fire or was previously wounded on the*
> *boat and we assume he lost consciousness and disappeared ... He*
> *was quite a young chap – about 21 – of a damned good sort.*

Arthur Young was sensitive and sensible. He realised not just that the Harrisons needed to know exactly what had happened to a 'damned good chap' like Maurice, but also that he himself needed to write about it. Arthur seems to have intuitively hit upon the way to cope with the loss with which he and the Six Troop survivors grappled.

Meanwhile, back in Britain the survivors of 2 Commando also had to cope with the sudden loss of more than three-quarters of their comrades. When we think about 'the bereaved' in war we usually don't include the comrades of the dead, even though they perhaps had been closer to each other than their families. At Plymouth the survivors ate in an echoing dining hall at mess-tables set for hundreds who were never coming back. A photograph taken that day shows a cheerful group of survivors (including Six Troop's) grinning for the camera, presumably on request. The predictable reaction came in the dark. That night they slept in barracks, many sobbing in the darkness, re-living the terrors of the raid in their dreams. One survivor explained simply, 'we were home and they were not, and we wept for them'.

The 'left-out-of-battle' party of 2 Commando in Ayr knew that their comrades had embarked on an operation, even if unaware of the details. Both the commandos' rear party and the townspeople of Ayr read of the raid in the morning papers on the twenty-ninth. The commandos' war diary—always inclined to the taciturn—simply noted, 'Gloom over town'. David Paton, 2 Commando's medical officer, remembered how when he led 28 survivors through Ayr from the railway station to Wellington Square people gathered silently on the pavements and wept, shocked at the loss of so many men who had been so vigorously among them just a few weeks before. The raid affected the unit's morale for months to come. An officer who joined it later in 1942 described being greeted by the adjutant with a large poster covered with photographs of the unit's officers before the raid. He was told—surely depressingly—that of the 22 shown in the photographs only three had returned.

The loss of so many discomfited the survivors. At the end of June two of Bill Spaul's friends visited his mother in Guildford. 'They don't seem to like their new Officers', she confided to Clive Burn,

Survivors of the raid photographed by an official photographer at Plymouth in the days following the raid. This group, who were clearly urged to smile for the camera, included men of Six Troop, and all were deeply traumatised by the ordeal.

'or the new men'. 'No doubt they have all settled down now', she added hopefully. The father of Reg Fursse, one of the seven of Six Troop who made it back to Britain following the raid, wrote to Phyllis to bring her up to date on Reg's doings. He let slip how in the weeks after the raid when he was home on leave Reg had been visibly 'very sad and upset at the terrible loss the Troop had sustained'. He had been 'very reticent and quiet', and his parents 'did not care to question him on the matter'. The parents of Jimmy Prescott, another survivor, also wrote to Phyllis. They too frankly described their son's grief at how 'so many of his personal friends were lost'. They probed more deeply than the Fursses and learned that Jimmy was 'most distressed … he said he felt he shouldn't have returned either'.

Mora Hope-Robertson, the Church of Scotland welfare officer ministering to the troops in Ayr, soon picked up word of the action from the tense mood at 2 Commando's headquarters at Wellington Square. She immediately wrote to Micky, though at the time she could not have known if he were alive or dead, captive or free, wounded or unscathed. Mora told Micky how they were all 'sitting on tenterhooks'. She felt especially for Morgan Jenkins. She had visited Jean Butler, Star Hotel proprietor and friend of many in Six Troop, but they 'could but weep on each other's shoulders – literally'. Unable to imagine Morgan a prisoner, she pictured him 'sitting under a haystack somewhere in France, planning to blow up the nearest goods yard'. She wondered what the raid had been like. 'Were you scared stiff and was Morgan slightly drunk and swearing loudly all the time?' But in the end, she knew speculation to be pointless: 'it's so hopeless to talk when I know nothing'. Few families or friends would know much for months; some never.

<hr />

'BEHAVED SPLENDIDLY': INTERROGATION

As they had been warned, the captured commandos faced interrogation. Some were questioned on the morning after the raid at the dockside— some at the moment the *Campbeltown* exploded. Others faced interrogation at La Baule or in the prison camp at Rennes; most, like Peter Westlake, were interrogated individually by German officers, and, after they returned in 1945, again by British officers to determine what they had said. At St Nazaire they knew not to give more than their name, rank and serial number; though as we have seen, some were tricked into saying more or let slip more than they should have while bewildered. Most of Six Troop's men remembered their training. Some faced intimidation. Willie Bell was told 'that if I did not answer all questions I would not be allowed to send or receive mail, parcels, etc.'. Others saw through the ruses they had been warned of: Stan Rodd recalled that 'They use falsified documents of operational orders' to try to kid men into believing that there would be no harm in confirming something that the Germans supposedly already knew. Paddy Bushe confidently told interrogators when he was liberated in 1945, 'Yes, I was questioned by a German officer ... [but] answered none'.

Commando and naval officers made the least rewarding subjects for interrogation. Philip Dark recorded his interrogation, in hospital at La Baule. Given a cigarette, he was asked:

> *'You are an officer?'*
> *'Yes.'*
> *'I don't suppose you intend to tell me anything?'*
> *'No.' A slight pause.*
> *'All right; you may go.'*

Hitler took the raid as a personal insult. He sent his senior interpreter, Dr Paul Schmidt, to Brittany: Micky recognised him from Nuremberg in 1935. Schmidt's reports of his five-minute interviews gave a very different picture to that given by the men of Six Troop after their liberation. He reported finding sailors and commandos willing to talk, and responding very differently to the reticence of Paddy Bushe. Although constrained by the politics of the Reich—the army and navy refused to allow Schmidt, a mere civilian, to put questions about military matters—the Foreign Office interpreters got a great deal out of the prisoners. Schmidt ('very polite and proper', George Davidson recalled) found most men talkative, except young officers such as Micky. In spite of their briefings, some prisoners tried to match wits with their interrogators. Schmidt asked Stan Rodd how the British expected to win 'when half the oceans are dominated by the German and Japanese navies?' Rodd retorted, 'Yes, the bottom half': a cheeky claim given the naval losses of the previous months. Schmidt admired the prisoners, who he thought made 'an excellent impression, and behaved splendidly', all confident of Allied victory despite their individual fate.

'NO PRECISE FIGURES OF CASUALTIES': THE RAID REPORTED

Soon the first reports of the raid appeared in British newspapers, written with remarkable speed by Gordon Holman and Ted Gilling (who must have returned as disorientated as any of the survivors). Ignorant of almost anything that had happened on land, the reports gave a vague impression of success. Gordon Holman's highly coloured and selective reports appeared in the *Daily Telegraph*. He had gone in on the *Campbeltown* and had escaped on a motor launch, and later rightly received the Croix de Guerre. Artists used his description as the basis of lurid drawings in the *Illustrated London News* in April. Stories based on Holman's reports appeared in British and later American newspapers and magazines, regarded as authentic because he had undeniably risked as much as any of the attackers.

All of the Six Troop families craved news, hoping that in the general press reports they would glean something of their men's fates. It was a vain hope. Wartime news was so closely managed that little of real value reached them. The authorities attempted to limit news to official channels. They gave survivors of the raid a printed notice telling them that they would be allowed to speak to uniformed war correspondents but that 'You will not speak or write to anybody else of any matter ... The lives of others depend on your silence', they were warned, 'IF YOU TALK, YOU WILL REGRET IT'. Soon major newspaper stories carried Mountbatten's warning that 'Commandos who talk' faced 'drastic action'.

If families desperate for news were disappointed by how little was said publicly, Combined Operations Headquarters wanted even tighter controls on coverage. Within four days of the raid Mountbatten had convened a meeting at Richmond Terrace at which senior intelligence and public relations officers dissected what had gone right and wrong in its reporting. They resolved to combat 'certain undesirable tendencies' in the press coverage of Chariot. They considered ways of ensuring that more positive news got out without compromising security. Editors were to be offered 'Confidential Guidance' to ignore the German communiqués that had undermined cautious British reports. Future raids needed what they called, with a worrying lack of irony, 'a genuine propaganda plan'. They decided on tighter control of cameras on future raids, to permit only biddable service photographers rather than uncontrollable press photographers to film men returning from raids, and to warn returning commandos and newspaper editors against breaches of security. They decided to divulge 'no precise figures of casualties'. Families would learn little from the papers, however thoroughly they searched.

All the same, word spread as survivors arrived home on leave. The inevitable rumours arose. Men let slip snippets to relatives or boasted in pubs and one way or another details leaked out. Many regarded a rumour overheard in a bus as more reliable than the official bulletins. As Mora Hope-Robertson wrote to Micky, 'the real news ... not just the stuff they tell you on the wireless and in the papers ... comes in slowly'. The security services picked up some of these rumours, in places as widespread as Greenock (near Glasgow) and Southampton. A telephone call, presumably detected in routine surveillance (possibly from a telephone box near a base used by many men), recorded a man (perhaps shocked by what he had seen) telling friends how, 'There were a lot that didn't come back. It was a hell of a mess. Half of the motor launches got smashed before they could land.' The identity of the speaker and the location of the telephone was censored even in the Combined Operations Headquarters file. In another, less excusable, case, a sailor sporting the ribbon of the Distinguished Service Medal supposedly for his part in Operation Chariot had described his part in the raid in a pub in Edinburgh a couple of months later. He had unwisely chosen to score a pint off a sergeant in a Field Security unit, but evaded arrest.

Despite senior officers' mania for security, it is clear that details about St Nazaire leaked if not before then certainly after. Just over a week after the raid a friend of Clive Burn's (perhaps a tenant of the Duchy of Cornwall) had written from the Scilly Isles giving a surprisingly accurate analysis of the assault:

> *It appears that owing to the heavy cloud conditions at the time, the air support was not able to be on the spot according to plan & that the A[nti] A[ircraft] defence was able to direct their fire on the M[otor] L[aunches] instead, which were mostly sunk …*

The significance of this snippet for the Burns was, of course that it meant that 'those who got ashore', like Micky, 'were unable to be taken off'. Despite the management of official news and the fragments winkled out of a host of letters, Clive had begun to reach an understanding of what had really happened.

'ALL MY FRIENDS KILLED': SIX TROOP'S DEAD MEN

Micky's most pressing worry, expressed in his first letter as a prisoner of war, was 'not knowing what has become of so many of my soldiers'. In keeping with the promise he had made to his men when he briefed them on the *Prinses Josephine Charlotte* on the sunny days before sailing from Falmouth, he felt he had to find out what had happened to the troop. He asked his parents to 'move heaven and earth' to find and send him news of them. He hoped that some were wounded and held elsewhere. There were about one hundred and thirty-five commandos and sailors at Rennes, but within days of the raid he knew that about ninety-five wounded remained at La Baule.

Almost all of the Six Troop families spent months in a limbo of unknowing. Even three months after the raid Micky knew only that Tommy Peyton,. Morgan Jenkins and Maurice Harrison were dead, and that Albert Lucy had died of wounds. He named six known to have been captured. But that still left up to eighteen unaccounted for, and Micky named eight of them: Lenny Goss, Reg Tomsett, Bill Spaul, Peter Harkness, George Hudson, Norman Fisher, Bobby Burns and Robert Woodman. Their families faced the same ordeal, beginning with a telegram. Each read 'believed to be missing in action': no one yet knew or could confirm deaths. Three years later Clive Burn would know Peter Westlake's father well enough to confide how Six Troop's men's parents would 'all remember that terrible night and those awful weeks of anxiety' that followed the delivery of the telegrams. The Burns knew because they had shared the worry. Soon after the telegram, they had all received a letter—actually Army Form B.104-83—reading:

> *Dear Sir or Madam,*
> *I regret to inform you that a report has been received from the War Office to the effect that (No.) .... (Rank) (Name)*
> *...*
> *(Regiment)*
> *...*
> *Was posted "missing" on the*
> *..*

Molly, Maurice Harrison's sister, recalled her mother's distraught reaction. 'Well, you can throw that stuff away', she said, gesturing at glasses and tableware: she was never expecting to entertain again. In a house in which laughter had often been heard, 'she was never going to laugh again'. But Maud Harrison heard nothing to confirm or challenge the news for months. The long uncertainty exhausted both Maud and Molly, the only child at home, who worked in local government as a secretary. Maurice's father, Samuel, a former singer who worked in music recording, withdrew into his grief, but Maud needed to talk. 'She used to sit on my bed at night and I had to try and

A GPO telegram boy delivers a telegram to an apprehensive woman. All the Six Troop families dreaded this moment—and faced it.

comfort her', Molly remembered. After soothing her mother, Molly would be able to cry herself. This, she remembered, 'went on for quite a while', night after night.

While Clive replied to most letters (using the Duchy's typists, who mercifully kept carbon copies), some families preferred to correspond with Phyllis Burn. Maud Harrison in particular developed a rapport with Phyllis, and they exchanged letters in spates as news or hints came to light. Their first exchange, in June, arose from the telegraphese forced on prisoners' sending messages on small letter cards. In writing to his sometime girlfriend Dinah Jones, Micky mentioned 'Harry killed'. But was this a 'Harold', or did it mean Maurice Harrison? Phyllis, who understood 'how much Mickie valued Maurice's friendship', felt obliged to pass this snippet on to Maud. She replied to thank Phyllis for taking the trouble, agreeing that 'Maurice and your son were such good friends and so near in spirit'. (Dinah, overwhelmed, sent Maud a kindly letter and a huge box of flowers.) Grief drew together people who would otherwise never have met.

Proximity to sorrow seemed to lend all affected insights not open to those less troubled, and Maud knew that 'you will understand how we are feeling'. Clive, who had been away on Duchy business in Cornwall, returned to offer his consolation. He thought that a letter from Micky conveying more concrete news of the deaths of Maurice (and Tommy Peyton) had been stopped or otherwise gone astray. He visited Combined Operations Headquarters again (the patience of busy staff officers who had begun planning what became the disastrous raid on Dieppe needs to be noticed) but learned nothing new. What Clive and Phyllis could offer was exactly what Maud needed so badly. Phyllis told Maud—a devout Catholic—that she had visited Buckfast Abbey and had lit candles for both Maurice and Micky. 'I know how much you thought of your boy', Clive wrote, 'and my thoughts have been with you in your desperate sorrow since I heard the news'.

Bob Woodman's mother, Agnes, known to the files only as 'Mrs Woodman' also replied to one of the circular letters Clive began to send to Six Troop families. In an undated letter (addressed in an unschooled hand to 'Dear Sir or Madam') she too confirmed that all she had heard was that her Robert was missing. Nonetheless, 'I'm confident that my son is still alive somewhere', she concluded. Snippets in Willie Bell's first letter written in captivity may have been passed to Mrs Woodman to give her hope. Willie had told his father that he had seen Bob 'in the water after their boat was sunk' though Willie 'can't tell whether he was rescued or not'. Willie meant 'rescued by our motor launches': he was already pretty certain that Bob was not a prisoner. It wouldn't have sustained Mrs Woodman's hopes for long.

News came to the Gosses' home in Brixton by telegram. Lenny's sister Jo had just returned from London after being evacuated to Cornwall. At fourteen, she was able to leave school and go to work. 'I was the one who answered our door when the bell rang', she remembered nearly fifty years later. She took the telegram to her mother. 'I don't think I shall ever forget that day as long as I live.'

Alex Gibson in Renfrewshire learned of his son Bill's death in what he described as 'a very nicely worded letter' written from Mora Hope-Robertson at Ayr. It was the second such letter Alex had received: his younger son and namesake had been an air observer, killed in August 1940. We have already read snippets of Bill's last, powerful letter, written from the *Prinses Josephine Charlotte* in Falmouth harbour. But it seems that Bill did not post it direct to his father. He left it to Mora Hope-Robertson to post if he did not return. She had delayed sending it—because she, like everyone else, waited, hoping for 'missing' to turn into 'captured'—but eventually, in early June, she posted it to Gibson's family. By a misguided kindness, a desire to soften the blow, Alex Gibson was not to read his son's last words for a further two months. He now read how Bill knew he was to go on a raid 'virtually suicide', but one whose 'repercussions will be very far reaching'. He read of Bill's admiration for Micky, and for his comrades, especially Peter Harkness. Bill had asked his father to write a 'wee note to my Irish girl'—Anne Brien—'to let her know what has happened'. And he was at last able to read his son's final words to him. 'You've been the best pal I've ever had', Bill had written.

> *Well Dad dearest, I'll close now. Don't worry and don't be too unhappy, remember what you always told me to keep my chin up ... I can only hope that by laying down my life the generations to*

*come might in some way remember us and also benefit from what
we've done.*

'I'm proud of my son', Alex wrote to Clive, 'and glad that it was in
such a noble attempt he lost his life'. He invited Clive to offer Bill's
letter for publication (Alex had recently read the propaganda booklet,
Combined Operations: the Official Story of the Commandos) and wondered
if it might be suitable. He thought that Clive's contacts in Whitehall
could place it. Clive, who showed that he had understood Bill's letter by
paraphrasing it, described it as 'a magnificent letter', but protectively
thought it 'too intimate' for publication. Both together, but also in a
very real sense alone, the Six Troop families faced the uncertainty of
not knowing their sons' fates.

'TO RAISE NO FALSE HOPES': THE CASUALTY BRANCH

More than any other kind of news, the notification 'missing' threw
families into a terrible uncertainty. Did it mean 'dead but they won't
or can't tell me' or did it mean 'alive but they don't know where'? In
fact, the War Office invariably had no idea except that they had not
returned. Not for weeks—not until well into the summer of 1942—
would families be given more definite news, and some would wait until
year's end before learning the worst. Many would cling to the flimsiest
of hopes, building on scraps of news, hearsay and supposition.

Half a dozen agencies had a part in the bureaucracy of grief. The
Red Cross, the various army records offices (especially the Rifle Record
Office in Winchester), 2 Commando's orderly room and Combined
Operations Headquarters all had a hand in the business. But central
to the process was the War Office's Casualty Branch. The Casualty
Branch was one of the War Office's busiest departments. Early in
the war it had been shifted out of London: ironically to Liverpool,
which suffered a blitz comparable only to the capital's in the winter of
1940–41. The office occupied the Blue Coat School, one of Liverpool's

oldest schools, itself bombed in 1941. It maintained records of what the army called 'casualties'—a technical or even bureaucratic term covering all of the fates war can inflict upon those drawn into it. In practice servicemen could be listed as dead—killed in action or died of wounds—wounded; or captured.

The spring of 1942 had been one of Casualty Branch's busiest times. With the Japanese conquest of South-East Asia over 60,000 British servicemen and some women had become prisoners, the great majority in the fall of Singapore in mid February. Defeats in North Africa in the course of the year would impose a heavy burden on its clerks, typists and supervisors. St Nazaire, with just 169 dead and 200 prisoners, was not to be compared with disasters in Hong Kong, Malaya, Singapore, Burma and Tobruk. To families, understandably concerned with the fate of individuals, the Casualty Branch's necessary bureaucracy became a frustration.

The Casualty Branch's clerks faced a dreadful task with inadequate means. Those with whom it dealt were wracked by loss or distracted by anxiety. Its staff relied on a grim and unbending procedural rectitude, which in truth was necessary in people whose job was to tell relatives over and over that their sons and husbands had died. At first sight heartless, its internal history—commissioned as a guide against the likelihood of having to do it all again in the event of a third world war—explains its methods. It almost persuades that, in the absence of a caring, sharing, counselling philosophy, its brisk approach to mass grief doled out in family-sized portions was perhaps at least fair.

In communicating with casualties' families its first aim was to be 'immediately intelligible to distraught and often illiterate' relatives. The complexity and circumlocution of officialese circa 1940 acted against this sensible and humane ideal. Clerks habitually wrote in the passive tense, and the branch's officers set a stern standard of proof. They resolved to 'quote no unverified information and to raise no false hopes'. Friends and comrades had no such scruples, of course, a discrepancy which made the Blue Coat School clerks look unhelpful, unimaginative and unkind even as they strove for discretion and probity. While the grieving families deserve the greatest compassion, in reading the correspondence one cannot help feeling sympathy for clerks who each morning must have looked at the files in their in-trays with mounting distaste. Serving in a tanker in the North Atlantic or a bomber over the Ruhr was worse, of course, but it cannot have been easy working in the Casualty Branch.

While communicating in stodgy prose and formulaic expressions (despite encouragement to word letters simply and concisely, 'shunning ... official clichés') the clerks knew the emotions their letters responded to and indeed provoked. They knew that anxious relatives were prone to criticise tardiness and vagueness in letters, and learned that some relatives blamed the War Office for the deficiencies of military documentation. The adjutants of units in action, for example, often failed (for understandable reasons) to record exact places or dates of death or burial, shortcomings which looked less excusable when put down on paper by a civilian clerk writing from an office in Britain. Accordingly, the letters—known as 'notifications' in the branch's jargon—were phrased as royal messages: 'The Queen and I offer you heartfelt sympathy', they began. Typed by civilian secretaries in Liverpool, they were shipped south to be franked in London to give the illusion that they had been posted from Buckingham Palace.

Everyone understood that a 'royal message of sympathy' was needed rather than or as well as rapid, efficient notification of news. Months before the war's outbreak Whitehall officials had pondered many of the implications of the war they knew would come. Among the myriad details of mobilisation and re-armament, they considered 'our intentions in a future war with regard to the expression of the personal sympathy' of ministers and the King. In the spring of 1939 an interdepartmental committee engaged in prolonged and, it has to be said, somewhat pedantic debate on who should be notified of deaths, how and in whose name: the sovereign or the relevant secretary of state. Drawing on the precedent of the Great War, some members of the committee anticipated that the next war would be different, though its members disagreed over what they should do about civilian casualties. The file grew to about three inches thick by the time it went to Cabinet within days of the outbreak of hostilities. In the confusion after Dunkirk all orderly procedure fell apart for a time. Orderly procedure ran up against powerful human emotions.

The Blue Coat School clerks discovered that not all 'families' were united in grief. Death sparked or exposed breaches between parents and daughters-in-law especially. Understanding supervisors had their clerks write to both. Their intention was to efface any suggestion that the missing 'have been forgotten, and still more that proper respect has not been shown to the dead'. Inevitably, though, the Casualty Branch found, a small number of correspondents, 'usually bereaved parents or wives whose sense of loss became an obsession wrote abusive letters and could not be satisfied'. Families unable to face the fact of a death notice often resisted accepting an official word. Some remained convinced that they could recognise the missing in photographs taken in prisoner-of-war camps, or believed against all the evidence that their man was alive but suffering from loss of memory. The fodder of stock plots in pulp fiction or supporting films at the pictures, these sad claims were, the Casualty Branch found, 'repeatedly made'. In every case investigated, the claims turned out to be false. As we will see, though, for Six Troop, a German photograph would be crucial for two families.

Casualty lists had been published in the first months of hostilities. Soon, their magnitude—on one day in June 1940 over three thousand men died aboard the bombed transport *Lancastria* off St Nazaire—led the publication of lists to be curtailed. Or rather, the publication of other ranks lists to stop: *The Times* still listed officers, with obituaries for the well known, including several commando officers killed at St Nazaire. Surprisingly for a country supposedly experiencing a profound egalitarian revolution from 1940, the discrepancy in attention paid to dead officers and their men 'appears to have passed unnoticed' as the branch's official internal history commented. Death notices inserted by families in local and provincial newspapers met the need formerly filled by official casualty lists. There the full impact of the trauma can be seen.

Half-heartedly seeking to explain its process, the War Office considered engaging a popular and effective speaker on the wireless (perhaps J.B. Priestley or the *Brains Trust*'s Professor Cyril Joad) to explain its procedures, but even the branch's own history admitted that it was 'not in the least keen'. Even a vague attempt to describe how families learned of their men's fates 'without encouraging false hopes or undue depression' faltered, and a public explanation was thought 'really best left unattempted'. The secrecy of the St Nazaire raid made the circulation of news even less likely. The Casualty Branch employed 'Hospital Searchers', who would scour wards and medical records for individuals posted as 'missing': a legacy of the Great War, when men driven mad and dumb from shell shock might languish anonymously in hospitals. Among the few exceptions to the rule were the casualties of the raids on St Nazaire and, later in 1942, Dieppe. Searchers were denied the details of missing commandos partly for vague 'security reasons', but mainly because 'it was believed that many men were still at large in the areas attacked'. The Chiefs of Staff Committee placed a temporary ban on inquiries to the International Red Cross in Geneva for those men.

While hoping that missing men might turn up as evaders in the meantime, families were told nothing. Many were desperate to hear a particular name; like Morgan Jenkins's family.

'MR JENKINS ... KILLED AS WELL': MORGAN'S FILE

Of Six Troop's fourteen dead, only one had been married: Second Lieutenant Morgan Jenkins. None of Clive and Phyllis's correspondence had been with Mrs Doris (or Edna) Jenkins, and there are few references to him in the Burns' papers. Clive had written to Ronnie Mitchell, the adjutant at Ayr, asking for details of Edna Jenkins (the name by which he knew her), without a reply, it seems. In 1943, Lewis Roach sent Clive a cutting from the *South Wales Echo* suggesting that Morgan's wife lived in London, but the Burns do not seem to have found her. Indeed, though Micky and Morgan had shared a room at times it seems that Micky did not know that Morgan was married. The story of Morgan Jenkins's death remains separate from Six Troop's as it is told in Micky's parents' file, but it is in many ways representative of all of the casualties of the raid.

Lieutenant Morgan Jenkins, in a photograph that hints at his attractiveness.

Morgan's army personnel file fills in the gaps in the records kept by Clive and Phyllis. It holds no less than thirty separate entries between the 'Missing' notification sent on 1 April 1942 to the final 'Death file opened by Registry' almost exactly a year later. Morgan's sister Gwen received a telegram on 1 April, and Edna a letter four days later. For the rest of 1942, though, Mrs Jenkins received no word, because there was no certainty about Morgan's fate.

The War Office pursued investigations into the fate of men aboard Morgan's launch, ML 268, diligently. By July 1942 the War Office had received a photostat of a letter written from Rennes by Morgan's friend Second Lieutenant 'Tiger' Watson to his father about the raid. 'Morgan Jenkins (my mad Welsh friend) was drowned, poor old boy', Watson wrote. 'He could not swim. He was a good chap ...' It may seem strange that one of Newman's officers could go through more than a year's commando training and not learn to swim, but life is made up of small, tragic ironies.

The War Office already had Micky's letter referring to Morgan as dead. Neither officer's report, however, said that they had *seen* him dead. The War Office checked with both 2 Commando and with Combined Operations Headquarters to establish who Micky meant. Then it sent yet another query to Germany, an inquiry form to the International Red Cross to check with Charles Newman that the men said to be dead had been seen dead. In fact, it sent three inquiries, in July, September and November. The November query finally reached Newman in his prison camp in Germany.

Meanwhile Morgan's family in Wales had also contacted the Red Cross seeking news. On 6 January 1943 Madame Morier of the International Red Cross Agence Centrale Des Prisonniers De Guerre at Geneva sent a wire to Margaret, the Dowager Lady Ampthill of the British Red Cross. The Red Cross acknowledged the inquiry about Jenkins but reported that he 'does not appear on our records' but they had since begun an inquiry. (Morgan had not appeared in the International Red Cross's records because of course he had never 'arrived' in France at all: he had died on the water.) Lady Ampthill duly contacted Mr Dawkins at the War Office, optimistically writing that she was 'hopeful that Lieutenant Jenkins is still alive'. But the exchange left her in a quandary, unsure whether she should inform 'his relations'—that is, his Welsh family—'who made the first inquiry here'. Mr Dawkins replied that 'I cannot see anything … to suggest that Lieutenant Jenkins is at large'. Confirmation came soon after in a card from Sergeant Leonard Bayliss of 2 Commando, now in Lamsdorf prison camp, to his wife Olive in Greenwich. 'You remember Mr Jenkins,' he wrote, 'he was killed as well'.

After these investigations Mr Dawkins wrote to Morgan's wife in February 1943 breaking the news that ' … your husband was on board a motor launch which came under enemy fire, received a direct hit and sank after the petrol tank had exploded … The surrounding water was alight with burning petrol and there was a strong current running …' Mr Dawkins was directed to 'convey to you an expression of the sympathy of the Army Council'. Perhaps on these occasions formality lent a dignity to the blow.

<hr />

'WE WEREN'T ALONE IN SUFFERING': BEREAVEMENT AND BUREAUCRACY

The families of the dead were united in more than grief. Having learned or assumed that their sons were dead, the families expected to receive what were known as, in the jargon of these things, their 'effects'; their belongings. Most seem to have expected to receive a parcel of letters, personal items such as photographs or perhaps a pipe, or keepsakes men had left in their various billets in Ayr. A commando had indeed had the sombre job of collecting the effects of all those posted missing—prisoners as well as those who would be declared dead—and making them up in neat brown-paper-wrapped parcels. But when would they be delivered to families? Already in late May, more than a month after Micky's fate had been established, Clive Burn had had reason to complain to Ronnie Mitchell, 2 Commando's adjutant, that 'the War Office refuse to give up Michael's kit', even though Clive had clearly been nominated as Michael's next-of-kin.

Clive, already thinking ahead to Micky's first winter in captivity, anticipated that it could take three months to get the kit to him. In April he began writing to Ayr to find out how he could gather up Micky's belongings (characteristically 'scattered all over the place'). Ominously, he sent off letters—to the Station Hotel, to the adjutant, to one of the few surviving officers and to Six Troop men who had not gone on the raid. Clive was perturbed to receive no word, but in the meantime he had more pressing matters to consider. He had an urgent reason for wanting to get hold of the kit. For the families of the dead and missing, though, their sons' clothes, photographs, letters and 'effects' were literally their last link with their loved ones. For them the matter became especially pressing. Clive understood the profound importance of these items—perhaps because as an officer in the Great War he had signed over 'effects' to bereaved families—and he acted with determination. 'It is an appalling piece of red tape': Clive was already working himself up to a campaign for the sake of other families.

Dorothy Peyton, by late July convinced by letters from Micky and Colonel Newman that Tommy had been killed, found that the Casualty Branch demanded more than the word of a man who had seen him dead. 'It does not seem to convince the authorities', she noted with sad irony. Clive found it inexplicable and at first seemed patient. However, soon letters from other families fuelled his determination to act. It seems that if he could not bring home missing sons Clive decided that he could at least be instrumental in sending back their letters and spare clothes. Even that poor substitute consumed energy. By July Clive's letters to 'Room 259' at the War Office had become terse. Tommy Peyton, he pointed out, was 'obviously "missing"', and Mrs Peyton was just as clearly his next-of-kin: why could not Tommy's effects be returned to her? 'I should have thought someone could take the responsibility without any inquiry to give the necessary instructions.'

Official reluctance to deem missing men 'killed in action' left many families with nothing to sustain them but hope. While by the first anniversary all of the missing commandos had been declared 'missing presumed dead', the Admiralty still clung to hope. A proposal to the Board of Admiralty in January 1943 to presume the missing were dead was defeated by the Second Sea Lord, Vice-Admiral Sir William Whittle, who felt that 'the possibility still exists that some of those included in the list of missing may be alive in France'. He sought a three-month extension: in fact it was not until 1 June 1943 that the 71 dead of HMS *Campbeltown* and the motor launches were declared 'killed in action'. Perhaps the Second Sea Lord's caution had been justified. The remains of 20-year-old Ordinary Seaman Harold Bott of the *Campbeltown* had been found on a beach, having floated about in the Atlantic for nearly a year. He was buried at sea, and commemorated in Portsmouth on the navy's great memorial to the missing.

The deaths of their loved ones tested the bereaved families' commitment to the war effort. Dorothy Peyton admitted to Clive that she wondered 'if it was right to risk all those wonderful men's lives with such a poor chance of even getting ashore'. Tommy had died when ML 192 exploded: he had never reached French soil. German propaganda—and inept British reports—fuelled doubts like these. German scepticism— dutifully reported in the British press—fostered the view that however heroic the commandos and sailors had been, the raid had been at best only a partial success.

As they began to realise what the task that Micky had wished upon them entailed, Clive and Phyllis reflected often on their relative good fortune. 'We are amazingly lucky ... when you compare us with others who have suffered', they mused, comparing their state with 'people with no news ... or even for that matter Singapore'. The Burns' reflections illuminate the resilience of individuals and families and of a nation. As Molly Harrison said, thinking of neighbours in Streatham who had also lost sons or brothers, 'we weren't alone in suffering'. The ordeal the Burns were helping the Six Troop families through was replicated time and again throughout the war—when a destroyer went down with all hands on an Arctic convoy; Lancaster crews got 'the chop' over Berlin; prisoners laboured on the Burma–Thailand railway: eventually the notifications would go out in bundles from the Blue Coat School. Then another lot of parents would feel the worry and the tears and the black, impotent emptiness. By being so close to it Clive and Phyllis knew very well what they had missed.

Six Troop men who had returned to Britain called at times on their friends' parents: Sergeant Jack Heery visited Isabel Wyles to speak of her William (Bill Spaul), and Bill Watt visited Edith Penfold to talk about Fred Penfold and called on the Burns to ask after Micky. Survivors serving in 2 Commando occasionally dropped lines to those captured and the families of the dead. This contact comforted Isabel Wyles. On the first anniversary of the raid she gratefully told Clive, 'they don't forget'. But when the survivors of 2 Commando moved to the Mediterranean in 1943 these visits stopped: the Six Troop families only had each other.

"Commando film is
winner ... best
this kind yet
THE N
OF K
PRODUCED BY
MICHAEL BALCON
THOROLD
EALING STUDIOS
Red Cross Food
on his postcard

CONDOLENCES:
THE SIX TROOP
FAMILIES

'A GOOD 50–50 CHANCE': MICKY'S FATE

Listening to the BBC's nine o'clock news bulletin had become a wartime supper ritual for millions of Britons. As the chimes of Big Ben died away on the evening of Saturday 28 March listeners heard 'Here is the News'—the script capitalised the noun—'and this is Alan Howland reading it'. The very first item informed them that 'details are still awaited of last night's small combined raid on St Nazaire, the U-boat base on the French Atlantic coast'. That was all: one sentence in a bulletin that went on to give news of 'continued fierce fighting' in Burma, air raids on northern Australia and the Philippines, and Princess Elizabeth's confirmation. A brief reprise later in the bulletin promised a 'further communiqué ... as soon as our forces return'.

The phrase 'combined raid' in the BBC's bulletin gave the game away to those attuned to the subtleties of wartime news and its code words. It alerted the families and friends of commandos all over Britain that their men might have gone into action. Telegrams, phone calls, postcards and letters over the following days would reassure many that their man had not gone on this raid. For about two hundred and fifty other families, the following days would bring telegrams from the War Office's Casualty Branch. Micky naturally became Clive and Phyllis Burn's first concern.

A French doctor had examined, X-rayed and treated Micky's wounds in Rennes. He experienced no complications and healed rapidly. 'I really have been very lucky', he wrote. He was luckier than many. 'Anyhow, you won't have imagined that I am dead',

Micky wrote to his parents a few days after capture. But that is of course exactly what Clive and Phyllis and all the other parents of the missing did fear.

As soon as he heard the BBC news on Sunday evening Clive Burn presumed on having been introduced and went straight to see Charles Haydon at Combined Operations Headquarters at Richmond Terrace. As ever, he followed the principle of 'going to the top'. Haydon confirmed that survivors had returned, but not Micky or Tommy Peyton. The next day Clive telephoned again, to be told that Combined Operations Headquarters had assumed that they had been captured or were still at large. Snippets of Haydon's reassurances found their way into letters the Burns sent to other families that week: Phyllis told Maud, Maurice Harrison's mother, how 'there is always a chance they might have got away into the country in all that chaos'. On the Tuesday, 31 March, the Hon. Sir Piers Legh (Master of the Royal Household, known to his fellow courtiers as Joey) wrote from Buckingham Palace, conveying the King and Queen's concern at Micky's being posted missing. 'Their Majesties', Joey Legh continued, 'express the fervent hope that you may soon hear reassuring news'.

Ted Gilling, one of the two war correspondents on the raid, called, immediately after having seen King George. Gilling had established a connection with Micky from their shared background as journalists. However, he told Clive a story so speculative and in fact wrong that it suggests only that eyewitnesses—even eyewitnesses supposedly as reliable as journalists—are not to be trusted. Micky, he said, had been in 'landing craft No. 2' which had been set on fire near 'the beach', and that Micky and his men had reached the beach and charged, armed with knives and possibly bombs. Gilling could not guarantee that he had seen this, but seemed 'quite confident', Clive wrote in the diary he kept for Micky. Gilling (whom Clive thought 'very sound') gave Micky and Tommy 'a good 50–50 chance': accurately, as it turned out.

All this happened nearly a week before the War Office's Casualty Branch in Liverpool had even drafted the official notification that Micky had been posted missing. While such notification precipitated worry in most families, its arrival at 10 Buckingham Gate caused no discernible response. Clive filed it in the growing pile of unofficial letters and cables and the Burns returned to the task of playing all their Whitehall, diplomatic and military contacts for anything they could give out. By 10 April Clive's network had paid a dividend. Brigadier Haydon himself had written with a list of Six Troop's survivors (five of whom had been in ML 156; Jack Heery had been in ML 443). Either way, Clive was able to confirm that six of Micky's men (Prescott, Fursse, Heery, Dawson, Watt and Tucker) had returned safely and he had Ronnie Mitchell's assurance that he would let him know of other news immediately. Later another (Lloyd) turned up: seven had returned out of 29.

Clive mobilised his friends and contacts shamelessly, able to do what less well connected people could not (though in this case he also used those connections for their benefit too). He contacted Canon Martin Andrews, whose Devon rectory Micky's commandos had visited in training. Andrews had 'had a feeling that St Nazaire was Micky's show'. He motored over from Stoke Climsland to Moretonhampstead military hospital to speak to a commando officer wounded in the raid. (Presumably as a clergyman he had been allowed into the ward.) The wounded officer could confirm nothing, but gave the reassurance—false, as it happened—that 'most of you had got ashore'. Andrews had met most of Micky's men before the raid. He admitted that 'words are poor things' but comforted the Burns with the notion that they would 'always be remembered'. 'This epic attack', he predicted, '... will live as long as England'.

While Micky's fate remained uncertain the Burns received over three dozen letters from well-wishers. The letters at first seem conventional; trite almost. Some include telling lines that suggest the stereotypical stiff upper lip. Bernard Hornung, one of Clive's Sussex Yeomanry comrades, for example, expressed the hope that 'this will help you to put a brave face on all your feelings': on first reading, just what one might have expected from stoic, reserved Englishmen. A letter from Clive's brother-in-law Tudor Crosthwaite, gives the flavour:

*Just a note to say how terribly sorry I am for the anxiety you,
Phyllis and your family are going through and how I share in
that anxiety for the safety of such a gallant fellow as Micky.
Don't write ...*

And then it dawns. This is not just what nice people wrote because
it was the conventional thing to do: they wrote like this because they
knew that this was what families in Clive and Phyllis's situation *needed*
to hear. They needed to know that what they were feeling was not
unique, that others acknowledged their anxiety, and shared it to the
meagre extent that we can share another's burden. Tudor Crosthwaite's
words were not merely conventional: they brought to Clive and Phyllis
the solace they needed. Bernard Hornung was 'distressed to hear ...
of the anxiety you are living through' and said how he 'long[ed] with
you for news'. These were no empty phrases: they meant what they
said. Would that all the anxious families of Six Troop could have had
this comfort.

Clive's mind worked analytically even as his emotions dwelt
on the awful possibilities. While he still did not know if Micky was
alive, he was able to ponder that he had now heard two stories. There
was Ted Gilling's about Micky and Tommy Peyton swimming to
the 'shore' and attacking up the 'beach', and another (presumably
heard directly—there is no letter) that his 'landing craft' reached
its objective and that the troop landed 'and were seen attacking the
beaches' (though naturally there was no 'beach'). Exerting control
of his emotions—indeed, possibly finding solace in the collation of
hopeful stories, even though they cannot both have been true—Clive
was able (like many men, especially of his time and background) to
examine his partial knowledge seemingly dispassionately. Except of
course we notice the growing file of letters: no one truly detached
would have written dozens of letters to concerned friends. Clive's
way of dealing with his anxiety was to write, write, write. And in one
of them (to Canon Andrews, who had also survived the Great War)
he confessed that he 'cannot help being desperately anxious'. Still,
like the lawyer he was—or perhaps anyone in such a position—Clive
rationalised what he knew in the light of what he wanted to know.

In the continuing absence of news, he reasoned 'the longer we are without news the better'. If Micky had been captured news must take a long time to travel via Geneva. If he was on the run, the delay must be even longer.

One of the consolations of the waiting was that so many of those who wrote to the Burns said things about Micky that perhaps revealed him to his parents in a new light. Letters came from people beyond the family and court circle—people whom the Burns had not met and who might otherwise never have met—who disclosed aspects of Micky's character that they might never have known. Given the wayward young man that Micky had been, these revelations would have come as a reassuring surprise. Not knowing if he were alive or dead, they may have regretted learning these things just too late.

On a more trivial level, aspects of Micky's past caught up with his parents when Clive was dunned for a bill from the High Street garage in Moffat. Mr Adamson, friendly but firm, pressed Clive for an unpaid bill for another hire car. Clive paid up with resigned good humour. As he explained to 2 Commando's new adjutant, 'Michael has always hired cars and leaving them unusable by the roadside has gone from the District'. Months into his captivity and a year after bilking Mr Adamson, Micky was writing to his father apologising for the financial mess Clive had to mop up. No sooner had the garage been paid than Clive had to settle a tailor's bill of Micky's, at least ten months overdue.

The letters arriving at Buckingham Gate show how widely Micky was known and liked. More than that: they show how Micky's circle exemplifies the transformation of wartime Britain. Rifleman Maurice Roe, for whom Micky had arranged a dangerous job with the Special Operations Executive just before leaving for St Nazaire, wrote to offer his sympathy. Explaining that he had served under Micky since joining the Territorial Army before the war, he described him as 'an officer that we men held in highest esteem'. Clive not only replied courteously and at some length but he asked him to visit when next he came to London. For all his position as a servant of the Duchy of Cornwall, Clive was no remote royal official. Still, not since the Great War had he encountered ordinary folk as he did during the saga of his son's wartime ordeal. If George Orwell, the perceptive and hopeful observer of British wartime life, was right, the war worked a social revolution of sorts. Clive and Phyllis's correspondence documents that change in relations between governors and governed. Orwell might not have agreed, but the revolution in the case of Micky and his friends was a product not of deeper forces of patriotism but also, more simply, of personality. Micky's ability to strike goodness and friendship wherever he went lights up these cross-class encounters. Tony Smith, who had also served in Norway with him and had learned of Micky's capture when he visited 2 Commando at Ayr, told Phyllis that it was 'friendships like Micky's which make this war seem more worth while'.

On 10 April Clive wrote a long letter to Charles Haydon summarising what the Burns knew and did not know, and what they hoped and feared. Clive professed himself a 'born optimist' and while conceding that 'a stray bullet may easily have hit him in the hellish fire they probably had to go through' both he and Phyllis remained hopeful. They based their hope on nothing more than intuition: 'It is odd', he wrote, 'but both my wife and I do not believe that he has been killed'. Haydon, who had served through the Great War and seen his commandos embark on hazardous raids, might have suppressed a realistic frown. In the event, though, the Burns were right. They learned of Micky's survival in an extraordinary story of coincidence, good fortune and daring.

<hr />

'A WEIGHT OFF OUR MINDS':
MICKY'S FATE DISCLOSED

A couple of days after receiving Clive's optimistic letter, Charles Haydon telephoned him to say that he had come by a copy of the German newspaper *Das Reich*. (According to a British prisoner of war who read it regularly in captivity, it was 'a very superior publication … designed for the educated classes'.) The cover of the 5 April issue featured a large photograph of rifle-carrying Germans shepherding commandos into captivity. Haydon and other officers at Combined Operations Headquarters thought that the man in the centre of the photograph looked like Micky. The next morning Clive visited Richmond Terrace and confirmed the identification. There was no question of who it was: 'one of the best pictures he has ever had taken', Clive wrote excitedly to one of Micky's old schoolmasters. He took the photograph to Buckingham Gate and both Phyllis and Alan (home on sick leave from the navy, recovering from mumps) agreed. 'Thank God', he wrote, 'that takes a weight off our minds'. The Butlers at the Star Hotel in Moffat also later sent a clipping from a Glasgow paper, *The Bulletin* of 22 April, which had reproduced the *Das Reich* photograph: dozens of people were literally looking out for Micky. Phyllis even received a letter from Dorothy Cocks ('Michael's first nurserymaid', she explained) passing on a cutting she had seen in a newspaper reporting that he was alive and a prisoner.

The news took a weight off many people's minds. Clive and Phyllis industriously and joyfully sent letters and telegrams to all of those who had written over the previous month. Among the papers now in Micky's possession are four dozen letters to relatives, family friends, former comrades, business associates, school friends, even courtiers at Buckingham Palace. All are dated within a few days of the news reaching Buckingham Gate. Though many had included lines to the effect 'Don't trouble to answer this' or 'No need to answer' in their letters, Clive replied to them all. The Duchy of Cornwall's secretaries must have typed furiously for a few days: surely gladly, because Clive was popular among Duchy staff.

Not all prisoners of war could have had such a wide and exalted circle of friends, but Clive's well-ordered correspondence suggests that every man who went into captivity—or every man who was killed—came attached to a circle of affection and concern. Dozens of such messages delivered by letter and telegram, a handy teenager or exchanged in bus or butchers' queues, must have passed every time a man was posted missing, killed or captured. Such expressions of concern, anxiety, relief or grief must have been common in wartime: though surely never commonplace.

Just a day short of a month from the raid Clive received a telegram from his son-in-law, the diplomat Lees Mayall in neutral Berne. Though it took three days to arrive, the telegram reported that Micky was officially 'Prisoner … slightly wounded but well'. Clive later described—with what degree of exaggeration for comic effect is uncertain—that Mayall had even 'hauled the German Consul off the Golf Links and got wires sent in every direction' before learning his whereabouts. Having been able to discover Micky's fate within a month, at least partly by making the most of their contacts within Combined Operations Headquarters and the British Embassy in Switzerland, the Burns probably found the confirmatory telegram from the Casualty Branch a week later and the letter the next month from the War Office something of a formality. Other families, they realised, had not been so fortunate. Almost the last sentence of the diary Clive kept of his month-long search for news of Micky ends 'still had no news of Tom Peyton': nor would anyone for months to come.

Meanwhile, in an astonishing coincidence, Ella van Heemstra re-entered Micky's life. One day in early April cinema-goers in Arnhem, in the Nazi-occupied Netherlands, watched the German footage of dirty, wounded and bedraggled commandos surrendering in the streets of St Nazaire. Ella was startled to see her dear friend Michael Burn on the screen, walking along with his arms raised in surrender. She grabbed the arm of the man in the seat next to her—who happened to be a German officer—saying (in English) 'It's Mickey!' She covered her surprise, but then returned to the cinema to make sure that she was right. Clandestinely the cinema manager, a Jewish woman, bravely cut a few frames from the film that Ella then had a photographer enlarge. On 22 April she contacted the Dutch Red Cross, which got a message to the Burns through the International Red Cross in Geneva. Addressed 'c/o The Times, Fleetstreet London EC' Ella's message, in pidgin English-cum-telegraphese, read:

> *Saw Mickey newsfilm, thought you might like know he well, looked very fit, same old Mickey! Personally delighted old friendships sake. Shall send him parcels.*

Though sent within days of seeing the film, the message seems to have taken a couple of months to reach London via Geneva. Phyllis, who may have known of Micky's liaison with Ella, though perhaps not how close they had been, sent a short and not altogether useful reply: 'Many thanks for your news of Mickie. He writes quite happily. Will welcome parcels or letters.' She ended 'Has changed address this month', though without telling Ella what the new address might be. Perhaps despite her gratitude Phyllis was not so happy at Ella and Micky renewing their friendship.

<hr />

'I DON'T THINK ANYONE KNOWS':
THE FAMILIES' UNCERTAINTY

The first Six Troop parents to learn of their son's fate had actually been Arthur Young's: mercifully, they had not long to wait. On 1 April Lord Haw Haw, the Irish renegade who broadcast propaganda from Germany, reported Arthur Young's capture and Phyllis was able to pass on the news the same day. Soon after, Mr Young saw a photograph in the *Evening News* showing 'Heroes left behind at St Nazaire'. He recognised his son Arthur 'being helped along 3rd on right'. Two months later, with the arrival of Micky's second letter from captivity, Phyllis and Clive learned that Arthur Young had saved Micky's life, supposedly by towing him ashore by the hair. The news arrived while Clive was away on Duchy business and Phyllis immediately wrote to Arthur's mother. 'You can imagine how grateful I feel to him', Phyllis wrote, 'for having got Michael out of the sea'. The Burns asked their son-in-law Lees Mayall to keep an eye out for Arthur and made sure that he received regular parcels. 'I only wish we could get news of so many others', Phyllis ended sadly. That absence of reliable advice dominated the lives of the Six Troop families for most of 1942.

Clive and Phyllis already knew what Micky expected them to do when 2 Commando went into action. Within days of learning of the raid Clive and Phyllis had begun the task they were to fulfil for the rest of the war. Transcending his own wounds and the fact of his capture, Micky's first thoughts were for the men of his troop. 'I had built my whole life around them', he told his parents, 'I can't really bear to think of them as killed'. He asked his parents not only to try to learn of their fates, but more importantly, he wanted Clive and Phyllis to 'try to keep in touch with the families', though warning, as if he knew the worst, 'don't raise their hopes'.

As the weeks passed, news and what the services call 'intelligence' gradually came to light. One of the more embarrassing sources was those who, like Arthur (contrary to their training and orders), spoke on German wireless programs broadcast to Britain. Though discouraged, listening to German propaganda was not actually illegal. Files in the Ministry of Information show how many listened in and how hard it would have been to prevent them. Perhaps two-thirds of the population listened occasionally, continuing pre-war habits of tuning in to continental stations presenting more lively programs than the BBC. Several million listened regularly, many hoping for news of captured loved ones. Interrogating prisoners at St Nazaire, Hitler's interpreter Paul Schmidt had learned that many Britons tuned in to German broadcasts, to the BBC at 9 pm and to Lord Haw Haw at 9.30; though they did not believe all they heard. While he would not listen himself, Clive had them 'listened to by various people on the chance that your name comes through', as he recorded in his diary. Listeners early in April found that chance had come up when the Germans broadcast the recordings made after the raid.

A month or more after the raid almost all of the Six Troop families (except the Burns and the Youngs) remained ignorant of what had happened to their sons. Their desperate need to know remained unfulfilled. Fundamentally, the Casualty Branch's policy, it admitted in its internal history, was 'to suppress or gloss over harrowing details'. In fact, many families wanted to know the details; or at least something. Soon Clive became a beacon for the families of missing commando officers—presumably because as a senior lawyer and royal official well placed in London, he might be able to open doors closed to those not in the know; as indeed he was and did.

The Burns' obligations of sympathy extended beyond Micky's troop. The mother of Robert Burtinshaw of 5 Commando (who had led both the impromptu revelry en route to St Nazaire and one of the demolition parties and had disappeared in the raid) wrote to Clive begging to be told anything he unearthed. Phyllis, having met some of 2 Commando's officers when she had visited Micky at Paignton in 1941, inevitably corresponded with their families. Phyllis wrote to the now pregnant Cécilie Birney, who as late as December wrote that 'David is still missing'. (David Birney, 2 Commando captain, had chaired the court of inquiry into Morgan Jenkins's accidental wounding at Paignton. He had been killed in the St Nazaire raid and buried at Escoublac: not that Cécilie knew.) Later in the war, especially after 2 Commando again suffered heavily at Catania in Sicily, the families of other 2 Commando dead contacted Clive, again trying to recover their sons' or husbands' belongings. Though he usually referred them to the 2 Commando Next of Kin Assistance Committee they still wrote, as did a widow, to say how it was 'comforting to know that there is someone to whom you can turn'. But the committee's secretary's disillusionment with 'Red Tape' deepened as families struck the same delays that Clive had met in 1942.

Six Troop families gained socially prominent allies in finding the details they sought. One Friday in April Isabel Wyles's supervisor called her to the works office in Guildford, where she worked in what she called a 'bomb shop', and she was introduced to Princess Marie Louise, Dorothy Peyton's royal lodger. The Princess told Mrs Wyles that she would do everything she could to discover what had happened to her son, Bill. She explained that the mother of one of the officers captured was 'a great friend of hers'. An overawed Isabel Wyles misunderstood and assumed that the Burns were friends of the Princess rather than Tommy Peyton's mother. So flustered was she by meeting even minor royalty that it was only later—perhaps in telling her work-mates—that Isabel realised that the Princess was probably looking for details of a commando called Wyles. In fact, she had remarried. 'I'm ever so sorry to trouble you', she wrote, but 'my son's name is Spaul' and not Wyles. 'I'm very proud my son was in the Commando', she told Ronnie Mitchell in Ayr. Unsure of what to do, the 2 Commando orderly room passed her letter on to Clive Burn, already the centre of a network of loved ones, all anxious for news. Clive reassured Mrs Wyles that both he and the Red Cross (and its head, the formidable Dowager Lady Ampthill) knew that Bill Spaull was her son and that as soon as news arrived they would tell her.

At this time, three weeks after the raid, Clive Burn was still able to hope that the troop's missing men would turn out to be captured. He hoped that Bill Spaul was 'all right although probably a prisoner' and that details probably took some time to come through the Red Cross. Clive realised that it was only an extraordinary chance that had confirmed Micky's fate. As news of the losses spread from families to acquaintances letters arrived from their sons' friends, often people they did not know. Tom Roach's landlady from Ayr wrote encouragingly, saying that 'if anybody will get away from that raid it would be the Captain and Tom'.

It took another three months before Isabel Wyles received any hint of Bill's fate. In July Nicky Finch (of another troop in 2 Commando, who had been photographed with Peter Westlake on the morning after the raid) sent a postcard from a prison camp to tell her that Bill had been killed in the raid. 'But you know Mr. Burn', Isabel wrote (in a letter written while so overwrought that she forgot to date it) 'I don't believe it, I just can't'. The Casualty Branch's habitual caution gave her false hope. She sent the card to Mrs Peyton, who in turn sent it to the Blue Coat School. The Casualty Branch's clerks told her that they needed to check with the captured commando in Germany and in the meantime Bill Spaul was still officially posted 'missing'. Isabel Wyles seemed to prefer the uncertainty of 'missing' to the terrible certainty of 'killed'. Clive did not seek to question her hope. 'There have been cases of men who were thought to have been killed, but who have come back', he wrote. Thinking of the pictures he had formed from news reports and Micky's letters, he found it easy to hope that 'in the confusion of St Nazaire a mistake could very easily have been made'. A week later the Burns had received further word that Bill Spaul (and Bill Gibson) had been killed, and Isabel's hopes and spirits plunged again.

By then, about mid July 1942, having corresponded with many families, read the news bulletins and spoken to officers such as Charles Haydon, Clive Burn had begun to realise that a central problem was the survivors were overwhelmingly men who had not landed. 'I don't think anyone knows ... what happened on land', he wrote to Isabel Wyles. No one who had reached Britain seemed to know anything beyond the dock wall at St Nazaire. 'We can realise your desperate anxiety', he concluded. Not until November did Mrs Wyles write to say that she had confirmation that her Bill had indeed been killed in the raid. 'It all seems so hopeless', she wrote. She still felt 'I just can't believe it'.

Two months after the raid Gordon Holman's book *Commando Attack* appeared. Some of the St Nazaire families bought it. Mrs Janet Burns, whose son Bobby had been posted missing without any further details, certainly read it. She found a book larded with platitudes: Holman encouraged his readers to think that Germans were often 'fanatically brave' but that they 'depend[ed] on mass attack' rather than individual initiative. Though light on specific detail for obvious reasons, he did describe what seem to have been the death throes of ML 268. But Mrs Burns read enough between the lines to realise that 'it must have been just hell', and she knew that 'the boys who are still alive today are lucky'. The lucky ones did not include her Bobby, and she was to wait many more months for more than Gordon Holman's generalised gloss.

Mrs Burns had to wait until early 1943 partly because her Bobby had been one of the men on ML 268 who had probably been drowned or burned within seconds of its explosion. Like dozens of other men, his fate was probable but not confirmed. But it was also simply because Bobby's paperwork was out of date. The War Office's notification had been sent out within a week of the raid, but to Bobby's father, apparently estranged from Mrs Burns, and to an outdated address. There was no Mr E. Burns at 3 Amersham Road, and the letter was returned to sender. The Rifle Record Office at Winchester (also responsible for contacting relatives) asked the Metropolitan Police to check. A police inspector, no less, made 'extensive enquiries' but found the address to have been a café unoccupied since before the war. The Ministry of Food, which issued ration cards and kept records on everyone, could not trace him either. Not until Mrs Burns wrote to the Rifle Record Office 'terribly upset' at the lack of official notification did Burns's family learn that Bobby was 'missing'. Bobby's father appears nowhere in his army file.

As well as helping families to seek details and bear with the lack of details, Clive himself bore news of death to waiting families. Albert Lucy had died in hospital at La Baule later on the day of the raid, though the news, transmitted from the French Red Cross through Lees Mayall in Berne, took exactly three months to arrive at his home in Kentish Town. Mayall, knowing of his in-laws' interest in the raid, sent the telegram privately to Clive, who contacted the Lucys himself. How did Clive get this news to the Lucys? Did he write, telephone or call on them? Knowing of his sense of duty and his maturing compassion, we can be sure it was a task he discharged faithfully. More than any single person in Six Troop's extended family, Clive seemed to be carrying the burden of their grief.

'PLEASE, NO LETTERS':
TOMMY AND DOROTHY PEYTON

The Burns and Dorothy Peyton had been 'in continuous communication' since the first days after the raid. Knowing Tommy as Micky's friend and fellow officer Clive made strenuous inquiries after Tommy as much as his son. Dorothy Peyton lived with anxiety. As she told Clive, she had already spent almost two years worrying over her older son, John, captured in France in 1940. Now she faced the agony of uncertainty following a telegram informing her that Tommy had also been posted missing. With all the families the tension of not knowing ate into their resolution. Like many others, Dorothy had received a vague telegram from the War Office. She had received Tommy's last letters within a fortnight of the raid, forwarded by a brother officer from Ayr: after that, silence. She had

had vague reassurance in a message from Robert Ryder, the naval force commander, whose wife Dorothy knew; but nothing definite. Two months after the raid she wrote to Clive to tell him that 'I have heard nothing at all ... I do just wonder what is happening'. Dorothy Peyton's particular worry was not just that Tommy might be dead rather than evading capture, but that 'they' knew and would not tell her.

Press reports fuelled Dorothy's anxiety. Newspaper stories had described how British officers had denied that the *Campbeltown* contained explosive charges and had bravely escorted German officers aboard as it sat in the Normandie Dock with the acid eating into the fuses. Dorothy naturally wondered if her Tommy had been one of these men: it would explain why his body had not been recovered. The story was a fable: military intelligence officers found no substance for it, and in any case, Micky had seen Tommy's body floating in the river the night before. But confirmation of his death did come. In June his name appeared in an official casualty list as 'killed', but without details. In the absence of definite advice she placed a notice in the personal columns of *The Times*. 'Please, no letters,' she added. Dorothy Peyton observed the form of a notice in the right newspaper but she did not parade her grief, and visiting it even six decades later seems intrusive.

'It naturally hit her hard', Clive Burn recorded in the diary he was keeping for Micky's return. Clive's immediate response—this was within a few days of his assuming the role of counsellor to Six Troop's bereaved—was to invite her to lunch: 'I will try and cheer her up', he thought. Dorothy was not to be so easily cheered up. Her letters hint at how suppositions, explanations, hopes and fears must have gone around and around in families' minds. If Micky and Tommy had been together when Micky came ashore, Dorothy reasoned, then Tommy's boat could not have been blown up. Ignorance fed grief: 'I would so love to have details of how he died', she wrote. Despite her notice in *The Times*, Dorothy Peyton actually *did* want letters: but only particular letters from particular people, and they were not forthcoming. She too wrote to Charles Haydon, telling him of Tommy's pride in his unit having been chosen for the raid and of his last letter 'full of comfort & the very highest ideals'. But she needed to ask 'just what was he doing when he was killed? ... May I ask you, if you know, to tell me?' Haydon could tell her nothing more.

Eventually—not for three months—Dorothy Peyton received word from Colonel Charles and from Micky in Germany that Tommy had indeed been killed, but virtually at the start of the action, and before his motor launch had even touched land. This was, she told Clive, 'a most frightful blow'. Dorothy at last faced the loss of her son: 'I shall not see Tommy again', she wrote. 'He meant so very much to me ... life has taken on a particularly lonely phase without him.' Dorothy Peyton's letters make heartbreaking reading because she hoped for so long that Tommy would have been spared, while we know all the while that he was not only dead, but that his body had drifted away and was lost. Tommy Peyton was truly missing. Clive sought to console her. 'It must be a relief to know that Tom was killed at once', he wrote, 'I think I'd prefer to know that his grave is in a British ship and not in a foreign land'. Tommy's brother, John, in Warburg prisoner-of-war camp in Germany, heard of his death just as an elaborate escape attempt failed. Confined to its bleak barbed-wire enclosure, John could only walk the perimeter fence, 'almost drowning in the misery of it all': sadly, he recalled, 'tears were not possible in such a place'.

Meanwhile, Dorothy Peyton also faced the struggle with a seemingly uncomprehending or unsympathetic bureaucracy. Despite the notice in *The Times*, the Casualty Branch's Mr Dawkins wrote advising her that 'unfortunately' while Micky and Colonel Newman had declared themselves 'certain' of Tommy's death, he had to insist on having a more exact account before he could declare Tommy dead or leave him posted as missing. (Or rather, that is what he meant: characteristically, Mr Dawkins couched his letters in passive, indirect prose.) He advised Dorothy that it could take up to eight weeks to get word back from a prisoner of war and 'the period may be extended if it is necessary for the International Red Cross Committee to refer to another prisoner'. Once 'conclusive evidence' of Tommy's death had been received, he wrote, 'you will be notified'. Sadly, and, it seems, unforgivably, his letters ended with no expression of regret either for

Mrs Peyton's loss or for the additional pain that this cumbersome process imposed upon her. Weeks later Clive was writing to another civil servant in the War Office reiterating Micky's and Colonel Charles's statements and wondering why their testimony 'does not appear to be sufficient evidence for the War Office'.

Reluctantly, Dorothy faced the responsibilities of her position despite her sorrow. Rather against her inclination, for she wanted to keep her grief private, she agreed to hold a memorial service for Tommy. She recognised that Tommy's many friends and especially 'the village people for they knew him from a baby' wanted to pay their respects. The service was held at nearby All Saints' in Ascot Heath, a confident Victorian Anglican church, its warm red brick illuminated by brightly coloured, gold-trimmed frescos. The service drew mourners from all stations: Princess Marie Louise as well as Bill Spaul's mother, Isabel Wyles. She was listed in *The Times* between representatives of Tommy's schools (Heatherdown Preparatory and Eton) and Clive and Phyllis. Perhaps the Ealing girls who had admired Mr Tommy attended, but they were not listed by name or number: nor were the 'village people'.

The memorial service at least allowed Dorothy to meet the Burns, who travelled to Ascot for it. While Mrs Peyton had written to Clive, relying upon his ability to finagle details out of a daunting officialdom, it was to Phyllis that she talked at the service. Here she emphasised that in dealing with the Casualty Branch she needed 'Michael's actual words' to prove to sceptical officials that he 'saw Tommy actually killed or dead'. Clive, who by this time had known for several weeks that Micky had seen Tommy's body, seems to have decided after meeting her that she could both stand to receive Micky's actual words, and that without them she faced an impossible task in retrieving Tommy's effects from the War Office. Clive at last quoted Micky's actual words: 'Tom Peyton my second in command was killed. I saw him dead myself, killed outright just as we landed.' However painful it was to picture her Tommy floating face down in the cold black water, his body drifting out to sea, lost, Dorothy at least knew the worst. 'All details are <u>much</u> more comfort', she reassured Clive, 'than knowing nothing'.

Clive and Phyllis Burn escorting King George and Queen Elizabeth on a visit to Lambeth to inspect war workers, including Phyllis's Women's Voluntary Services workers.

In making contact with Micky's men's families the Burns had assumed a burden which they felt they must shoulder, because Micky had been in command of his troop. Phyllis, a woman who had never had a paid job, who had so much felt overshadowed by her family, blossomed under the responsibilities she took on. 'She came into her own during the war', her future daughter-in-law explained. She led the Lambeth organisation of the Women's Voluntary Services from the war's outbreak to 1943, and, her daughter-in-law remembered, 'turned out to be a very clever administrator'. Her scrapbooks, and the warm testimonials they include from those who worked with her and for her, show how fully Phyllis responded to the expectation she embraced.

The war changed Clive Burn too. As a lawyer, a man not given to showing his feelings and uncomfortable with displays of emotion, Clive might seem to be a man singularly ill-equipped to deal with the steady trickle of letters, each of them full of sorrow, between if not on the lines. Far from evading the demands these letters brought, it is obvious that through the summer of 1942 Clive increasingly became able to respond to other parents. Not only did he not ignore their pain, or pass to his wife any 'difficult' or 'emotional' letters: he faced and responded honestly to other parents' feelings. To Dorothy Peyton, whom by now he knew, he was able to confess that in pondering how to reply to another letter going over and over the events of those frenzied minutes in the Loire estuary, he stumbled upon what counsellors came to call 'empathy'. 'I tried to imagine my own reactions to this sort of news if our positions had been reversed', he wrote. He was still worried that giving Mrs Peyton full details might 're-open the wound': but he sent them anyway. The disclosure did not cause Dorothy Peyton to collapse. Now, she wrote, 'I feel absolutely [sure] that my Tom is <u>not</u> alive'. When he read through the thick wad of paper in 1945, Micky found that his father had answered each letter fully, dictating replies to 'Miss H', his secretary. 'My father's letters never sounded, and never were, perfunctory', he reflected.

'SO CLOSELY RESEMBLED ... ST NAZAIRE':
THE NEXT OF KIN

A few weeks before the raid the Directorate of Army Kinematography (the 'K' spelling an affectation of the time) finished and released Thorold Dickinson's film *The Next of Kin*. Made by Ealing Studios for the War Office, it had begun a year earlier as a twenty-minute training film but ended as a full-length feature drama complete with a score by William Walton. Cinema trade papers summarised the plot as a 'spy story with a commando raid climax'. The raid, on a Breton port in which dozens of attackers die, reinforced the message that careless talk costs lives. Its last twenty minutes showed the fighting unusually graphically, with blood and bodies—both German and British. The title, which came to Dickinson in his bath, echoed the common line in wartime bulletins that 'the next of kin have been informed'—of casualties. Thorold Dickinson, a leading British auteur with a finely developed sense of his place in the creation of Kinematic art, co-wrote and directed the film. His dramatic recollections of the making of the film over the next 30 years have largely shaped the film's interpretation by social and film historians.

By March 1942 *The Next of Kin* awaited release. No sooner had newspapers begun to promote the film than the Ministry of Information decided that 'it will not be seen by the general public'. Newspaper readers might have inferred that its withdrawal might have been because 'certain scenes are said to be harrowing'. *The Next of Kin* is said to have attracted two interventions by Churchill; but this story comes mainly from Dickinson himself. Neither the National Archives nor the Churchill Papers seem to include any record of his interest. Dickinson described how Churchill had learned of the film weeks before the raid on St Nazaire and ordered it withdrawn because 'its subject matter so closely resembled the forthcoming raid on St Nazaire'. (At one point in the film, Dickinson recalled, 'there was a shot of an officer pointing on a map to the coast of North-West France at very little distance from the German submarine base at St Nazaire'.) Churchill supposedly ordered the film to be withdrawn in the meantime. After the St Nazaire raid the film's realistic scenes of combat attracted Churchill's attention again. He supposedly sent

Film publicity artwork for *The Next of Kin*.

around a couple of brigadiers to ask Dickinson to 'tone down these deaths'. Dickinson, becoming a doyen of the British film industry, often lectured and reminisced about this to film students. He described how slicing twenty seconds off shots in the battle sequences made all the difference artistically, and kept the censors happy.

When the film was released, a month after the raid, critics approved of Dickinson's realistic representation of battle and soldiers generally thought that he had it right. (A report of a test screening at the GHQ School of Battle described how 'other ranks were most expressive during the fighting on the Dockside'.) But historians of film and social history have relied unduly on Dickinson's memoirs in understanding how his audiences received the film. He often told a dramatic story of how the manager of the Curzon cinema in London, where the original version first screened, had brandy on hand to revive patrons, especially women overcome by the film's realism. He claimed that one woman insisted that the battle sequence had depicted an actual battle, denied Dickinson's explanation that it had been fictional, and had to be referred to a psychiatrist. Thorold Dickinson's highly coloured memoirs seem melodramatic—he was, after all, a film writer and director. It seems far-fetched that battle scenes could have been taken to be realistic or even actual, but the *Daily Herald* was giving out that the War Office had censored the film as 'so frightening that not even troops were to see it'.

But for a couple of hundred families the film was not just a gripping cautionary tale ending with an unusually realistic battle scene. As the *Daily Mail*'s film correspondent wrote, 'in some of its incidents "Next of Kin" resembles the recent combined operation against St Nazaire'. This story appeared within days of Clive and Phyllis Burn hearing of Micky's survival, but while most of the St Nazaire families remained ignorant of their sons' fates. For several weeks from May 1942, apparently now to Churchill's urging, the 'Hush Hush Film' screened in over 4000 cinemas in Britain. Over three million people saw it in its first six weeks. By July it had been adapted for broadcast on the BBC as 'cine-radio'. It seems likely that some of the Six Troop families saw or heard it. Who knows what they felt as they heard a vivid description of a botched commando raid or saw the bodies of commandos lying in their own blood on wrecked landing barges on the Breton coast? Perhaps the film showed the real next-of-kin nothing worse than they had already imagined.

'THIS CRUEL BLOW': THE WORST NEWS

Gradually news reached families that their sons were no longer 'missing'. Only in mid July was Lewis Roach able to tell Clive that he had heard officially that his son Tom had been posted killed in action. George Hudson's sister, Violet, told Phyllis that she had also been making 'every possible enquiry' but even in August had no official news, though 'each day we hope will bring us good news'. Violet Hudson had heard in a roundabout way—from a captured commando who had written to Ronnie Mitchell—that George was in a prison camp: but the report turned out to be mistaken. George was dead.

Parents sought each other out. Violet asked after Lenny Goss, Reg Tomsett and Morgan Jenkins. Edith Penfold travelled from Clapham to Streatham to visit Maud Harrison. She found her 'very grieved. I could see she has taken it very hard.' The Tomsetts met Lillian Goss when they visited London from St Helens. Reg and Len had been friends, and their bereaved parents found comfort in their shared loss. From prison camps Six Troop's survivors sent letters to their parents to ask after missing comrades. John Cudby's father wrote to Clive 'rather anxious to know of one of my son's pals', Bob Woodman, whom he had met when John brought him home to Workington at Christmas 1941. Mr Cudby hoped that Bob had not been in the raid and innocently asked after him. Peter Westlake asked after Maurice Harrison and his father John passed the query on to Clive. The sombre news came back: Bob Woodman was dead; so was Maurice.

When the Tomsetts travelled to London to call on Lillian Goss they also visited Buckingham Gate to see the Burns. Arriving unexpectedly, they met Phyllis and in 'a long talk' confided to her their belief that Reg was still alive. Mr Tomsett had done what many parents must have done. He had scanned the few German photographs published in British newspapers and became convinced that he had seen Reg alive in one depicting the burial service at Escoublac. That meant that he could not have been killed, didn't it? Clive, who had missed the Tomsetts' call, wrote to disabuse them, but gently. He hoped that they were right, but counselled them not to 'jump to such a conclusion without there being good grounds for it'. The Tomsetts' reaction was exactly what the Casualty Branch had seen so many times. Ironically, they had to be persuaded of the impossibility of their hopes by the father of one of the very few missing who had been identified from a photograph.

In the first week of July 1942 Clive felt certain enough to work his way down the list of next-of-kin that Micky had left him, writing to them one by one to pass on the scraps of news he had collected, piecing together the fate of his son's men. The replies he received disclose the distress that families had suffered for just over three months. Mabel Fisher, Norman Fisher's mother, had heard nothing since 2 April. 'I have been nearly frantic over it', she confessed. Norman, whom she had brought up alone since he had been three, was 'all I have got in this world', she wrote, 'God could not be so hard to take him from me'. Mrs Fisher was 'hoping and praying that he is a prisoner'. A month later, when Edith Penfold visited her, Mrs Fisher was 'still waiting ... very sad'. She may never have known that poor Norman took nearly a month to die in the German hospital at La Baule. (Mrs Fisher seems not to have contacted the Red Cross, unfortunately—because Norman had died in France, it might have been able to help.) Mrs Janet Burns, Bobby's mother, also wrote to thank Clive for writing. She had received an official notification that he was missing but nothing about her 'very dear boy' in the three months since. She promised to pass on anything she heard and hoped for the same in return.

As letters and cards began to arrive from survivors in prison camps in Germany through the summer of 1942, captured men were able to give families the details they so desperately sought. Late in 1942 Maud Harrison received news of Maurice in a paragraph from a letter from Stan Rodd describing 'the last time I saw him'. Maurice and Stan had been in ML 192 when it exploded. Stan had been swimming for the shore. 'I helped him half way to the shore', he explained, 'and then he left me. I did not see him after that.' Maud Harrison at least knew that Maurice had died in the water, but because the information differed in minor details from that contained in a card from Fred Penfold, she found it 'all very confusing'. Inevitably, those who comforted the anxious parents held back distressing details. By August, when Edith Penfold visited Maud Harrison, she already knew, from Fred's letters and from reading between the lines of various reports, that the commandos' launch had exploded in what she described as 'a dreadful inferno'. Nevertheless, Mrs Penfold seems not to have told Maud that Maurice might have been burned to death rather than drowned. 'No doubt that we are all saying [so] to ease her anxiety and make it seem he didn't suffer', Edith later acknowledged to Clive.

Maud Harrison's confusion deepened in November when she heard from Clive via a letter from Willie Bell's parents that he had seen Maurice drowned. Still, as with so many bereaved families, the absence of a body was hard to comprehend. 'If they were so near shore', she mused, 'it seems so strange that Maurice has not been found'. As Mrs Penfold recognised, 'it must be terrible [to be] still in the dark', more than seven months after receiving the telegram posting him as missing. In fact, Maurice's body had been washed ashore and he had been buried at Escoublac. (Sadly, neither the Germans nor the Swiss thought to visit the cemetery to record the names on the temporary crosses erected over their graves.)

From his prison camps Micky shared his father's distress at not being able to offer his men's families any definite word of their sons' fates. 'He is doing all he can to find out about his men', Clive reassured Mabel Fisher, 'but I expect he has as great a difficulty as we have'. Clive trusted that 'the news when it comes will be good', but it seems that he knew by July that all those who had survived, even if they had been captured, had been accounted for. Clive, whose son was safe, if behind barbed wire, found himself writing defensively as he corresponded with families who could rest on no such certainty. 'I don't think my son knew what was happening to the rest of that gallant band', he explained. But in the main Clive, a man who had previously found more than the conventional expression of feelings difficult, learned to offer consolation without indulging in empty hope. He offered Alex Gibson, who by July knew that there was no hope, 'my very deep and sincere sympathy in this cruel blow'. For the rest, it was a matter of waiting.

Some parents waited months more for confirmation of their fears. By November cards from prison camps—necessarily terse— both confirmed fears and brought reassurance. Fred Penfold sent a card from Germany describing to Lillian Goss how her Lenny and Reg Tomsett had been killed by a shell striking ML 192. He saw from the other end of the launch: 'they did not suffer or feel anything', he reassured them. Edith Penfold, who sent Clive long and informative letters recording her letters and visits with several London families, seconded Clive's sympathetic realism. She heard from her Fred's fiancée that Maurice Harrison, Norman Fisher and Reg Tomsett 'were all killed at the same time as [Lenny] Goss'. By that, she explained clearly, she meant 'instantly', when ML 192 exploded. Edith wrote to Maud Harrison and Mabel Fisher, but asked Lillian Goss to contact Edith Tomsett. (In fact, Edith was wrong about Norman Fisher, adding inadvertently to Mabel's uncertainty.)

The Tomsetts' ordeal continued. They were still tormented by the hope that Reg was alive and had been photographed. Mrs Goss wrote to Mrs Tomsett, whom she had met the previous July. She apologised for bringing such sad news but confirmed that Fred Penfold had seen Reg die. 'I was hoping they would turn up somewhere', she confessed. That was all she felt able to write. A letter from the War Office arrived in the same post, verifying the news. The Tomsetts could still not believe it. 'My wife and I still have a very strong feeling that our boy is alive', Mr Tomsett told Clive on Remembrance Day. Fred Penfold's account was a shock, of course, but they could not bring themselves to abandon all hope. They wondered 'whether a mistake has occurred'. They still had the photograph from the newspaper, and they insisted that the soldier in it 'bears a very strong and striking resemblance to our son'. What did Clive and Phyllis think, he asked? Clive, reluctant to compel the Tomsetts to let go of their hope, half-heartedly suggested that an enlargement of the photograph might help to resolve the Tomsetts' belief. But the tone of his reply—phrases like 'tragic news' and 'help you in your sorrow'—suggest that he saw them as clutching at straws. Eventually the waiting ended. By the year's end private letters from the survivors in camps and official notifications from the Casualty Branch came together to eliminate any hope. Ironically, while photographs had proved to be crucial in Micky's case, Clive knew that, as Lees Mayall had remarked, 'photographs are such bad evidence'.

For the families of the dead, part of life ended with the news of their son or husband's death at St Nazaire: as it does for all those who receive such a telegram, a telephone call or a knock at the door. The families began to depend upon each other, and no one can fail to be struck by the kindness shown by these fearful and grief-stricken parents for each other. As Edith Penfold observed to Clive (her son Fred survived but she visited nearby mothers who were still waiting for news) 'no one can know better what their anxiety is' than those who shared it.

<hr />

'EXACTLY A YEAR TO THE DAY':
THE FIRST ANNIVERSARY OF THE RAID

With the approach of the first anniversary of the raid many families' thoughts turned to St Nazaire. For Dorothy Peyton 'those ghastly days' became 'more vivid than ever', and like many she felt the need to write to those who shared her pain. 'I was going over my son's letters a few nights ago', Lewis Roach told Clive Burn, 'I do often read them over ... I can't help it'. A year had naturally failed to efface either their grief or their hunger to learn more. Lewis Roach was 'longing' to meet Micky; 'I am sure he could tell me a lot', he felt. From Ireland Mary Bushe wrote thanking the Burns for remembering the anniversary. She agreed that 'Paddy and your son will be thinking of that date too', and reflected on the good fortune she and the Burns shared: 'it was from sorrow to joy' for them at least.

For some families the anniversary brought renewed sadness, when a year on those still posted missing (fourteen of Six Troop) were at last declared 'killed'. A year to the day that the force left Falmouth, Mrs Janet Burns, Bobby Burns's mother, received her second official notification from the War Office Casualty Branch. She had at last learned that 'the motor launch he was in came under enemy fire and had a direct hit and sank'. The War Office, though slow, had been thorough, contacting Micky through the International Red Cross. Officials were now quite certain of Bobby's death. 'Naturally, I am awfully distressed', she admitted. Having had no news for so long, the Burns 'began to feel that he was in hiding'. She and her daughter now dwelt on 'the lovely memories of a very dear loveable boy'. Like other bereaved families they made contact with others in their situation. Janet Burns, in Brockley, had written to Mabel Fisher in Acton, whom she knew from the Queen's Westminsters Territorial Army network.

Peter Westlake thought of his family. 'Exactly a year to the day' since his capture he wrote to his parents confessing to feeling 'all hot and cold when I think of all you must have gone through' since they received the 'missing' telegram. Late in March Clive sent a circular to both the families of the dead and the survivors in camps in Germany, suggesting that they observe the anniversary formally but privately. Clive and Phyllis—significantly the letter names 'my wife and I'— wrote to Stan Rodd proposing, 'we should give up the minute before the 9 o'clock news on March 27th to commemorate the anniversary … in appreciation of all you did on that grand night'. The BBC evening news bulletin, which changed so much for so many, was a fitting symbol for a moment of reflection and remembrance in homes across Britain. Practical as well as sympathetic, Clive accompanied his letter to the prisoners with another consignment of cigarettes, and told them not to bother writing to acknowledge their arrival. 'Just mention it in your letters home', he urged, 'we are in touch with your families and they let us know your news'.

By the time of the anniversary Micky and Clive had become the poles of Six Troop's collective memory. Micky himself, his father wrote, was 'desperately sad' at his men's deaths, and Clive expressed his determination that at least 'their memory will not die'. He wrote to all the families of those killed and captured to ensure that they knew of an advertised anniversary broadcast. Hoping that the coming anniversary would not revive sadness, he wrote 'in sympathy with your great and abiding sorrow'. Many replied, thanking him, as did Alex Bell, for his 'kind and thoughtful letter'.

On 27 March 1943 the BBC made a 'St Nazaire Anniversary Broadcast', delivered, not by a sailor or a commando who had returned, but by Captain A. Cleaver Jones, an American air force officer serving in Combined Operations. Though it had been carefully crafted (by Hilary St George Saunders of the Combined Operations public relations staff), those listening closely to the broadcast—especially the families of the killed and captured—were not all impressed. They recognised it as propaganda. Alex Gibson was unhappy that 'it was clear that he had not been an eyewitness … but merely giving a story from facts that had been collected for him'. Still, Jones gave a copybook account of the raid and its success. He described how in 'one of the shrewdest blows' the *Tirpitz* had been denied a port on the Atlantic by the *Campbeltown*'s explosion. Jones mentioned the three Victoria Crosses awarded after the raid to sailors. 'Doubtless the number would have been greater if more of the soldiers had returned', he explained, but 'it is the general practice of the Army not to award decorations to officers and men taken prisoner'. This cannot much have eased the minds of anxious families: were their men slighted heroes?

Perhaps a more comforting message came from Gordon Holman, who had become the resident press expert on Combined Operations. He published an article on the first anniversary, directed not so much at the readers of the *Evening Standard* but 'in the nature of an open letter' to those who had survived the raid. It is very likely that families posted clippings to commandos now serving far away—2 Commando was to fight in Italy in 1943—and to those in captivity. Holman admitted (in a story thoroughly vetted by the Combined Operations censor) that the ' "inside" story of your heroic achievements' had still to be told in full. Holman directed part of his story to those who had, as he put it 'only had a single ticket for the party'—the men who had been captured. He reminded them that they understood better than the man-in-the-street why they had received no decorations, but hinted very broadly (again, in an officially approved story) that 'there must surely be some high reward awaiting' the captured commandos on their return. This was a message that families and survivors could cherish, wherever they were. 'You are constantly remembered', Holman reminded them.

By the first anniversary of the raid the entire tenor of the war had altered. Axis defeats—at Stalingrad and Alamein, in the Atlantic, and in Papua, Guadalcanal and Midway in the Pacific—signalled that the initiative had at last shifted to the Allies. 'I do trust that your hopes that the end is in sight are right', Clive wrote to Lewis Roach, 'it will be a long hard fight but they are getting a taste of what is coming to them'.

Over the anniversary itself many families dwelt on the events of a year before. Isabel Wyles, who had finally accepted her William's death, confided that 'they are never very far from my thoughts', and that on the anniversary itself she had been 'shedding a few tears'. The anniversary notice prompted the Tomsetts to write again to Clive to say that the War Office had confirmed that Reg had indeed been in the cemetery that the German photographers had recorded, but as a corpse rather than a mourner. They made clear their determination to visit his grave as soon as they could after the war. The Commando's Next-of-Kin Fund, which became active from 1942, following the losses at St Nazaire, gave bereaved families, and especially mothers, ways of helping their dead sons' comrades. Isabel Wyles had collected £39 for it in the first three months of 1943, partly by raffling a commando badge among the 'girls' in her 'bomb shop'. 'I can't do any more for my own boy', she told Clive simply, 'so I must do what I can for his friends'.

Soon after the Ministry of Information published *Commandos in Action*, its official account of the raid on St Nazaire and of the more controversial British–Canadian attack on Dieppe in August 1942. If German radio propaganda had insinuated that the raid had failed, *Commandos in Action* triumphantly refuted the charge. One and a quarter million copies were printed, and in the USA the Book-of-the-Month Club selected it as its June 1943 offering.

Though vindicating the raid the book did not attempt to conceal the cost. Its account of the fighting on shore was based on the reports of three commandos (who had evaded capture to reach home): otherwise, 'none of the troops who went ashore came back', *The Times* reported, dampening the spirits of those nursing lingering hopes. Over two hundred raiders remained as prisoners.

KRIEGIES:
SIX TROOP'S
PRISONERS OF WAR

'REPORTED PRISONER OF WAR': RENNES

'Well, here I am a prisoner of war', Micky's first letter home began, 'very much to my surprise'. He reflected on how lucky he had been, and hoped that his parents would not have to wait long before learning of his fate. The letter arrived exactly three months later, on 1 July. Fred Penfold had also written to his parents in Clapham on 1 April. He too confessed that he had not expected to be captured: it had been 'the last thing he expected to happen', his mother told Clive. A commando officer later reflected that the lecturer on evasion and escape in Falmouth harbour 'might as well have talked to the mess-deck tables ... no one could imagine this happening to them'. What had happened was that they had become *Kriegsgefangener*: prisoners of war, what they called 'kriegies'.

Captured commandos and sailors gradually gathered at *Stalag* 133 at Rennes, the capital of Brittany, some 60 miles north of St Nazaire. Held in a French army barracks, whose primitive, stinking latrines confirmed their prejudices about French plumbing, the prisoners were looked after by French colonial troops, Senegalese and especially Indo-Chinese. Friendly and willing—they bought the St Nazaire prisoners toothbrushes from the canteen with their own meagre pay—the colonial prisoners were to fare much worse than the newcomers. About half of the 15,000 Africans captured in France had died by the war's end.

Life at Rennes had been, as John Cudby had told his father, 'rather monotonous' because they were 'locked up quite a lot'. Their rations were meagre and grim (Micky's cooking, he described in a letter from Rennes, was 'imaginative but unpractical'). The Germans seem to have taken no chances with a desperate lot of commandos. Indeed, in accordance with their training, from the beginning some men planned to escape. At Rennes Corran Purdon tried to get out in a wicker laundry hamper, defeated by French officers unwilling to risk reprisals on their families, while Billie Stephens tried prising panels off a door in the hospital. Both would try again in Germany: Stephens would eventually reach home; Purdon would end up in Colditz with Micky. But Colonel Charles discouraged his men from risking escape: he had lost enough of them.

On 23 May, two months after the raid and almost a month after Micky's fate became clear, Lees Mayall sent another telegram to his father-in-law. He had done some more sleuthing with the International Red Cross and had learned that as well as Micky, Arthur Young and Willie Bell a further five of Micky's troop had been captured. They were Stan Rodd, Fred Penfold, Peter Westlake (given as Westlane but the error was obvious), John Cudby and Paddy Bushe. Micky's first letter sparked another round of letters to the families on his list. Clive wrote to Mrs Bushe in Tipperary, the mother of the other man in the photograph published in *Das Reich*. Through Clive's letters the families of the captured men joined the families of Six Troop's dead. For the time being not everyone knew whether they were waiting or grieving. Edith Penfold kept in touch with 'several mothers who are still waiting for news'. Soon the two networks tended to separate. 'Hope obtain information other members of troop', Mayall's telegram ended optimistically.

As the Germans processed the captured commandos and sailors they gave each of them a number, their *Gefangenummer*: the number that now, more than their army number, identified who they were in the German prison camp system and in the corresponding British, Swiss and Red Cross records. Six Troop's were eight men among the 160,000 British Empire prisoners in Axis hands in Europe. Their numbers suggest something of the order in which they were handled. Fred Penfold, Peter Westlake and John Cudby, at 18567, 18569 and 18570, must have been processed virtually one after another. They had probably already worked out that survival as a prisoner of war depended on sticking together. Micky was a few places behind Cudby in the queue to be processed, at 18599, with Willie Bell, Paddy Bushe and Stan Rodd within sixty other places, perhaps standing in different lines. Somehow Arthur Young's number—11673—placed him out of sequence with the others, probably because he had been taken with other wounded to La Baule and then treated at Rennes, and had been among the last batches of wounded prisoners to be sent on to Germany. Arthur was still at La Baule in late June, but they seem to have all caught up just before the prisoners were divided into camps for officers and other ranks.

Establishing what happened to the captured commandos is complicated by a surprising dearth of records. The Casualty Cards in their army personnel files record 'Reported PRISONER OF WAR' and then 'confirmed' a few days after the raid, and usually a notation 'Stalag VIIIB' in the summer. But the next entry is 'Arrived UK' with a date in April or May 1945. Four of the eight filled out sketchy interrogation reports on their return to Britain, which together do not add more than a dozen snippets. What happened to them in between?

At least two Six Troop families had already lost sons as prisoners in Axis Europe. Dorothy Peyton's older son John and Lewis Roach's son, Tom's elder brother, were prisoners. All the families began a dispiriting round of waiting for letters, from their men, from the Red Cross, the War Office and anyone who might be able to assuage their hunger for reassurance. So great was this desire for news that from May 1942 (just when the St Nazaire men's families needed it) the War Office published a free monthly magazine, *The Prisoner of War*. Soon after a book, *Prisoner of War*, appeared. In it, journalist Noel Barber (whose own brother was a prisoner) gave families reassuring advice on where they were, what they did, what they ate and how they were treated.

Through the summer of 1942 the speed of postal deliveries increased, so that it was taking up to a month for letters sent from prison camps to reach families in Britain. Reading between the lines of Micky's letters, which were still dwelling on the fates of his men, Phyllis perceptively observed (in one of her many letters to Maud Harrison) that 'I think Michael is only just getting over the first shock of it ... trying to remember what really took place'. Clive, too, realised how hard his men's deaths had hit Micky. Confirming to Peter Westlake's father, John, that Maurice Harrison was indeed dead he acknowledged that 'he was a great friend of my son's and he is very upset at his death'. It sounds conventional, but it came as an unexpected admission from the father Micky had known before the war changed all their lives.

Forty thousand British troops had been captured in the fall of France in the summer of 1940, another 15,000 in Greece in 1941 and 50,000 in North Africa, the Mediterranean campaigns including many troops from Australia, India, New Zealand or South Africa. Airmen drifting down into occupied Europe and Germany joined them with every bomber raid, along with a trickle of merchant and Royal Naval sailors taken in the Atlantic. They were held in dozens of camps in Italy and Germany. The German army's system of *lager*—prison camps—divided prisoners by service and rank. Officers went to *Offizierlager* (*Oflags*), other ranks to *Stalags*. Because the St Nazaire commandos were at first regarded as marines (they had after all arrived by sea) they went first to a naval prisoner-of-war camp, a *Marine lager*—*Marlag*—at Sandbostel, near Hamburg.

'QUITE WELL AND CHEERFUL': SANDBOSTEL AND WESTERTIMKE

Over the spring of 1942 commandos and sailors began to be moved to Germany. Officers had travelled in third-class carriages with an armed guard in each, their men in cattle trucks. The journey took five days, with much shunting and waiting on branch lines while trains carrying more important cargoes steamed past. Their guards had issued food for three days but many ate it all in the first. Hungry, unshaven and filthy, they wearily stepped out of the train to find themselves at Sandbostel, on a sandy plain on Luneburg Heath in north-west Germany.

The first parties arrived at Sandbostel exactly a month after the raid. 'It is great that all the boys are in the same camp', Paddy Bushe's mother wrote to Clive, 'they'll be a comfort to each other'. The naval camp shifted mid-way through the St Nazaire prisoners' time there, from Sandbostel to nearby Westertimke. It is not always clear whether descriptions and anecdotes refer to the old camp or the new. Westertimke had better amenities (such as stoves) but the chilly east wind still blew sand into prisoners' faces and their rooms, and the two thin blankets issued to each man did not keep it out.

'We are settling down well', Lieutenant Commander Sam Beattie, *Campbeltown*'s captain, reassured his wife soon after his arrival, but the early days of captivity proved to be a trial. The St Nazaire men at first tried to stick together. Officers took on various jobs to make the camp work. Micky organised the meagre first aid stores, but lost the job to Philip Dark when patients found that he had dispensed laxatives instead of aspirins. (The laxatives were unnecessary: on largely liquid diets, prisoners found that the buckets placed in passages outside the barrack rooms were often urgently needed.) Charles Newman shared a room with eleven other officers, including Sam Beattie, Bill Copland, Philip Dark and Micky. The strains of crowding, lack of privacy, and unhandy tyro cooks sharing one stove caused squabbles, smoothed by Newman's personality and example. They held joint church parades on Sundays, with Newman taking the service and Beattie reading the lessons. (They had a prayer book but no hymnal. They tried to reconstruct hymns from memory; to their embarrassment, Sam Beattie found, usually only getting as far as the first couple of verses.)

Many remembered the words to other songs. The captured commandos remained in good spirits. In his novel *Yes, Farewell*, Micky had his character Alan Maclaren describe the demeanour of men captured in a raid on the French coast in 1942. He described their 'cheerfulness and enthusiasm', marching along the sandy tracks of Luneburg Heath singing and whistling 'the songs of freedom'—the 'Marseillaise', 'The Wearing of the Green', 'John Brown's Body', and even the 'Internationale'. The commandos' morale remained high at Sandbostel, presumably because they were all together—Micky even continued the 'E.P.' for the surviving men of his troop. They built a large emblem in the sandy soil, with the words ST NAZAIRE in large letters. This, Bill Copland wrote, was partly to '"rub it in" to the goons' and partly ('somewhat optimistically') to show up on aerial photographs and so disclose their location. 'Strangely', he reflected, 'the Germans never made us shift it'.

The joint *Marlag-Milag* camp was among the most unusual of the Reich's hundreds of prisoner-of-war camps. It was the only camp run by the *Kriegsmarine*, and, except for the St Nazaire commandos, held only naval inmates. When the St Nazaire men arrived it held about 140 officers and 440 ratings, of both the Royal (in *Marlag*) and Merchant (in *Milag*) navies, as well as some Norwegian women civilians interned in their own little compound nearby. Reports on *Marlag* graded it as 'satisfactory' to 'good'. Lees Mayall told his mother-in-law, Phyllis (addressing her with unusual formality as 'Dear Mrs Burn') that his diplomatic counterparts at the Swiss Embassy in Berlin had visited the camp a few days after Micky arrived. The camp, she would have been relieved to learn had seen 'no really foul abuses of the Geneva Convention'. German sailors ran it with little of the deprivation and demoralisation so often seen in larger army camps. It had canteens for officers and ratings, offered football, cricket and softball, films and an orchestra, and for a time BBC broadcasts played over a loudspeaker (the latter possibly the result of astute bribery). The only complaints made by prisoners to the Red Cross seemed to be that 'lascars'—coloured seamen from Mauritius, India or Malaya serving in and captured with British merchant ships—were allowed to mingle in the European sailors' huts.

Many of the captured raiders had heard the *Campbeltown* explode and surmised that the dock had been destroyed, but they did not know if their success was known in Britain. The uncertainty weighed upon them. An incident in June gave them reassurance. While nothing was yet known in Britain of the commandos' fight ashore, the surviving naval officers had given full reports. This had enabled the Admiralty to recommend sailors for decorations, including three Victoria Crosses, the Empire's highest award 'FOR VALOUR', as the medal testifies. As well as the posthumous VC awarded to the commando Tom Durrant,

Robert Ryder (who had returned) and Able Seaman William Savage (who had died defending the motor gunboat 314 in the Loire estuary), a VC went to Sam Beattie, who had so skilfully steered the *Campbeltown* into the dock gates and had ensured the success of the raid. Beattie was among the prisoners at Westertimke. On Saturday 30 May the German admiral commanding the camp arrived in full dress in a horse-drawn coach and, before a parade of the prisoners, congratulated Beattie on having been awarded the VC. (He was 'very courteous about it', Beattie modestly told his wife.) Prisoners reported their reactions in letters passed to British intelligence. John Cudby described in a letter to his father 'a little celebration' the prisoners held. An officer described how he had 'never heard such hearty cheering', and how the prisoners had celebrated with 'Lager and our mouth organ band'. Both he and an unnamed sailor made the point that it showed that 'Britain realizes what a tremendous action St Nazaire was' and 'how the raid must have been thought worth while at home'.

At Sandbostel and Westertimke the St Nazaire prisoners saw their first Soviet prisoners of war, men unprotected by the Geneva Convention. The Red Army saw them as traitors for having surrendered and the Germans used them as expendable slave labour. Micky described them as 'gaunt and starved, wearing rags and tatters of old sacks'. They died in hundreds from starvation and disease, 'buried naked in heaps', Micky wrote in *Yes, Farewell*. Like most British prisoners, Micky deplored the Germans' treatment of the Russians. But he may not have been surprised. British prisoners avoided the Russians' fate because Germany essentially observed the 1929 Geneva Convention. 'The Geneva Convention is broken somewhere in Europe every day of every year of this war', Noel Barber told prisoners' families in describing 'This is how they live' in his book *Prisoner of War*. But the convention existed and for British prisoners—astonishingly, considering the nature of the regime in whose power they lay, it was observed far more than it was broken.

Micky himself bent the Geneva Convention in May to send a postcard to a man he addressed as 'Cousin Arthur', still in hospital at Rennes. Pretending that Arthur Young was related ('fortunately we are allowed to write to relations in other prison camps') he had 'a chance of thanking you for pulling me ashore that night at St Nazaire … I was about to sink'. 'Rodd, Bell, Westlake, Cudby, Penfold [he forgot Paddy Bushe] send their love', he wrote, and promised a reunion at Westertimke 'if not in Moffat'.

Later in May, Lees met the Swiss camp inspector who had actually spoken to Micky in Westertimke. He described how Micky was 'quite well and cheerful' and recovered from his wounds. This Lees was able to transmit to his relieved in-laws. Across the vast confusion of occupied Europe, in a prison in the Reich, it seemed that happenstance had again intervened in Micky's life for the good. A month after, though, Micky and the commandos would be separated from their naval comrades, and the two groups would not meet for the rest of the war. Before parting, Charles Newman and the commando officers told their naval counterparts that they would meet in London on the first 28 March after the war. In the meantime, in the early hours of 27 June, exactly three months after the raid, the commandos milled about before being transported to army camps in Germany. Their departure turned into a shambles: the prisoners had learned that they had no responsibility to impose order for the Germans' convenience. While men supped porridge and tea to sustain them on their journey the camp's security officer (named Gusveld, inevitably known as Goosey) directed his men to search the prisoners' baggage. 'How many officers are there here?', Goosey demanded of the nearest officer. 'I haven't the slightest idea', Micky replied.

'OUR ALL BEING ONE': CONTACTING PRISONERS

The large number of men in captivity demanded a massive effort. British Empire prisoners of war in Europe were looked after by the British Red Cross Prisoners of War Department. By mid 1942 the British Prisoners of War Relatives' Association had become a sizeable body whose members had a strong interest in the Red

Cross's work. (It was a curiosity of the British system that while men were cared for as soldiers by the army, once they were captured they became the responsibility of what was in effect a private body, albeit one partly funded and directed by the government.) By then, just as the Six Troop men reached Germany, the Relatives' Association (now swelled by the families of those captured by the Japanese at Singapore and in Asia) became restive at the improvisation hitherto accepted. Its council pressed for greater government responsibility. The government was spending about half the £15 million that seemed to be needed to sustain them. Much of the support sent to prisoners came from voluntary contributions and from parcels sent by family and friends. While parcels were physically the most important, letters nourished men emotionally.

It was easy to write to a prisoner of war. Anyone could buy a flimsy Prisoner of War aerogramme at a post office for threepence, and they went by airmail. Until their transport system collapsed under Allied bombing in 1944–45 the Germans delivered practically everything without restraint. With luck, letters could reach Germany in under a fortnight. Replies could be received more swiftly from prisoners in Silesia or Saxony than from servicemen in, say Burma or Persia. Micky received letters not only from his parents but also from many friends and relatives, and from survivors of his troop, notably Jack Heery, who also wrote to the families of his dead comrades. To Heery he wrote in 1944 how he was 'so glad you're OK'. He knew that he was safer in Colditz than Heery was fighting with 2 Commando, and wished that he were either 'locked up safe like us' or wounded 'just badly enough to fight no more'—a couple of fingers, say. Jack Heery had been Micky's political mentor through the 'E.P.'. 'I've written a good deal and developed', he assured him. 'You're quite often in my mind.'

Officers from 2 Commando also wrote to the families, at least until they left for active service. This meant a great deal to them: Isabel Wyles told Clive and Phyllis that 'even if my son was only in the ranks they don't forget'. At least as long as mail deliveries continued in Germany, the post remained astonishingly efficient. By mid September 1942, in less than six months, Fred Penfold had received 36 letters, 'so he seems quite contented', his mother reported.

It was harder for prisoners of war to write home, but as long as Germany both observed the Geneva Convention and had a postal and railway system able to distribute mail, letters or postcards could arrive within as few as three weeks of being written. Indeed, British intelligence agencies relied on the regularity of the German postal service and the organisation of the German system to maintain a regular secret communication with prisoners. Like the great majority of prisoners, however, Micky had not anticipated capture and had not arranged a code. (In retrospect it seems curious that men sent on operations with a high chance of being captured were not ordered to devise a simple code.) Even so, Micky found ways of signalling his awareness of the war's progress. In July 1943 Clive wrote to Willie Bell's father, Alex. He told Alex that he had received his first letter from Micky in three months. Micky had described his camp, Spangenberg, as enjoying 'lovely weather' but—confusingly—also very wet. 'I gather he means wet underfoot as a result of the bombing of the dams', Clive thought: the RAF had destroyed three of the Ruhr dams in the celebrated 'Dam busters' raid in May.

With Micky known to be a prisoner but with little else to go on, Clive, like every other parent, tried to imagine how he would adapt to life in captivity. After giving Fraser Browne (one of Micky's masters at Winchester) an account of Micky's part in the raid—an embroidery of Ted Gilling's garbled description—he speculated on how he would fare. 'I can see him lecturing on Shakespeare', Clive wrote, 'or annoying the nazis with his insolence ... and always with the idea of escape in his mind'. Among the letters sent to the Burns expressing relief at Micky having survived, even if a prisoner, there are many jocular references to expecting him to get away. Like the overwhelming number of prisoners, Micky never tried to.

Just as Clive developed a special relationship with some of the bereaved families, so he found friendship among the fathers of his son's captured men. He and John Westlake, though always opening their letters with a formal salutation, developed a friendship. Mr Westlake was a journalist ('looking in on Printing House Square most days')—and as a court reporter he and Clive shared an interest in the law. He also knew the journalist Gordon Holman, who mistakenly told him that Clive was a colonel. John Westlake addressed him as 'Colonel Burn' until Clive told him to desist. (John Westlake had spent the Great War with the Army Service Corps on Salisbury Plain; Clive had been a captain in the Sussex Yeomanry, and gained a great deal of credit with Westlake for not insisting on it, as he might have according to etiquette.) 'You flatter me', Clive replied, 'I never obtained that exalted rank and in fact dropped all Military rank as soon as I could after the last War'. Unlike most of Micky's men's families, the Westlakes were securely middle class. They sent drawing materials from W.H. Smith and tobacco from Harrods or Whiteleys, all emporia that the Burns patronised. Soon John was calling on Clive and they met for the inevitable lunch. Clive was comfortable with the clubbable Westlake, whose familiarity with Micky's world stood him in good stead. John had never met Micky but his Fleet Street friends assured him he was 'a most brilliant young fellow without having the least bit of side'. It seems that war continued to reveal to Clive aspects of Micky's life and character, and he warmed to John Westlake accordingly.

The scarcity of letters from the seven other men of Six Troop captured at St Nazaire obliges us to infer what their experience would have been like from reading letters, diaries, memoirs and recollections by other prisoners of war. Much of their experience can be imagined. At New Year, for example, Padre Ellison Platt, a Methodist minister who kept a detailed diary in Colditz, would look at the clock at 1 am (knowing that Britain was an hour behind Germany) and think of his family. 'Then I knew that they were thinking of me', he wrote, 'and I knew that they knew I was thinking of them'. Surely every prisoner mused about what his loved ones would be doing at some time.

Micky asked his mother to send Mrs Harrison a copy of Tolstoy's *War and Peace*. 'He says', Phyllis wrote to Maud, 'a book like that will mean more to people who have lost people they loved than any letter': though he did write as well as sending an idiosyncratic, though well-meant, gift. Mrs Harrison replied that it was 'a lovely thought' of Micky's, hoping (somewhat doubtfully) that 'it may help us as he means that it should'. Even more precious to Mrs Harrison was a diary that Phyllis found among Micky's effects (part of which had at last been sent on, though from 2 Commando rather than through the

War Office, which was still resisting Clive's appeals to compassion and common sense). Phyllis at first assumed it was Micky's, but as she began reading it she realised that it must have belonged to Maurice, and she sent it on. It was in fact Maurice's record of the weeks before the raid; today one of the few substantial sources about Six Troop besides Micky's papers.

Many of the families of the dead wrote to those captured. They sought out their addresses (including the all-important prisoner-of-war number, which regulated the direction of post) and wrote to men asking after any details of their loved ones' fates. The prisoners' families too kept in touch. Mrs Penfold in Clapham wrote to Mrs Cudby in Workington, again, with Clive acting as the intermediary. Writing, to their sons or someone else's, gave the Six Troop families a sense of connection. As Micky wrote to his father, 'maybe it gave you something of the feeling it gives me here, of our all being one'.

<hr/>

'AN ENEMY WE SHALL FIGHT FOREVER': CLIVE AND THE RED TAPE

Just as Clive had become a counsellor to the families of Six Troop's dead, he took on the task of helping the families of its prisoners of war practically. For example, as a solicitor he was able to advise the Inland Revenue on Willie Bell's income tax, though even he found the rigmarole for claiming allowances based on Willie's pay 'all too complicated to worry about'. Clive also wrestled further with the Casualty Branch in getting the prisoners' kits released. Families wanted to send clothes and personal gear to their sons—Mrs Penfold frugally confided that 'it is useless buying more when they already have things in their kit'. Here was a practical outlet for Clive's anxiety, a task he attacked with passion.

Within weeks families had begun writing to the War Office's Effects Branch to ask when they might be given personal items their sons had left behind. Prisoners were denied personal items they needed and would have difficulty replacing behind barbed wire. Here begins a small saga of unthinking insensitivity that would be repeated over and over again: not just for the dead of St Nazaire but for the tens of thousands of families of those killed or captured in 1942, notably the casualties of the loss of Singapore and the collapse of the Empire in South-East Asia. The Effects Branch's inflexible adherence to rules put Clive Burn and various families to inexcusable trouble and needless pain at a time they needed all their emotional energy. Clive began to warm to this task.

Early in May 1942 Phyllis had written asking for Micky's effects to be released. After receiving an unhelpful reply, Clive also wrote, suggesting that 'with a little elasticity this red tape could be cut'. Impatiently, on the same day he also telephoned, with results recorded by a hapless Effects Branch clerk in Liverpool. Clive simply asked for Micky's effects to be sent to him. The clerk, Mr Rogers, advised that 'unfortunately he was unable to do that'. 'Mr Burn', he recorded in a note for file was 'extremely rude in his remarks'. Mr Rogers called for his supervisor's help, and Mr Bloom explained that 'we had no power to issue an officer's kit to anyone but the officer himself'. At this, Mr Bloom noted:

> *Mr Burn would not listen to my further remarks but shouted in a loud voice about red tape and what he intended to do, finally closing the one-sided conversation by slamming the phone down.*

Far from ruining his campaign by this outburst, Clive's temper and his letter (on Duchy of Cornwall stationery) together galvanised the War Office to actually change its policies. The War Office convened a series of meetings, first in Liverpool and later in London and Cheltenham, involving progressively more senior officers and officials. It became clear that the Effects Branch, perhaps overwhelmed by the quantity of notifications it processed, was hiding the problem of prisoners' effects under the cloak of bureaucratic detail. Mr Bloom claimed that the Effects Branch had 'a statutory duty ... in regards to the kits of officers killed but no authority to deal with the property of the living'. His colleagues urged him not to take such a legalistic attitude. Other officials, attuned to the prisoners' needs rather than procedural rectitude, minuted that 'The procedures suggested [by Mr Bloom] will not satisfy people like Mr Burn', and rather than ignore or contest his representations, the War Office's officials conceded they needed to alter them.

Extraordinarily, Clive's written arguments and intemperate telephone call actually induced the Army Council to revise its Instruction on the disposal of the effects of captured personnel. Despite the Effects Branch's lingering disagreement ('Cas P.W. is not an officers' "lost property" branch', an official waspishly minuted) a new Instruction recognised the sense in not waiting for the owners of these effects to ask for them. It determined that effects (except clothing that was bloodstained or likely to cause distress) would be forwarded to next-of-kin even if their owners had not asked for them.

Accordingly, Clive established that the War Office would accept an 'indemnity' from the families authorising Clive to act on their behalf, and in July sent form letters to all the families except Arthur Young's. Still, the victory entailed further frustration. A few days later, having learned that the War Office required a particular form of words, he was exasperated to have to ask families to complete another form. John Cudby's father naïvely supposed that 'they will be attending to them', but the matter was to drag on, and in August 1942 Clive advised Mr Cudby to contact him if nothing happened. John Cudby was typical in not receiving his kit from 2 Commando, via the War Office until well into November: over six months after Clive bearded the War Office. Fred Penfold's mother told Clive in exasperation in August that none of her son's belongings could be found, and she had to buy new gear anyway. In the event the summer of 1942 saw British prisoners in Germany receive plentiful supplies of clothing, and several of Six Troop reassured loved ones that they had more than enough clothes for their first winter in captivity.

The families of men 'missing' endured frustration still longer. The Infantry Records Office continued to advise that 'so long as a man is missing no action will be taken as to the disposal of his personal property'. Despite Clive's intervention, then, the War Office's reluctance to send families their sons' effects lasted—unbelievably—

beyond the first anniversary of the raid. On 31 March 1943, Lillian Goss pleaded with Phyllis to help. 'They will not send me his things', even though 'they have records ... What shall I do?' Clive promised to 'get hold of the individual who is dealing with the question'. By now his patience had worn thin. 'This maddening ghastly red tape is an additional enemy we shall fight forever', he wrote in exasperation. He eventually succeeded, but in the end all Mrs Goss received were Lenny's tobacco pouch and some documents.

'THE PARCELS ROUNDABOUT': SUSTAINING THE PRISONERS

Prisoners lived for parcels: indeed, without them many would have died. The Germans' greatest neglect in observing the Geneva Convention was in food. Paradoxically, while the Germans threw the responsibility for feeding prisoners adequately onto their enemy (through Red Cross parcels) it gave prisoners' parcels the highest priority in the German transport system. As long as German railways could deliver parcels prisoners would not starve. They came from several sources. Fred Penfold was eligible to receive them from his parents, from the Burns, the Red Cross, the Royal Fusiliers next-of-kin association and the 2 Commando Next of Kin fund, as well as a local Lord Mayor's Fund charity.

Ten days after Clive and Phyllis had confirmed that Micky was the prisoner of war on the front cover of *Das Reich*, Clive thought to look again at the photograph. 'With you is another fellow', he wrote in the diary he kept for Micky, 'I hope it will be possible to find out who the man is'. It was in fact Paddy Bushe, the only member of Six Troop to come from Ireland, and the Republic at that. Clive wrote to Bushe's widowed mother, Mary, who lived in a village near Thurles in County Tipperary. Mrs Bushe had already accepted an offer that the 2 Commando fund 'adopt' Paddy, as she put it. She was upset that as a poor widow, living in a remote village far from the help of the

Red Cross, she could not send Paddy what he needed. She was, as she told 2 Commando's Next of Kin Assistance Committee, 'a widow in poor circumstances, and am suffering from Chronic Neuritis'. She had little to spare: 'I have to pay rent, rates for my cottage and never have money to buy clothes for myself'. While Eire enjoyed better food than the United Kingdom, clothes and tobacco were rationed or expensive, and Paddy specially asked for undervests, underpants, shirts, socks and tobacco. Later the Royal Ulster Rifles Comforts Fund sent him parcels too. Mrs Bushe was frustrated that she had heard so little from her Patrick. 'I have no further information', she complained, 'Patrick gave me none on the two cards I had from him'. Her Patrick turned out to be a negligent correspondent, it has to be said: he sent few cards to Thurles and she wrote less often to the Burns.

Micky received his first parcel late in July, perhaps because Lees Mayall pulled strings in the Embassy at Berne. After that he, like all British and Empire prisoners in Europe, was supposed to receive two each month. Still, it was a comfort to Lees's 'dear Mother-in-law', as he oddly called her, to know that Lees would be 'able to keep up a regular supply of some sort'. In fact, a huge organisation existed to get parcels to prisoners of war. The clumsily named British Red Cross and St John of Jerusalem did most of the actual work of supporting prisoners and their families, while the War Office's Prisoner of War Department co-ordinated official policy. (It was mildly ironic that Lady Edwina Mountbatten headed the organisation responsible for succouring men whom her husband's Combined Operations outfit had put behind barbed wire.) As Clive had already discovered, a formidable bureaucracy also bedevilled the administration of comforts for prisoners of war.

Phyllis soon began arranging to send parcels to the prisoners. The Burns contacted most families (all but Paddy Bushe's mother, for whom arrangements in Eire differed, and of Arthur Young's, who always seems to have been different to the rest). She offered to buy chocolate, soap, socks, clothing, or wool for the men to knit their own sweaters, and of course tobacco and cigarettes. The mechanics of what to send, how and how often preoccupied prisoners' families. The rules were both complex and strict. Many items were forbidden and those that were posted had to be packed and labelled in very particular ways. *The Prisoner of War* monthly newsletter sent to all prisoners' families devoted many pages to explaining rules and revisions and answering families' anxious questions: from the practical ('What knitted garments are most useful?') to the fanciful ('May skis be sent to prisoners?') *The Prisoner of War* gave reliable advice.

Letters so often mention the sending and receiving of cigarettes that we might imagine the prisoners to have been chronically addicted to tobacco: and so many were. Cigarettes could be sent in unlimited numbers. They became the common currency of the prisoner-of-war camp (tins of Nescafé came a poor second). Peter Westlake was 'only an occasional smoker', but welcomed deliveries of cigarettes because they gave him the wherewithal to buy or barter for what he needed. Camps often had a regular 'mart' where approved stallholders traded goods for cigarettes, regulated by price-lists. When Fred Penfold received three shipments in August 1943, totalling 1400 cigarettes, he became for a time a well-off kriegie. Able to trade with fellow prisoners for treats, he added to his Red Cross rations to buy the means to enjoy a party to mark his twenty-third birthday. Clive regularly sent parcels of cigarettes and tobacco to Micky's men, giving them not only the consolation of a smoke (and its consequences) but also a capital start in the camp economy. 'Non-smokers became the capitalists', a prisoner explained, 'able to buy anything'. Indeed, the economist Fred Mulley based a classic economics treatise on currency on his observations of a *Stalag* cigarette-based market.

Clive regularly sent each of the Six Troop prisoners a gift of 300 cigarettes and a pound of tobacco (a fact only disclosed when Mrs Bushe mistakenly tried to send tobacco direct to Paddy rather than despatching the parcel through a registered wholesaler, as Clive had done). All the families had to learn the ins and outs of sending parcels. The Westlakes had so many problems with their first parcels that John Westlake visited the big British Red Cross depot at Finsbury Circus for first-hand advice. The Westlakes had spent £7 on an earlier parcel, and discovered that it had cost them seven more clothing coupons than they were allowed. Articles in official books and magazines explained the complexities of the rules. If the Westlakes, well-off, on the spot and confident enough to visit the depot to get advice, had trouble, how were widows like Mrs Bushe in rural Tipperary to get on?

What Red Cross officials called 'the Parcels Roundabout' involved everyone following instructions exactly. Violating British or German rules ran the risk of denying their own loved one, and perhaps all prisoners, the comfort a parcel brought. However carefully a parcel was packed, it was unpacked and examined. Clothes included had to tally with the coupons issued: if not, it was sent back. Then the Red Cross volunteers, mainly young women, checked for contraband. Money, stamps, stationery and playing cards were forbidden. Volunteers rejected toothpaste or anything in tubes that could contain messages, and any food besides chocolate. (Though a mainstay of escapers, chocolate was permitted—the Westlakes sent their entire ration to Peter.) Every week the Red Cross returned hundreds of homemade cakes to disappointed well-wishers. The volunteers searched for hidden messages—in the toes of socks or in slippers or gloves. They destroyed even innocuous messages, including codes embroidered on clothes.

Once checked and repacked in layers of corrugated cardboard and waterproof brown paper (tied up in the 200 miles of string the depot used each week) the parcel began its long journey. All European prisoners' parcels travelled through Lisbon, and in huge quantities. Five million cigarettes a week went in consignments from registered tobacconists, 100,000 food parcels from Canada alone, plus bulk shipments of beef from Argentina ('official' Red Cross parcels included food, though family parcels could not). All this went in brilliantly lit Red Cross–marked ships—Swedish, Portuguese and even Swiss registered and crewed. Each ship's voyage from Lisbon to Marseilles had to be documented and specifically permitted. The Red Cross supervised the shipment from Marseilles to Geneva by rail, and there made up consignments for hundreds of individual camps, transport to which was in German hands. The journey from Finsbury Circus to the parcels hut of a *Stalag* could take up to five months.

Small wonder then that regulations soon upset the families' plans. Phyllis found that she could not buy pyjamas or even knitting wool without coupons, but between her work, the help of the grandly named Princess Marie Louise's Knitting Party and the families' own efforts, parcels began to leave Britain for Germany. Soon all of the prisoners' female relatives were knitting: 'Peter's grandmother is a tremendous knitter of socks', Mary Westlake told Phyllis. But knitting, however inconsequential it may have seemed, was vital. Everyone who knitted—on the bus, by the fire or the wireless—felt that they were actually contributing directly to their man's welfare: and so they were. Every monthly issue of *The Prisoner of War* included a pattern for a woollen jumper. Parcels took so long to arrive that woollies posted even at the height of summer would reach their recipients just in time for winter.

Every three months prisoners' families were allowed to send a ten-pound parcel, and were able to send underwear and warm clothing to help men meet the bitter European winter. These parcels might also include chocolate, books, tooth- or hairbrushes, shoes and socks. The rules for what they could include and how it was packed were strictly enforced. Oats, though easily transported, were forbidden because they could be hoarded and used to sustain escapers. Families without the means or the initiative to send such supplementary parcels left some prisoners without. Many huts pooled parcels, but not always, and inequalities fostered envy, feuding and in extreme cases theft within messes and barrack huts.

The Bells appreciated the Burns' kindness. 'These acts of generosity', Alex Bell wrote, 'help to compensate for the anxiety we feel'. Willie himself also wrote to them to thank them 'for all you have done for me since I was taken prisoner'. The gifts did not stop as more pressing concerns intervened: that December the Burns sent Willie Bell precious razor blades and a cheque for ten shillings, and presumably similar gifts for Micky's men in other camps.

Clive regretted that being separated from his men prevented Micky from continuing the educational and vocational scheme he had begun in Scotland in 1941. He hoped that the men would continue themselves. 'The main thing', he told John Cudby's father, 'is to keep them interested in the future'. Already by July 1942 Willie Bell was asking his father 'for books to study'. Most of Micky's men craved books as much as tobacco, chocolate or letters. Like thousands wondering what they ought to send, his brother-in-law Lees Mayall agonised over what books to choose. Apart from the difficulty of finding English books in Switzerland, he thought it a waste of time to send 'light and quickly-read novels'. He knew (perhaps from his Swiss contacts) that Micky wanted books on economics. By the middle of 1942, Lees had sent two food parcels and a consignment of books, including the works of Goethe, perhaps an attempt to engage the sympathies of the camps' German censors.

Both Germans and British regulated the supply of reading material, one of the prisoners' most pressing needs, especially in non-working camps. The British would not allow technically minded prisoners books published after 1939, for fear of inadvertently disclosing technical intelligence—the German censors examined all books routinely. The Germans prohibited many books on security grounds. Atlases were banned, of course, but also music, presumably because scores could conceal codes. They also forbade hundreds of books for ideological reasons. *The Prisoner of War* advised families that 'quite obviously' it was pointless to try to send books criticising the Nazi regime and works by Jewish writers—Freud, Jung and Einstein were singled out. But, more surprisingly, it named books by G.B. Shaw, H.G. Wells, J.B. Priestley and, of all things, Lancelot Hogben's *Mathematics for the Million*, as 'likely to offend'. On top of these weighty considerations was the question of individual taste and desire. Fred Penfold was asking for 'more books' from the autumn of 1942, but in his next letter he explained that he wanted ' "thrillers", anything exciting'. Conversely, Peter Westlake, in the same camp though it seems in a different working party, wanted 'the latest Penguin fiction' and 'not detective stories please'. Most other ranks, though, found that they were not to be given much leisure to read.

'FIT AND WELL AND WORKING HARD':
THE LAMSDORF WORK PARTIES

From Sandbostel the seven other rank prisoners of Six Troop were transported south-eastwards across Germany to *Stalag* VIIIB at Lamsdorf in Silesia, east of Dresden. Each time they moved, their families only caught up with them weeks or even months later and the move disrupted deliveries of letters and parcels. Lamsdorf was at the time the largest prisoner-of-war camp in Germany. It was a vast, barbed-wire enclosure in the midst of a sandy plain, with up to twenty thousand men occupying bunks in large, often bug-ridden and stuffy huts, each holding several hundred inmates. 'Twenty thousand', journalist and author Noel Barber observed, made Lamsdorf 'as big as Windsor, Bexhill or Hartlepool'. He told a story that two brothers from Birmingham, captured at Dunkirk and on Crete, lived in the camp for more than a year before they bumped into each other at a club for Birmingham men. This huge 'other ranks' camp belied the British Army's assumption that men needed officers to think for them. With officers segregated in *Oflags*, under the Geneva Convention other ranks elected leaders known as 'Men of Confidence'—go-betweens. Lamsdorf's prisoners were led by Warrant Officer Sid Sherriff, its 'Man of Confidence'. A Welshman, a member of the Royal Welch Fusiliers, Sherriff had the hardest job in any of Germany's camps—he was responsible for up to thirty-two thousand prisoners in Lamsdorf and 300 nearby work camps. Sherriff aroused the admiration of those who saw him. One prisoner remembered him as 'a leader in every sense', a man who retained dignity, personal smartness and his integrity. 'If ever a man deserved a decoration for gallantry in the face of the enemy', a prisoner recalled, 'it was Sid Sherriff'.

Lamsdorf had a bad reputation at first. By the autumn of 1942, when the first commandos entered it, parcels were also arriving, along with replacement uniforms and boots, and books. Peter Westlake ('very fond of sketching', his mother explained) asked for Indian ink and drawing paper. If he received them he may not have had much chance to practise, because Lamsdorf existed to supply the Reich's industries with cheap labour. It was not a brutal camp, but it was cheerless and dreary, with inadequate, monotonous rations, where prisoners were harassed by petty restrictions and frequent roll calls. The Germans' intention seemed to be to make the holding camp uncomfortable so that working parties seemed attractive. In effect it was a huge transit camp for prisoners moving from one work party to another. But thousands of prisoners remained in the main camp, so large that supervision by the Germans could never be as close as in smaller camps. Indeed, a recaptured Colditz officer who spent a night at Lamsdorf while being escorted back to the fortress learned that the other ranks had several tunnels operating undiscovered. They were used not just to get intrepid men away but also to allow others to visit nearby villages and factories to trade for food and sex.

Under the Geneva Convention 'other rank' prisoners could be obliged to work. The remit was hedged about with provisions and safeguards, but essentially prisoners represented a cheap if unmotivated (and therefore inefficient) workforce. They were to become commandos of a different kind: *Arbeitskommando*—working parties. Up to fourteen thousand British Commonwealth prisoners, most soldiers, worked in the area. Willie Bell's father astutely observed that 'it must be a trying experience for them ... being prisoners after having such strenuous training'. Lamsdorf was a camp of workers: the midday meal there was always called 'dinner', never 'lunch'.

By September 1942 all the Six Troop other ranks had arrived at Lamsdorf and most were posted to some of the hundreds of work parties operating in the surrounding area. (Until late in the war Silesia remained the main German industrial area safe from bombing, though as the American offensive against oil production got underway prisoners died in raids on refineries.) Arthur Young, in a letter to the Burns (who had counselled him not to 'waste' his precious letters writing to them) described how the Six Troop prisoners at Lamsdorf had been split up between working parties. Many were put to land reclamation, housed in makeshift hutted camps in flat sandy clearings. Parties also worked as builders, plumbers, farm or factory labourers, on roads, and in mines and quarries: more or less in that order of desirability.

Work brought some compensation: better rations, modest but useful pay (70 pfennig a day, about nine pence) and the chance to fend for themselves. As Willie Bell told his family, 'I am still fit and well and working hard'. By the winter of 1942–43 Peter Westlake was working in a sugar beet factory (to distil alcohol). He asked his parents not to worry, though John Westlake was not sure after reading Peter's letters. 'He mentions the number of hours he works', he wrote, 'but these have been blacked out [by a German censor] and we wonder if they are rather long'. *The Prisoner of War* tried to explain to their families exactly what prisoners did in work camps. Always inclined to put a cheerful construction on its stories, the newsletter described men on work details as 'the happiest prisoners', though their happiness evidently depended on the sort of work to which they were put. Mr Westlake found the magazine 'a great comfort'.

Work parties received mail and parcels less often but could scrounge food more easily, especially on farms. The worst jobs were in salt mines or especially coal mines, abhorred for obvious reasons. Men often worked nine-hour shifts for six days at a time, and because they rarely received work clothes, lived in filthy uniforms. Prisoners knew that they were 'slaves' and detested helping their enemy. German supervisors learned that the normal condition of a prisoner-of-war work gang was malingering. Losing tools, 'misunderstanding' instructions and working fitfully and sloppily (shovelling ballast away from rather than under railway lines, for example) became their private contribution to the war effort. Men on especially arduous or dangerous work parties, however, resorted to self-inflicted wounds (scalding water produced painful but impressive blisters), even breaking fingers to secure a few weeks' respite in the main camp.

Many other rank prisoners on work details enjoyed opportunities denied their senior non-commissioned officers. Chocolate, coffee, soap or cigarettes from Red Cross or private parcels gave them openings for trade. Some bartered for eggs, ham or white bread. Others traded goods for sex. German women risked punishment for both parties for *Volkschande* (degrading the German people), but the many women transported to the Reich as forced labourers presented less-dangerous opportunities. On farms or in factories couples could find barns or rooms (one example: in a paper factory in the Bohemian mountains, some desperate Polish women were known as 'table-enders', from the furniture on which they coupled with prisoners). Even large camps gave other ranks chances denied their superiors. Prisoners could, if they tried, find Ukrainian or Polish slave workers willing to coerce women slave workers, and British prisoners told unsavoury stories of women servicing gangs one after another in the toilets for a bar of chocolate or soap for each time.

Prisoners' letters from Lamsdorf are chatty but vague: 'very fit and well at present', Peter Westlake writes in September 1943, 'still finding life as interesting as ever, hoping to see you some time next year'. Noel Barber explained to their families one of the characteristic phrases of prisoners' letters. Rarely was anything 'good', but almost everything was 'fair': 'We get fairly good food', they would write: perhaps to write 'good' would tempt fate. Their standard fare became coarse black bread, turnip and cabbage in quantities, ersatz cheese (made from fish waste) and red jam from sugar beet and turnip. Monotonous German rations gave amateur cooks the incentive to use tins and packets from food parcels ingeniously. Practice winnowed out the inexpert and challenged those with flair. Men's standards were not exacting. Crushed biscuit with grated cheese and dates could end up crisp and be called a cake or soggy and become a pudding.

Peter Westlake's letters to his parents from Lamsdorf are numerous and detailed. Though hardly candid, letters written in January 1943 convey the flavour of the kriegies' life. He was in a party working outdoors in the snow ('picture a scene from a Christmas card'), one of 60 prisoners but including a teacher, a commercial artist and some professional men ('a galaxy of talent'). They returned from work about three in the afternoon, 'with a healthy glow and feeling as fit as we have ever felt'. A fortnight later he wrote again.

Dear Mother and Father,

... Before I give you the latest news – such as it is, I think I had better give you a list of the more important items to include in

future clothing parcels. Apart from chocolate, every parcel should contain solid toothpaste, boot polish and dubbin, razor blades, sewing and darning material, socks, shaving soap and a tooth brush. Other items to be sent now and then are brilliantine, soap … leather soles size ten, fancy shirts for summer … In the next parcel I should also like a pair of sandals, shorts and swimming trunks … At present very well off for clothing, although book and tobacco parcels will be much appreciated.

Finding life very pleasant with my third working party, plenty of books to read, a very decent crowd of fellows and very warm and snug quarters, very well indeed. Still quite happy and contented, but longing and looking forward to the grand times ahead.

Deepest love

Peter

This is a curious mixture. Peter takes for granted—and would have been foolish to mention—that the regular arrival of Red Cross food parcels supplemented the basic German rations and kept them fit and well. He relies on his parents' parcels for all the items that allow him to keep clean and shaved, to maintain health, cleanliness and self-respect: even to dress his hair with brilliantine. Men work hard in Lamsdorf, but they are housed in bearable accommodation in the depths of a central European winter. He is expecting to remain a prisoner for a long time—into the summer, when he expects to be able to wear 'fancy shirts' and sandals and go swimming. Captivity sounds like a strenuous working holiday—perhaps he intended to reassure his parents. But at the end he lets the cat out of the bag: he is still a prisoner and is 'longing' for home.

'AT LAST WE HEAR SOMETHING':
STUART CHANT'S RETURN

In May 1943 *The Times* had reported that 'none of the troops who
went ashore came back', but for once Micky's old newspaper had been
wrong. Five men—all other ranks—had evaded capture and made it
home, all to be decorated for the sort of initiative commandos were
expected to display. As early as 8 May 1942 the British Military Attaché
in Madrid had reported the arrival in Spain of Corporal George
Wheeler. In mid June there was news of the arrival in Madrid of two
more, and another two followed. Three St Nazaire commandos also
escaped from Lamsdorf and reached Switzerland, and Billie Stephens,
who had commanded Micky's launch in the raid, got out of Colditz.
And besides these evaders and escapers, another commando returned,
though more contentiously.

The Geneva Convention allowed the repatriation of wounded or
disabled prisoners or medical personnel. In October 1943 German
prisoners were taken to Barcelona and 5000 British Empire prisoners
were taken to Stockholm, returning home from those neutral ports.
The BBC reported their arrival in Leith. Listeners, many the families
of those returning, followed their progress with what Ministry of
Information investigators described as 'almost with bated breath':
wireless broadcasts of their arrival 'brought tears to many eyes'.
Among the repatriated was Stuart Chant of 5 Commando, who had led
a demolition party from *Campbeltown*. Though no longer fit to return
to fight with the Gordon Highlanders (he had been badly wounded
in the leg), Chant was a source of both intelligence and propaganda.
The first officer to return from St Nazaire, Chant's account added to
the meagre stock of knowledge about the events in the docks.

Once debriefed by Combined Operations Headquarters, Chant
was allowed to tell a version of his story publicly. The Ministry of
Information cleared his story for release in February 1944 and well-
wishers sent copies to the Burns in case they had missed it. Chant's
account, represented as verbatim but actually carefully crafted,
corroborated the story told in *Commandos in Action*. For the families
of the dead and captured men of Six Troop, though, it gave them
few details of men they had known or heard about. In describing the

difficulties faced by the protection parties (such as Micky's men on ML 192) Chant told of how Micky's motor launch 'was hit and blown up' and its occupants thrown into the water. (He was not allowed to say that some had died in the explosion.) But he repeated how Arthur Young grabbed Micky by the hair and dragged him along until they reached the Old Mole. There Micky, armed with a few grenades, made his way across the docks to join the fight. Young and the wounded who had made it to shore (though he did not say how) were captured by the Germans. Chant described how a man beside him had been shot and killed while in the act of surrendering. The detail was hardly likely to reassure those who had lost men in the raid, and must have re-opened painful speculation among the bereaved. Gordon Holman, who had returned from St Nazaire to write the upbeat book *Commando Attack*, interviewed Chant for the *Daily Telegraph*.

The newspaper stories brought Chant letters and requests for meetings from many families. Clive, both as Micky's father and the link between the Six Troop families, met him 'two or three times'. 'We taxed him terribly', he told Stuart's mother, Kate, 'plying him with questions'. Mary Westlake presumed in a letter to Phyllis that 'it must have given you great pleasure to meet an officer so recently in touch with Cptn Burn', but from Chant's perspective the Burns were just one family among many who wanted to meet him and ask after their sons, captured or killed. It was a wearying business, but he explained that 'I have written to all I can ...'

Chant's stories, both the sanctioned version published in papers and the ones he told to loved ones, gave families insights into what their men had gone through. Glimmers of that news reached the men still held in Germany. 'Dear Young', Clive wrote, 'at last we hear something of the fighting on land'. Chant's return at last opened a curtain that had fallen as the launches landed or blew up on the night of the raid.

With his gammy leg Stuart Chant was not to return to active service, but he was still able to serve the war effort. Indeed, compared to most repatriated prisoners, whom Clive correctly described as 'complete wrecks', he was relatively hale. It is odd that the Germans, themselves so expert at propaganda, did not think that his reports would be an asset. He was used again as a propagandist, in the United

States, and even wrote—under heavy tutelage—an article on the raid published in the *Reader's Digest*. Indeed, St Nazaire featured heavily in the American press, a reminder that Britain was still able to inflict blows on Nazi Germany. The propaganda war continued, with the prisoners of war among its pawns.

'ONE OF THOSE HITLER HOLIDAY CAMPS': HOHENFELS

Under the Geneva Convention sergeants were excused the need to labour. Some sergeants went out with their men, for exercise, to maintain solidarity and self-respect, or for variety and to take the opportunity to trade or even escape. Others chose to remain in camp. Stan Rodd managed a transfer from Lamsdorf to *Stalag* 383 Hohenfels, just when it changed from an *Oflag* to a camp for non-working non-commissioned officers, in September 1942.

Stan, whose father sent Clive regular budgets of Stan's letters, was said on the first anniversary of the raid to be 'going on alright'. A year later Mr Rodd reported that Stan 'seems to be keeping well and he looks fit' in a recent photo he'd sent. Stan remained there almost until the war's end. Hohenfels, near Regensburg in Bavaria, was regarded as being one of the best camps in Germany. We know a great deal of its interior life from Donald Edgar's memoir, *The Stalag Men*. When Edgar arrived there in 1943 he was 'agreeably impressed', especially after the cheerless barrack blocks of Lamsdorf. As a former Hitler Youth camp its accommodation resembled chalet-like huts, standing between vegetable plots, with prisoners rarely seeing sentries, who stayed outside the wire. Though hardly 'one of those Hitler holiday camps', as a fellow kriegie called it, Hohenfels was clean and well run by its 6000 sergeants and warrant officers.

Regular parcels and an efficient messing and cooking system, the absence of work and the presence of capable and responsible organisers made Hohenfels as bearable as camps could become. When the YMCA's European Secretary visited in mid 1944 he said that he had not seen any better camp. With greater leisure and energy, Hohenfels prisoners mounted more theatrical performances than any other. In the year from February 1943 its two permanent theatres staged 200 performances (including four revues, ten plays, three music festivals and two operas or musicals). They entertained an aggregate of eighty thousand patrons, in a camp no more than 6000 strong. One troupe specialised in Gilbert and Sullivan and once the commandant so enjoyed *The Mikado* he waived *Appel* (roll call) for three days. Its production of *The Merchant of Venice* was professional enough to justify borrowing full costumes from the State Theatre of Berlin (though that may have been merely an opportunity for anti-Semitic propaganda).

Prisoners of like inclinations tended to congregate together, and many huts cultivated a studious air. Donald Edgar, who translated Tolstoy's *Confessions* in Hohenfels, found his way to a hut more interested in serious study than playing cards or gardening. Its inhabitants used the camp library of over 6000 volumes, 500 of which were on loan at any time. Over 2000 men in Hohenfels obtained Royal Society of Arts or Matriculation qualifications in the camp, padres invigilating the examinations while even the Germans scrupulously refrained from reading examination scripts. Nevertheless, Noel Barber cautioned, 'this does not mean that all the camps have now been transformed into urgent seats of learning'. He warned families that many men studied 'to hide their personal tragedies ... so hard to detect in their cheerful letters home'. In many huts a man with a spare hour would still rather kip than swot.

Despite its reputation for liberality and scholarship, Hohenfels was still a prison camp, in which men lived cheek-by-jowl with a dozen or two others without respite. A cartoon series in the camp's monthly magazine, *Time*, 'I hate the man ...', reflected the tensions of their enforced communal life. The artist ('The Man with the Dagger') hated ' ... the fellow with the home-made stove', ' ... the man who practises in the hut', ' ... the fellow who smiles in the morning' or '... the man on the top bunk'. Every cartoon ended with the offender with a dagger in his back. The Man with the Dagger spoke for every prisoner tormented by smelly stoves, inescapable accordions, the relentlessly cheerful, or restless sleepers. Paradoxically, a hut might also embody greater liberty than any had found in civil life: Donald Edgar's hut tolerated an open homosexual liaison between a Guardsman and an Australian, even when their afternoon coupling shook the man reading on the bunk below.

Crowded together, though, men learned about themselves and about their country. Donald Edgar felt 'as if I was learning about a foreign nation, ill-educated, ill-fed, ill-housed and ill-led'. Like many, he asked himself, 'What sort of society ... are these men fighting for?' The Hohenfels prisoners debated those questions in *Time*, which published articles about 'that other war' on disease, squalor, idleness, want and ignorance, that had 'haunted Britain's mean back streets too long'. 'If we desire peace, and social and industrial advancement', prisoner number 6828 urged, 'then we must all ... play our part towards its realisation'.

Hohenfels was as bearable as it was, largely because of its 'Man of Confidence', Company Quartermaster Sergeant David Mackenzie, an Edinburgh schoolmaster. In his brief statement on his liberation, which like many other statements was as short as it decently could be, Stan Rodd singled out Mackenzie, who, he said, 'helped in every way possible'. Donald Edgar, who knew how difficult it was to stand between prisoners and guards, praised his 'sensible, firm leadership' of the prisoners and his 'subtle mixture of diplomacy and obstinacy' towards the Germans. Mackenzie, who early in 1944 had been elected Man of Confidence by 4319 votes to just 261 was a man (*Time* wrote) 'whose record of efficient and incorruptible administration' endeared him to his fellows.

Soon, as the bombing of Germany intensified, the prisoners could see the effects of raids on nearby Regensburg, and as in other camps deliveries of parcels faltered. Late in 1944 Bill Gibson's girlfriend Anne Brien (who wrote to her late boyfriend's comrades) passed on a snippet from Stan to Micky. Stan was 'still well and longing to come home'. Before Stan, David Mackenzie and his charges could return they would face their most severe test as the war's end approached.

'A LOT TO BE THANKFUL FOR ... ':
THE PRISONERS' FAMILIES REFLECT

As the months passed, it became clear that the Six Troop families had reached an understanding. Some families lacked the need or the means to maintain a correspondence. Mrs Woodman, Mrs Fisher and Mrs Lucy dropped out of contact, though they continued to receive the circular letters Clive despatched. Sadly, Edna Jenkins perhaps never knew that she might have drawn comfort and support from them. Others leaned on the arm that Clive and Phyllis offered—and they shared the burden. That bereaved families needed and appreciated their support is clear from many exchanges. Replying to another of Phyllis's patient and kind letters, Maud Harrison wrote that while she tried to face life in the spirit that her Maurice would have wished, 'at times this trouble overwhelms me and I am then truly grateful for any advice or help'. This the Burns offered uncomplainingly. The trouble they took to contact the families and help them deal with the uncertainty and the terrible finality of their sons' deaths is perhaps explained best by a short sentence in one of the dozens of letters that Clive wrote in 1942. In trying to comfort Lillian Goss he simply explained that 'They were my son's closest friends'.

The prisoners' families also realised by late 1943 that their sons were more fortunate than they had imagined. Peter Westlake told his parents that over the summer of 1943 life around Lamsdorf had become 'just one long holiday'. He had been allocated to a job in the camp laundry and went into a nearby town twice a week to deliver and collect bundles of washing. 'Actually we have quite a lot of freedom on working parties', he wrote reassuringly. The reality was not always so pleasant: the war crimes investigators' files show that at Lamsdorf guards struck men (on one occasion just before the Six Troop men arrived, prisoners were beaten with rifle butts for 'not working hard enough'). Men on isolated work parties were always more vulnerable to their captors' whims, and for every story of an indulgent or humane gang leader there seems to be a tale of a petty tyrant.

This contrasted powerfully with news from 2 Commando. In the summer of 1943 it had gone into action again, at Catania in Sicily and lost heavily at Salerno, near Naples. 'They have suffered a lot',

Stalag 383, Hohenfels. Prisoners-of-war lived a relatively comfortable life at Hohenfels.

Willie Bell's father reflected. In a letter to Phyllis he speculated that 'in all probability if our sons had not been prisoners they may by this time have lost their lives ...' Jimmy Prescott, one of Six Troop's seven who made it back to Britain after St Nazaire, told Arthur Young that 'the worst time they experienced was when they had to fight in the line' rather than in the raiding role for which they were trained and equipped. (At Salerno 2 Commando was used as infantry without having the numbers or heavy weapons for the task, and more of its men died there than in Operation Chariot.) In August Clive and Phyllis heard that Bill Watt, a Six Troop survivor who had visited them in 1942, had been killed in Italy. Fred Penfold's mother asked the Burns to write to the Watts, to send them 'a few words of comfort'. 'We have a lot to be thankful for', Willie Bell's father had written a month or so later. Thinking of her youngest son, John, recently qualified as aircrew in Bomber Command, Mrs Westlake went so far as to 'almost wish that he could be a POW too'.

For the prisoners 1943, and especially the summer, represented the most bearable phase of the war. Mrs Penfold described how Fred had marked his twenty-third birthday in Lamsdorf. 'The boys made a party in his honour', she told Clive, 'a grand party ... they had more food than they could eat so they invited others in to celebrate ... it was a grand day'. Though she did not say, it is likely that at least some of the six men of Six Troop in Lamsdorf shared Fred's birthday tea. Captured commandos were split up and sent to the dozens of work parties based on the camp, but they met at picture shows and when parties returned to the main camp for re-assignment. Peter Westlake also looked back on it as a time of 'a pleasant summer ... of exceptional freedom'. Manual work had toughened him physically (a surprising claim for a commando) while the opportunities for reading had 'stimulated my ideas and ideals', giving him 'a fresh vista of life full of interest for the future'.

Despite the prisoners' reassuring letters, families were never free of anxiety. In the autumn of 1944, Edith Penfold had an unpleasant scare. She heard through a soldier's wife that men who had been taken prisoner at St Nazaire had been posted to his battery, and they included one named as 'Penfold'. Mrs Penfold, distressed to learn that her son might have been repatriated but kept from her, wrote in confusion to Clive and Phyllis. 'I know I can always call upon you for advice', she wrote. Clive in turn wrote to the soldier, a Gunner Moore stationed at a camp at Nettlestone on the Isle of Wight. It all turned out to have been a misunderstanding: Moore had seen Fred, but in a camp before the raid.

News of the success of the Allied invasions of occupied Europe in mid 1944 unsettled the prisoners. Peter Westlake was finding it 'difficult to settle down to life as before, owing to the exciting events taking place in the outside world'. By late 1944 life for the Lamsdorf men had become more rigorous than it had been the year before. (For one thing the Allied invasion of southern France had disrupted the parcels route from Marseilles.) The few letters of Peter's that arrived allude to a deterioration in food and conditions, but indirectly for fear of the censor. Because they lived in the country they were able to find fruit and vegetables—more than German city-dwellers, perhaps more than many British civilians.

By October 1944 Peter was among a party of 50 men working in a stone quarry at Selzdorf, near Jena. Earlier in the year he had been driving an electric crane, 'but I am also quite good with a pneumatic drill and can swing a hammer as good as any navvy'. By the autumn he was responsible for issuing rations. He had to venture out into the local village to buy supplies (something increasingly difficult as the war's grip tightened) and had to juggle the deliveries of ration parcels from Canada, New Zealand and Britain. Still, he had not had a day's sickness all year, and claimed to be gaining weight, 'Like a young elephant'. Peter's 'combine' of three included 'Ted' and 'Tom': neither commandos it seems. The bonds of commando comradeship inevitably weakened in the *Stalags*, overtaken by the immediate mateship of being 'kriegies' together. Soon, their war would become even harder, as Micky was also finding.

RACE.

COLDITZ:
MICKY IN CAPTIVITY

'A SPECIAL SORT OF CAMP': SPANGENBERG

Lying in his bunk one night, surrounded by the glowing cigarette
ends of his room-mates, Micky had a sudden, swooping vision
for the opening shots of a film:

> A camera would swing across the battlefields, across the bombed cities,
> along the hills, into this quiet river valley in the heart of Europe,
> catching the ... derelict castle in one long held shot, and then dip inside,
> among the prisoners with their dreams; and so a story would begin ...

That castle was Colditz. Micky's journey there began as a German with
a submachine-gun shepherded him up a ladder from a ship's engine
room on the cold grey morning of 28 March 1942 and continued, as
we have seen, to the naval camps at Sandbostel and Westertimke.

In the summer of 1942 the Germans separated the St Nazaire
prisoners. Naval officers and ratings remained in separate compounds
at Westertimke. Except for escape artists like Billie Stephens, the
captured sailors from St Nazaire mainly remained there until they
were liberated in April 1945. In late June, they split up Micky and the
commando officers and their men. It seems that they had a chance
to farewell each other. Arthur Young told his family that Micky was
'cut up at being parted from us all'. As we have seen, commando
'other ranks' went to Lamsdorf in Silesia. Commando officers went to
Oflag IX AH at Spangenberg, in western Germany.

A few British other ranks joined the officers, as 'orderlies'; but
none of Six Troop's other ranks volunteered as servants, so the two
were separated for the rest of the war. Micky reserved some of
his monthly allocation of letters and cards to write to his men's

families. The families in turn wrote to the Burns to let them know that Micky had written. Micky's determination to stay in touch with his men meant that Clive and Phyllis received fewer letters than they would have liked. In November 1942, for example, the Bells wrote to say that they had received a postcard from Micky remembering him to Willie and they knew that even a brief mention would 'set your mind at rest ... seeing you haven't heard from him for 3 months'.

'I am now living in a castle', Micky wrote to his parents, 'as most of the best people do at this time of year'. Spangenberg, a fortress on a wooded hill overlooking the River Fulda near Kassel, held many senior officers captured at Dunkirk. Noel Barber quoted an officer from Spangenberg, who told his wife that it was, 'a rather special sort of camp'. It was secure—very few escaped from Spangenberg or even tried to—but it was reasonably comfortable. Articles and memoirs suggest that most had decided to accept incarceration for the duration. Jim Rogers, an engineer officer who later shared a cell at Colditz with Micky, noticed 'a dichotomy' between older and younger officers greater than in most camps. It was not easy to be a young Territorial officer in a staid camp, quite different to escape-minded camps like Warburg or Eichstatt. Tensions arose between officers: young against old, regular against Territorial: in fact Spangenberg was divided into two camps, an upper and a lower, one holding older officers, the other younger. Regular officers, Padre Ellison Platt recorded, remained 'exclusive to a degree'. He described them as suffering from 'Territorialphobia'. Younger officers impatient with senior officers willing to sit the war out welcomed the arrival of a number of active younger commandos. 'Everyone pleased to see new faces in the camp', a major recorded on Micky's party's arrival, 'particularly fresh young blood'.

Conditions varied greatly between camps and within camps over time. At one time in Spangenberg a prisoner could have ordered two or three bottles of wine a few days before his birthday, and apart from *Appels* and sentries the Germans hardly intervened. Searches in Spangenberg were notably less intrusive than at other camps. At the other extreme shortly after the St Nazaire commandos arrived there guards 'savagely attacked' two officers recaptured after attempting to escape. Still, the prison 'cells' at Spangenberg offered a glorious view over the beautiful hills of Kassel, to which vista British officers could gaze while orderlies brought their breakfast tea.

In 1942 days at Spangenberg revolved around lessons and lectures. A typical day's program, an inmate explained in *The Prisoner of War* magazine, resembled a university's, with a morning timetable taking in classes in Urdu, Engineering, Agriculture and Shorthand. After the inevitable *Appel*, signalled in Spangenberg by the beats of a hammer on a saw-blade, and lunch of fried meat roll and cabbage, he passed the afternoon at piano practice. Literary-minded officers contributed to a magazine, *The Quill*, recording the prosaic reality of their lives, escapist fantasy and their hopes and dreams for the future in gently humorous stories, verse and art. The commando officers soon became involved in camp pursuits: within weeks of their arrival they were performing a skit parodying *Julius Caesar*, with most of the cast, as an old hand recorded in his diary, 'composed of the St Nazaire crowd – really good fun'.

Spangenberg's inmates remained in contact with MI9, the Military Intelligence section responsible for liaising with prisoners. They sent coded messages among the hundreds of genuine letters posted each week from the camp. The head of its Escape Committee taught codes to officers reaching the camp. It was just as well. He recorded tartly that five of the St Nazaire commandos who arrived in Spangenberg had 'forgotten most of what they had learnt' in the weeks before they reached the camp: a sign of how little they had anticipated capture, perhaps. The five included Colonel Charles and Micky. After a vigorous refresher course 'they became members of the code team and', he reported at the war's end, 'did extremely good work'. Clive forwarded letters to the War Office's Room 311 for MI9 to inspect, though he may not have realised why. The German security staff at Spangenberg not only did not detect any of over 500 coded messages despatched from the camp, but had no idea that officers remained in constant contact with home.

By the winter, though, a reaction seems to have set in. Clive told Charles Haydon that he detected a change in the tone of letters from both prisoners and their families. 'They don't seem to feel that Saint Nazaire cuts very much ice' and thought that it might have been regarded as 'in fact, a bad show'. Clive asked Haydon if he could reassure the Operation Chariot prisoners that their sacrifice had been appreciated. (This may have sparked Holman's article on the anniversary reassuring the raiders that the raid had succeeded.)

Tensions evidently arose in Spangenberg. Micky even became something of a figure of suspicion, to Clive's anxiety. Looking at the photograph of him with his hands up, published in *Das Reich*, a fellow prisoner had commented that he would 'have to explain that when the War is over'. His reputation suffered when he began to give lectures on his experiences among the unemployed of Gloucestershire and Yorkshire from a stance a commando officer jokingly categorised as 'slightly to the Left of Major Attlee'. Spangenberg's older officers asked the Senior British Officer, Major General Victor Fortune, to stop him. Fortune asked Micky whether he planned to criticise the Royal Family, and on being reassured, declined to forbid him speaking. Fortune justified his decision by explaining perfectly seriously that 'at Winchester I once took five catches off his father's bowling'. (But Fortune was no old buffer: Tommy Peyton's brother, John, who shared a camp with him, recalled his courage and dignity.) As the autumn of 1942 closed in, the Spangenberg prisoners had more to worry about than Micky's allegedly subversive lectures.

<hr>

'NATURALLY VERY WORRYING':
THE REPRISALS OF 1942

Further British commando raids along the coast of occupied Europe provoked Hitler's wrath. In October 1942 he issued what was later called an 'extermination order' threatening that the 'sabotage troops of the British and their hirelings' were to be 'killed to the last man'.

The Germans began manacling prisoners because German troops captured in a raid on Sark, in the Channel Islands, had been restrained. The British government imposed counter-reprisals. (Clive thought that instead of restraining German prisoners in retaliation British workers should work an extra half hour a day, the best reprisal being more guns and bombs.) The Germans imposed the reprisals widely, though less harshly in the larger camps. When sergeants and warrant officers at Lamsdorf were restrained with string taken from Red Cross parcels they called out, 'How do we wipe our bums?' and fell about laughing, to their guards' consternation. Denholm Elliott, an actor even behind barbed wire, performed in *Twelfth Night* in work camps around Lamsdorf, holding his wrists out to have his handcuffs removed to enter on cue.

The reprisals also affected the officers in Spangenberg. They were stripped of rank insignia and denied towels, brushes, razors and even toilet paper. The Germans forbade walks, eating utensils and changes of clothing. Beards, one prisoner assured his wife, were warmer (they ran a beard-growing competition). A Swiss inspector found the sight of 400 bearded prisoners 'shocking' but thought their 'air of manliness and dignity' impressive. Another prisoner tested the suitability of German newspapers as toilet paper. (He found the virulently anti-Semitic *Volkischer Beobachter* less satisfactory than the liberal *Frankfurter Zietung*.) Prisoners spent 60 days becoming increasingly dirty and smelly. Though probably reflecting his son's more favourable account, Clive reported how the reprisals affected Micky. He was not manacled but was deprived of washing materials and, more seriously, books for about two months. It was, Clive thought, 'a stupid and senseless thing to do … it only breeds additional hatred'. Denied books, prisoners entertained one another—Micky delivered some fifty lectures, about one a day, while the reprisals lasted. Another effect of the reprisals was to delay postal deliveries.

News of the reprisals deepened many families' fears. In October Mary Westlake confided to Phyllis how 'I think about Peter so much during the night, and imagine all kinds of dreadful things, but with the day comes renewed courage'. Her husband John told Clive five months later how he and Mary had been worried to read in a Red Cross magazine that prisoners in Lamsdorf were still manacled.

'Peter's letters seem pretty genuine', they were relieved to note. They asked Clive's opinion. 'It seems a spontaneous effort', Mr Westlake thought, 'and not a letter written under coercion for propaganda purposes', as many people assumed. In fact prisoners were not coerced, but they wrote under several constraints. They had little novelty to report; they knew the Germans would censor their letters; and, most importantly, perhaps, they did not want to alarm their loved ones by including anything that might fuel the fears to which they knew families would be prey. Journalist Noel Barber warned families that 'cheerful letters home ... so often give a curiously wrong impression of life in prison camps'. Reading so many cards and letters from his son's men, Clive suspected as much. 'One always has a slight fear that they may be trying to makes things easier for us.'

Their families' anxieties increased when *The Times* reported that Germany might repudiate the Geneva Convention altogether. The report seems to have been part of the German propaganda campaign accompanying the reprisals. While Hitler idly considered abandoning the Geneva Convention more sensible officers deflected the idea. British officials knew that most Soviet prisoners had died in, or survived, appalling conditions without the protection of the convention. Prisoners' families knew only what they read in the newspapers, unable to distinguish between the factual and the fanciful, despite the positive gloss of *The Prisoner of War*. Rumours that the Germans might renege on the convention as their manpower needs grew and the burden of feeding and caring for hundreds of thousands of prisoners became an increasing drain was, Clive admitted, 'naturally very worrying'. Had the Germans abandoned the Geneva Convention, even by refusing to distribute food parcels, prisoners of war of the western Allies would have suffered similar fates to Soviet prisoners in Germany or Allied prisoners of the Japanese.

Hitler's reprisals also affected men of 2 Commando more directly. In September 1942 he had been outraged by another daring raid, on a hydro-electric plant at Glomfjord in Norway, and ordered that captured commandos be executed. Among the seven captured commandos had been Reginald Makeham, one of Micky's troop who had not gone to St Nazaire. They had been taken to the 'special' prisoner-of-war camp at Colditz in October. Held there with six comrades for a fortnight, he was then taken to Sachsenhausen concentration camp and executed with a bullet to the back of the neck before dawn on 23 October.

Soon after, the reprisals began to ease. Switzerland, the 'protecting power' administering the Geneva Convention in both directions, urged both British and German governments to moderate their stance. The Germans lifted the ban on writing or receiving letters in mid October (when prisoners received an average of 23 letters each) but still forbade washing or shaving and—a particular hardship for Micky—kept their books. 'What swine they are', Clive wrote with even-tempered contempt. The reprisals did little to damage the prisoners' morale: Micky reported that at Spangenberg officers remained 'in extremely good spirits'. When the commandant read out an order countermanding the reprisals regime on 28 November he was met by a dignified silence. The next day many officers paraded with only half their beards shaved off, a deliberate gesture of defiance.

'SHE IS A WAR CASUALTY': DINAH'S DEATH

Between the disruption caused by the increasingly heavy bombing of Germany and the lingering effects of the reprisals of late 1942, only in late January 1943 did Micky learn that Dinah Jones was dead. Her mother, Lady Evelyn, had written from Fakenham in Norfolk to tell him that she had died, on Christmas morning. She had fallen ill in August and was soon diagnosed with tuberculosis. In the limited space allowed by the 'Prisoner of War' aerogramme, Lady Evelyn summarised the swift course of her decline: 'many tests ... galloping TB ... lung collapse ... peritonitis'. She died without pain or distress early on Christmas Day. Dinah was not a commando and did not take part in the raid on St Nazaire, but those who knew her reacted to her death in the same ways as they had to Micky's men's deaths. Her mother certainly saw Dinah's death as attributable to the war.

When she fell ill in the summer Dinah had been working in a war-related job. 'She is a War Casualty Micky', Lady Evelyn wrote. 'Her body couldn't stand the strain of all she tried to do.' Lady Evelyn's tardiness in writing—over three weeks after Dinah's death—is explained by her and her husband's uncertainty about the nature of Micky and Dinah's relationship. 'She never told us anything about you – said "just friends"', but they suspected more.

Micky replied immediately, wishing he could offer his condolences to Lady Evelyn and her husband Jonah in person, to help 'make the loss less cruel'. He wrote warmly of Dinah, as honestly as he was able. He recalled her as being 'as pure and lovely as you believed her to be'. Dinah, he wrote, 'knew of my waywardness ... she helped me to save myself from these things'. Dinah's death came on top of the loss of the fourteen men of Six Troop. The experience gave him the maturity to respond to her death, as his mother noticed. Phyllis wrote to Lady Evelyn recognising that Micky had met the news 'with an understanding that I think would have been impossible before [his] recent experience'.

Lady Evelyn was in need of consolation. Her loss led her to seek solace through spiritualism. Like many of those bereaved in war, she had 'a well known medium' try to contact Dinah, and in due course passed on a message purporting to come from her. 'I am close to Mickie', the message read. 'Tell him I spoke and asked about him & that I think I am helping him.' Lady Evelyn was satisfied ('while we are naturally hoping for more evidence') she was 'inclined to accept it'. 'I think Mickie will have NO doubts', she wrote.

As news of this further loss passed among Micky's friends and their families it emerged that Dinah too had also written to many of Micky's men. 'She was of the greatest help and inspiration', Maud Harrison told Phyllis. Her daughter Molly, still grieving for her brother Maurice, wrote to let Lady Evelyn know of the comfort Dinah had brought: 'her letters were so sane and full of strength ... they did more to steady ... me at a time when my whole world was rocking'. Phyllis, who learned how Dinah had written or spoken to Micky's men's families, acknowledged how 'her steady faith and confidence ... helped us enormously'.

Dinah Jones, who loved Micky and became his 'girlfriend' in 1941. She died of tuberculosis on Christmas morning 1942.

Micky mused on this latest loss. Often, he wrote, 'my first thought is that I must tell Dinah, and then I remember …'. With time to spare in Spangenberg and other camps in 1943, Micky had time to think deeply about Dinah, and he told his parents more of his relationship with her. 'Although I was not in love with her', he acknowledged, 'she understood and made the last 2 years before we sailed very happy …'. Micky associated Dinah's love with his affection for his troop.

'She loved all the troop and that free life', he explained, 'I only wish Tom or Morgan or Maurice Harrison were here to talk about her'.

In November he wrote to Lady Evelyn, explaining that 'I hope you don't think because I haven't written that I've forgotten Dinah', and that he was writing about her. Among the poems he sent to his mother was 'To Dinah, who died on Christmas Morning'. More unfinished meditation than polished verse, it reflects Micky's attempt to make sense of yet another death. The soliloquy ends 'We came here to live, let us live,/ When the long war's finished'. Micky described to Lady Evelyn how he had asked Dinah to marry him after the war—disclosing that they were indeed more than friends—but that she had unselfishly decided not to consent until Micky desired it as fervently as she did. He did not disclose that he could not feel for Dinah as intensely as she for him. And when, after all, the long war had finished, on his wedding day (the fifth anniversary of the raid on St Nazaire), he wrote again to Lady Evelyn. Telling her of his marriage, he acknowledged that 'maybe all would have been different had Dinah lived', but affirming, in life as in verse, 'her spirit is with me always', as it still is today.

<hr />

'DEUTSCHFEINDLICH': MICKY'S TEMPTATION

In 1943 Micky would be moved on. Newman and several other commando officers would remain in Spangenberg, living a cramped and confined life so different from how they thought their war would go. Newman kept in touch with his old commander Charles Haydon, writing on the raid's second anniversary how 'we occasionally glean little bits of news ... and will be drinking a toast to you on the 28th'. By then the German authorities ordered Roman Catholic officers and orderlies from picturesque but overcrowded Spangenberg to Rotenburg, about ten miles south. Spangenberg, it seems, had no Catholic padre; Rotenburg did. Micky, having converted to Catholicism in Devon, now found his fate dependent upon his new faith.

Rotenburg camp, *Oflag* IXA/Z, actually occupied the Jacob Grimm school for girls. Its inmates were mainly senior officers, men wounded and disabled before capture and the 'protected personnel' who cared for them. Though moderately comfortable (its baths were good, and inmates enjoyed bed linen and laundry done by local women, who would even darn socks), it was not a happy camp. Senior officers occupied quarters known as 'Snobs' Alley', while 'very vocal and aggressive' Australian and New Zealand officers, resentful of being captured in Greece, vented their feelings against British officers (who were, after all, sharing their captivity). There was, as a perceptive Ordnance Corps lieutenant noticed 'the usual animus between regulars and civilians in uniform', as well as 'a number of cliques and coteries'. Soon after Micky arrived the camp's morale took a blow. Almost simultaneously, a tunnel collapsed, prisoners detected a collaborator and the Senior British Officer, Brigadier Claude Nicholson, died in a fall from a window that may have been suicide. (His is the only prisoner's grave in the cemetery at Rotenburg.)

While at Rotenburg in the summer of 1943 German officials invited Micky to turn traitor. Those who knew him well understood the political journey he had made in the 1930s: from apathetic apolitical waster, to Nazi sympathiser, to committed if unfocused and non-doctrinaire socialist. Canon Robert Quirk, his former housemaster at Winchester, had a schoolmaster's shrewd insights into Micky's character. He had remained in touch during Micky's journey and had written to the Burns to express his concern when Micky had been posted missing. When Quirk received a letter in the marathon of letters that Clive had sent in April 1942, he had offered a speculative insight. Like many, he expressed hope that Micky would prosper despite his situation. 'I expect Michael will win all hearts', he wrote, 'even among Nazis'. Canon Quirk thought that Micky had an 'ace to play ... his friendly interviews man-to-man with Hitler, & the photographs & book'. If a schoolmaster in Hampshire knew of Micky's Nazi flirtation, how much more likely was it that the Gestapo and the German Foreign Office knew too?

The Germans seem to have known that Micky had been fêted at the Nuremberg rally, introduced to Hitler and received a copy of *Mein Kampf* from the Führer's own hand (even if his losing it signified the point at which his feelings turned). They might have expected him to be amenable to collaboration (unless they had read *The Labyrinth of Europe*). They may also have noted how many titled correspondents he had attracted—in Spangenberg he reported that 'half the House of Lords have written'. As a former journalist they might have thought him a useful tool in the propaganda war. Instead, he had refused to consider not only collaboration but even to be tempted. He had protested against a British officer agreeing to investigate the site of the Katyn massacre (when on Stalin's orders his secret police, the NKVD, murdered over 4000 Polish officers). Micky had no idea who had killed them, but he argued that it would be 'disgraceful' for British officers to assist what would become Nazi propaganda: as it did. The Germans tried both enticing and threatening him, unsuccessfully. In 1944 an officer who had known Micky in captivity was repatriated and contacted the Burns. He wrote that Micky had been sent to a punishment camp because he refused to go to 'the so-called holiday propaganda camp'. The Germans stamped Micky's file with the red-inked DEUTSCHFEINDLICH: 'hostile to Germany'. It was a judgment that in the summer of 1943 led to his being sent to the most notorious prisoner-of-war camp in Germany, Colditz.

'THE BULLINGDON MESS': MICKY'S COLDITZ COMPANIONS

Micky arrived at Colditz in early August 1943. His escort led him from the railway station up a cobbled lane, towards a *Schloss* towering high above the pretty Saxon town, set picturesquely on a river surrounded by woods. A mixture of medieval castle, run-down Baroque palace and nineteenth-century hospital, it was to be Micky's home for the rest of the war. This was *Oflag* IVC, Colditz, lying in the centre of the triangle formed by Leipzig, Chemnitz and Dresden in the heart of Germany.

Colditz, one of three 'heightened security' camps among the hundreds in Germany, remains the most celebrated prison camp of the Second World War. (The others were *Stalag* 325 at Rawa-Ruska, in the Ukraine, and *Oflag* XC at Lübeck. Almost no one mentions the others, but there is a vast literature on Colditz.) It famously held many officers who had attempted escape from other camps and a small number of 'hostages', members of notable British political or aristocratic families whom the Germans thought might make useful bargaining chips if the war went badly.

And now Colditz held Micky. He described himself after sixteen months of captivity:

> *Your son at 30. I now weigh not more than 10 stone. My cheeks have fallen in like a landslide ... My hair around the ears has gone the grey of a distinguished stockbroker and has deserted the temples entirely ...*

His transfer to Colditz might have had some connection with his family's proximity to Buckingham Palace, but German assumptions or hopes about his pliability, based on his pre-war brush with fascism and his craft as a writer, seem sufficient. Fellow commandos had no doubt that Micky's arrival in Colditz had been 'something to do with his job as a writer'. Stuart Chant explained to a future historian of the raid how 'the Germans feared that he had some sinister propaganda value with us fellow prisoners'. Micky reached Colditz as an 'in-between arrival', that is, as an individual rather than in a group transferred from another camp. Arriving alone raised the possibility that he might have been a German plant or stooge. Colditz held enough friends and acquaintances, including St Nazaire commandos like Corran Purdon, to establish his bona fides.

Micky was so much accepted as genuine that he was allocated to what was nicknamed the 'Bullingdon' mess, named after the exclusive Oxford drinking and riding club, in which aristocratic undergraduates would play practical jokes whose effects they could efface with money. The group comprised, as Micky later explained, 'close relations of the Royal Family and several lords and lairds', the socially prestigious hostages known as the '*Prominente*'. They included Charlie Hopetoun, the son of the Viceroy of India, and Lieutenant Viscount George Lascelles, the eldest son of the Princess Royal and the Earl of Harewood. George Lascelles had been a 21-year-old Grenadier Guardsman, wounded and captured on a patrol in Italy. Ironically, Oxford's Bullingdon club had, to Clive's sorrow, blackballed Micky in 1930: 'not the type', they had decided.

He found himself part of a small group of British and Commonwealth officers, looked after by a small and more-or-less permanently disgruntled party of British other ranks working as orderlies. The castle had been occupied by recalcitrant Polish, French, Belgian and Dutch officers until late 1940, when the first British arrived. By mid 1943 only the British remained. While they regretted the loss of the cosmopolitan atmosphere (and the language skills that had helped successful escapes from a supposedly escape-proof camp) it became a much more cohesive community.

Colditz's setting was the most spectacular of any camp in Germany. Like Spangenberg it sat on a bluff, high above a river, the Mulde, and the town. It commanded, as even an official Red Cross inspector noticed, 'a beautiful view', with a good climate and facilities superior to other officers' camps. But few inmates appreciated either the view or their healthy situation. Though in a beautiful setting, a Red Cross visitor wrote, he sensed a 'permanent feeling of friction' within it, which 'does not make the camp a very agreeable one'. Another Red Cross official bemoaned that 'it seems impossible to establish a satisfactory understanding between the prisoners and the German authorities'. A third puzzled inspector noted the continual friction that characterised relations between the prisoners and the guards. Nobody, on either side, sought to improve the building's material state: 'the prisoners make havoc with the material equipment of the camp'. He reported that almost all the officers' bed-boards had been sawn up to make either furniture or to support increasingly desperate escape bids. British officers, Red Cross officials found, were 'all the time thinking of how to escape', though they made few bids, and no successful attempts, after the middle of 1944. From about the time Micky arrived Colditz became the Reich's most rigorous *Oflag*.

Soon after arriving in Colditz, Micky contracted a fever. As he lay sweating and delirious a vision came to him of how 'The Castle took to air, /And people climbed up steeples, and /Got out of bed to stare'.

Some verses of this long fantasy ('part Edward Lear, part *Alice in Wonderland*') appeared in his Colditz novel, *Yes, Farewell*, as the work of the character Jim Irving. The verses of what became *The Flying Castle* are, as Micky admitted, 'nonsensical symbolism'. (In sending them home he warned his parents 'you mustn't assume I've gone mad'.) But they are not pure nonsense: they express Micky's perception of his situation and the ideas that increasingly preoccupied him while a prisoner of war. Phyllis copied the verses out and they were displayed in an exhibition of prisoner-of-war art and literature at St James's Palace early in 1943, to mixed reactions from his parents.

Micky had suggested that his parents consult his former lover, Guy Burgess, about obtaining opinions on his verse—he had 'a contemporary mind', Micky explained—but whether Burgess helped is unknown. At Micky's prompting, Phyllis sought opinions from J.B. Priestley ('very promising'), Edward Marsh ('I must admit defeat'), Cyril Connolly ('not quite suitable for *Horizon*') and an anonymous but candid reader from Heinemann publishers: 'immature, if not adolescent … extremely obscure'. Clive confessed, 'I hate poetry unless it rhymes', but he at least consented to 'the literary "toughs" … being consulted'. Phyllis, who had always secretly hoped that Micky would become a poet, acted upon Clive's motto of always going to the top and sought an opinion from the leader of the literary toughs, T.S. Eliot. The material landed on Eliot's desk at Faber & Faber among what he described as 'the numerous other volumes of verse which I receive every week'. While preferring to give criticism in person—hardly possible in this case—and worried that his opinion might seem 'much more absolute than it is', Eliot thought Micky's 'versification … immature and often awkward', but that the verses showed 'a potential sense of form and point' with a natural sense of rhythm. Phyllis evidently included shorter verses as well as *The Flying Castle*, because Eliot distinguished his epigrams from the monotonous metre and fantastic imagery of the product of his delirium.

'I think he needs to devote his attention primarily to the craft rather than the art of poetry', Eliot counselled tactfully. Despite this faint praise, Micky continued to write and publish verse over the

Colditz castle, viewed from the River Mulde that flows through the town.

following 60 years. John Chrisp, a naval officer whose tendency to tunnel landed him in Colditz, remembered Micky as 'the castle poet'. Describing him as 'dreamy and impractical', Chrisp recalled him as 'a born optimist, one of the few men in Colditz who never got depressed'. Another member of the Bullingdon mess told the Burns that Micky was 'in tremendously good form … his fertile brain active with … much reading and study mixed with bouts of writing poetry when he feels the urge'. It is remarkable that Micky felt the urge in Colditz, and was able to muster the physical and mental stamina it demanded.

'LIKE A BAD HOTEL': LIFE IN COLDITZ

By mid 1943 Colditz held 169 British officers, about twenty from the dominions, with the addition of a handful of Americans and French officers, the only non-English-speaking inmates. About sixty orderlies served the 238 officers. The orderlies tended to begrudge having to act as servants to fellow prisoners: only the more canny realised that cooking in Colditz was preferable to labouring in a work camp, and tensions with and between orderlies punctuate prisoners' diaries. By the war's end the guard force had been increased from about two hundred to some five hundred. If nothing else, the prisoners obliged Germany to devote two-and-a-half times their number simply to keep them inside what was the most secure prison camp in Germany.

Micky's novel *Yes, Farewell*, written in Colditz, captures precisely the shabby atmosphere of the castle's grim corridors and its warren of small rooms:

> *The floors of the corridors were long planks, endways on, which creaked. Mice had made nests underneath; they came out through holes between wall and floor, where the angle-beams had been torn up for firewood. Cigarette ends and crumpled scraps of paper lay about. Rusty nails jutted from the rafters. In one corner where there had formerly been a stove, a disconnected pipe hung loose. The peeling discoloured walls looked as if they had smallpox.*

Eighteen sentry towers overlooked the castle, each with searchlights and machine-guns. Arc lamps illuminated the entire fortress, doused briefly during raids on nearby Leipzig and Dresden. Sentries with dogs patrolled the grounds. Below ground, sound detectors sought to prevent tunnelling attempts that had occupied so great a proportion of the prisoners' energy. Frequent and intrusive searches aimed to find escape materials, while prisoners were summoned to the cobbled courtyard at odd hours four and even five times a day, beginning as early as seven or as late as ten at night, obliging them to stand about being counted while some shouted catch-cries and abuse at guards. (The guards, known as 'goons', were given offensive nicknames—ones Micky recorded were 'Ropey', 'Dopey', 'Pieface', 'Snuffler', 'Eggs' and simply 'Bastard'.)

Micky later tended to deprecate Colditz, describing it as 'like a bad hotel': a characteristically tongue-in-cheek line intended to conceal the uncomfortable and tedious reality. Micky's letters to his parents are quite candid about it. In November 1943 he felt that 'the worst thing here' was physical restraint—'lack of exercise and sex'. A month later it was 'the squalor ... next to the lack of freedom and privacy'. He claimed he (and surely many other officers) had been prepared for the ordeal by 'the harsher side of public school life', with its combination of routine, bad food, intellectual pursuits and 'on the whole agreeable companions'.

Tedium fostered boredom and depression, and in some a descent into madness. Bored 'with each other and with themselves', they spoke in what Micky called 'parallel monologues'. Miles Reid, who claimed to be Colditz's oldest inmate and who knew Micky slightly through his father, wrote long, frank letters to his wife. He deplored how prisoners of war 'never lose the faculty of chatter'. Reid had been in Spangenberg, but thought that Colditz was 'the worst I've been in' for the 'endless streams of utter drivel' he had to put up with. Other prisoners withdrew from their fellows, in cycles of depression. In *Yes, Farewell*, Micky described their drugs as 'smoking, sleeping and self-abuse'. Few have had the honesty to mention masturbation: it hardly fits with the image of the clear-eyed escaper of the Colditz myth. Men sought release from this intense, claustrophobic world in various ways. Micky described the alcove occupied by his character Tug. On his bookshelves lay 'the tombstones of past crazes': handbooks on sailing from the time he was designing a yacht; books on farming, cars, German, French and Russian grammars, each the relic of a failed fad. Many prisoners became broody at times, often around meaningful dates: Christmas; birthdays; the anniversaries of capture or arrival in Colditz; wedding anniversaries. British prisoners were left alone to work it out. Most combated the ennui and tension with what Micky's friend Giles Romilly called 'cheerful aggressiveness'. Everything became the subject of perpetual wrangling between successive Senior British Officers and the camp commandant and his staff. Prisoners languished in a state of permanent, tense inactivity. Young officers especially sought to alleviate tedium by pushing their guards' patience to its limits. To Swiss inspectors their defiance seemed 'childish'.

The most valuable tonic remained letters from home, and from other interesting correspondents. Astonishingly, Ella van Heemstra was able to write to Micky from occupied Holland. At Christmas

1943 she sent him a photograph of herself, 'to remind you of the good old days!' Ella put on a brave face in describing the hardships of wartime Holland. Her family was well, she reported and Audrey was still able to dance and dreamed of performing after the war. 'We'll send you tickets for a box [on her] first night ... in London!' In 1944, though, hunger, sickness, Gestapo reprisals and the terrors of battle would bring the war to Ella's family and force them to flee as refugees.

'THE SCRIBE': THE SECRET WIRELESS

Colditz's earliest inmates subsisted on news cribbed from private letters until in the summer of 1943 departing French officers bequeathed to the British a wireless receiver hidden in the attic of the main block. Powered by tapping into the mains and then (as mains power failed under the impact of increasingly heavy raids) by an electric motor stolen from the church organ, the wireless gave the prisoners a nightly news service. In paragraphs added to the manuscript of *Yes, Farewell* after the war's end (because to have admitted it in captivity would have imperilled the wireless's security), Micky described how 'every evening they heard the British news'.

The wireless set was Colditz's only daily link with home. (It only received broadcast news; it was not a secret transmitter.) The Germans later knew that a wireless existed, but never discovered its hiding place. Only a handful of prisoners knew its location, under the eaves and actually inside the wall cavity of the block's attic. It was in an alcove in a room over the Bullingdon mess, though only Micky and a few others knew exactly where. The hiding place was no cubbyhole, but was large enough to hold three men, a table and chairs. Getting into or out of the alcove took five minutes, a particular danger if an *Appel* were called in the meantime. An 'army of stooges' guarded the approaches to the attic and gave some security from guards' searches. 'Camouflage men' or 'putter-inners' ensured that the trapdoor and the corridor leading to it was closed, and carefully restored to an innocuous appearance. References to the secret wireless appear in many Colditz memoirs, often differing in detail.

Two teams alternated on the task, working under a 'master stooge', Gris Davies-Scourfield, another Rifles officer. Two men operated the set in turn (Dick Howe and Jimmy Yule), while two scribes took turns to transcribe the bulletins: Lieutenant Jim Rogers, a former mining engineer, and Micky. (He was at last using the Pitman shorthand his father had urged him to learn.) They took down broadcasts verbatim, usually the BBC, sometimes German or French bulletins. Micky became known as 'The Scribe', at least partly for his work in transcribing hundreds of hours of broadcasts. This duty earned him his only mention in the official history of the fortress compiled after the war, and in Pat Reid's popular unofficial history, *The Latter Days at Colditz*.

Immediately after the broadcast, as the operators replaced the set and the camouflage men tidied up to leave the attic looking undisturbed, the scribes would dictate their notes to a group of 'readers', who visited the various rooms and read out the news, usually within an hour of the broadcast. Then both burned the shorthand notes and the readers' transcripts. Eventually prisoners ceased to try to conceal that they were getting news from outside the prison, and even discussed their differing versions of war news with guards, but the set was never to be exposed. Despite near-run alarms, in which scribes, operators and camouflage men jumped down a chute that ended two floors below, the clandestine wireless set operated daily for nearly two years without discovery. Prisoners reported that the feeling of being in daily touch with reliable (and increasingly heartening) news was, as the prisoners' own history of Colditz put it, of 'inestimable value in maintaining morale throughout the period'. Even Miles Reid, one of Micky's adversaries in Colditz (and another who finished a novel there), acknowledged 'our tremendous debt of gratitude' to the men who kept the wireless in operation. The encouragement of news became all the more important as material conditions deteriorated in the war's final winter.

The secret wireless receiver allowed inmates to follow the slow but inexorable progress of Allied victories. Positive news from all fronts encouraged hopes for a swift victory, and prisoners suffered agonies from disappointments and setbacks. With the landings in Italy in 1943, by New Year it was possible for Willie Bell's father to write to Phyllis on New Year's Eve that 'I trust the war will soon end and all the boys will come home': something they both wished for fervently. In the spring of 1944, with the invasion of France expected, prisoners 'spoke of the invasion as a kind of revelation to come'. Many allowed themselves to believe that 'a few days after it had been launched they would be free'.

News of the invasion came first from observing their guards' unusually unsettled behaviour. On the evening of 6 June the BBC confirmed the news: Allied forces had succeeded in landing in France. Maps of Normandy appeared on barrack room walls. Even German newspapers reported the invasion. By mid summer the prisoners were 'breathless with the speed of events'. For so long cynical of ever getting out, for a time, Micky wrote, 'they took it almost as a studied insult if there was not a victory each day'.

The wireless party continued to transcribe and spread news until the liberation. On the final day Micky simply left the wireless hidden as it was, leaving one of his notebooks on the shelf: a BBC television crew found it there nearly thirty years later.* Meanwhile, the tempo of Allied air raids on the Reich increased. When the Americans raided Dresden, 25 miles away, the windows in Colditz would rattle. It became clear, both from the wireless bulletins and from the sight of huge formations of bombers overhead that the war could not last much longer.

'ESCAPE OF THE MIND': MENTAL LIBERATION

Escapers were, as Jim Rogers said, the 'Kings of Colditz'. The castle's celebrity derives largely from the daring, skill and success of attempts to get out of it. Pat Reid recorded that by the end

---

* Micky and Jim Rogers both claimed the notebook discovered by the BBC film crew as their own. Henry Chancellor's 'definitive' history of Colditz gives the palm to Rogers.

of 1942 about forty officers had made just over seventy attempts to get out. In the camp's first three years 131 individuals made over one hundred and eighty attempts: only 30 successfully. Their attempts remain the essence of the Colditz legend. Among the four last successful escapers was Billie Stephens, commander of ML 192, who got away in October 1944. (The last man to get out of Colditz, a Canadian engineer, simply disappeared, probably anonymously recaptured then killed in Mauthausen concentration camp.) Clive's friend Sir Alan Lascelles wrote from Buckingham Palace to suggest that Micky 'will find his own way home some day soon'. Clive too was 'quite sure that he will not rest until he has made an effort to get away'. In fact, like the vast majority of British prisoners of war, Micky made no attempt at escape; at least in the physical sense, though a rumour went around his friends later in 1943 that he had got home. His former troop sergeant wrote from an officer cadet school in India to congratulate him. (He had taken up the offer that Maurice Harrison had considered and refused. Maurice might have died with the Chindits in Burma; or he might have survived.)

Having mostly ended up in Colditz because of failed escape attempts, escaping exercised a fascination for its inmates, irrespective of nationality. The most successful escapers proportional to their numbers were in fact the Dutch, one in three of whom attempted it. The British became more celebrated, but only one in 4.5 British inmates tried to escape. In the war's final year only fifteen attempts were made, and one of the last was to end in tragedy.

Some men became obsessed with escape, making repeated attempts, however foolhardy, until they made a 'home run' or died trying. One was the redheaded Michael Sinclair, nicknamed by the Germans the 'Red Fox'. Like Micky a former Winchester scholar and a Rifles officer, Sinclair had been captured at Calais in May 1940. He had escaped three times before being sent to Colditz, once evading capture for five months and getting as far as Bulgaria. He had got away again in November 1942 only to be recaptured on the Swiss frontier, and in September 1943 had attempted escape by impersonating a sergeant nicknamed 'Franz-Joseph' because of his distinctive side whiskers and resemblance to the late Austro-Hungarian monarch. This time a guard, nicknamed 'Bigbum', had shot him close to the heart while Sinclair already had his hands up. Three months later Sinclair and another officer took advantage of a three-minute lag in a guard change to make a hastily planned and audacious getaway. They squeezed through a barred window, scrambled down a wall and got away through a barbed-wire fence a few minutes ahead of guards blinded by their own arc lights. Five days later, they were back again. Extraordinarily, recaptured escapers invariably received light sentences in the fortress's cells which, though Spartan, at least offered respite from the irritations of the overcrowded barrack rooms. Rarely—notably when the Gestapo executed 50 men after the 'Great Escape' from *Stalag Luft* III in March 1944—did the Germans act like archetypal Nazis. All the prisoners admired Sinclair for his dedication, ingenuity and courage. But his desire to get out increasingly smacked of desperation.

In September 1944, Hitler transferred command of the prison camp system from the *Wehrmacht* to the SS's head, Heinrich Himmler. Later that month, the prisoners were paraded in the courtyard. After the count, unusually, a German officer had a quiet word to Willie Tod, the Senior British Officer from June 1944, and called off his guards. After the guards had gone Tod informed them flatly, 'Gentlemen, I am sorry to tell you that Mr Sinclair is dead. Fall out.' Admiring Sinclair as they did—no one had made more attempts than he had— they felt, as Padre Platt recorded that evening, 'a moment of extreme wretchedness'. Guards had spotted Sinclair climbing over the barbed wire enclosing the exercise field and fired as he ran for the fence. Sinclair was buried a few days later, the pall-bearers all members of the King's Royal Rifle Corps. Sinclair's escape attempt had been, as a sympathetic Red Cross inspector observed, 'an act of despair'. Others were to escape in less dangerous ways; in their minds.

Soon after Micky's capture Clive had imagined him behind barbed wire offering to 'lecture on Shakespeare, the Bible, literature or Street fighting' or 'organizing lectures for the Troops upon reconstruction and the future of the world so long as anyone will stand it'. Though Clive often seems to be a distant father, he saw his son clearly in many ways. This is exactly what Micky was to do. Despite the obstacles of hunger, ennui and depression, many turned to the mental escape of reading serious literature, studying for qualifications and even creative effort.

Many men in Colditz thought about the sort of world that the war would bring about. Padre Platt, Colditz's non-conformist clergyman, preached a sermon some time in 1944 in which he mused on how 'most people [in Colditz] are wondering what the state of things is likely to be in post-war Britain, America, Canada, Australia or whatever place they call home'. Platt urged Colditz's inmates to 'be better men'. He had an uphill battle. 'Cynicism', Micky wrote, 'was the castle's dominant mood'. Many had lost faith 'in England, in democracy, in human nature, and in their friends'. This disillusionment meant that 'a crust grew around them ... difficult and troublesome to break'. Micky's approach differed from Platt's.

As a journalist, he had become an expert in relations between states. As a prisoner, he had read and thought about economics as an engine of human social behaviour and mechanisms for its regulation. It had been relatively easy for Micky to take up serious study behind barbed wire. He began work in earnest, studying to a schedule, and in due course won a Diploma in Social Sciences (with distinctions in all subjects) from Oxford; at last fulfilling his youthful promise. Clive, as usual going to the top, had written to the Master of Balliol as early as June 1942. He sought his help in posting economics texts fuelling both Micky's degree work and his reflections on the state of the world. As well as literature sent by friends from *The Times*, the books Micky read in captivity included *The Theory of Full Employment under Capitalism, Inequality of Incomes, Trade Cycles and the World Depression*, and John Maynard Keynes's *General Theory of Employment, Interest and Money*. (Given the German prohibition of subversive books, it was an achievement for Micky to have read socialist economics in the Reich's most secure prison camp.)

Clive actively assisted Micky's ventures into political economy. Despite his constitutional Toryism, he caught the reforming mood of the war's years of victory. 'Planning, of course, is in everybody's mind', he wrote. He was glad that the government was planning for the post-war world, unlike in 1918. Clive sent him various official reports—including Beveridge's, the founding charter of the welfare state—that helped him to stay abreast of the political and social changes the war brought. This diet of economics called for the determination of what he called a martyr. It was always hard to find a quiet spot in the crowded barrack rooms and harder still to concentrate amid the clamour of other men doing odd jobs or wrangling to while away the time. Reading, reflecting and arguing, by this time, Micky later recalled, he was 'well on the way to Marxism'.

'Escape of the mind', Micky wrote afterwards, 'enables the escaper to possess another world for a prolonged period, while remaining physically where he is'. In Colditz Micky achieved this through his novel, *Yes, Farewell*, revealing another meaning to his nickname, 'The Scribe'.

YES, FAREWELL: MICKY'S COLDITZ NOVEL

'At least fifty novels' were begun in Colditz, Micky wrote, but 'they were like tunnels, a means of escape, usually ended halfway through'. From the autumn of 1944, many prisoners spent much of the day in bed, to preserve their strength and keep warm. That Micky found the energy to continue is a testament to the firmness of character that lay beneath the languid and fey exterior. Few novels were finished and published: among them Micky's *Yes, Farewell*. It reflects and draws on Micky's experience of Colditz but inevitably embroiders the reality to express the needs of fiction. Its central character is Alan Maclaren, a lieutenant captured in an independent company in Norway.

The book is structured in four parts. The first, set in the autumn of 1942, occurs over 24 hours in 'Castle Durheim', a thinly fictionalised Colditz (both the setting and many characters can be identified). Alan, Tug and Brian plan an escape. The second part traces the story of the ultimately unsuccessful escape. Alan and Tug separate from Brian (who makes a 'home run' only to die in Normandy). They meet two Russian escapers, Ivan and Mischa, who introduce the essential tension in the novel, between an idealised Soviet socialism and the jaded liberalism of pre-war Britain. Tug and Alan are caught just short of the Swiss frontier and, because they carry rings inscribed with Soviet stars (gifts from the Russians) they are taken to a Gestapo prison in Munich. Here, in the novel's third part, they meet Dr Tomavich, a Balkan history professor captured with partisans in Yugoslavia. Tomavich prompts Alan especially to consider what the war is for and against. At the end of the winter of 1942–43 Dr Tomavich is given orders to be transferred to another camp, at which he is likely to die. In a scuffle Tug is shot and killed. Alan is returned to Castle Durheim. There, in the fourth part, he sees the prisoners through new eyes. He takes up the study of economics, joining a Marxist discussion group and stopping a despairing friend, Jim Irving, from killing himself. Over the war's final year Alan develops a respect for the castle's prisoner-of-war orderlies—anticipating the 'proles' of George Orwell's *1984*—and deepens his commitment to a different way of thinking about society after the war. In the war's final winter two officers, the communist Morshead and Anstruther (a sort of composite reactionary character) debate communism and capitalism, a reflection (as we will see) of what actually occurred. In the spring the Russians (and not, as in life, the Americans) liberate the castle and Alan leaves to engage with post-war freedom, though he has said yes, farewell to the liberalism that, he thinks, has failed them all.

The novel sustained Micky over the war's final year. He later admitted that he became obsessed by it, failing to stop for meals, even when the prisoners were most hungry, resenting the war's approaching end because the manuscript remained unfinished. An orderly, Sydney Smith, a Royal Sussex Territorial captured at Alamein, proved invaluable by transcribing Micky's writing. In fact, he appears to have given Micky ideas for the chapters in which Maclaren spends time in the Gestapo cells. Smith had worked alongside Russian prisoners in a mine and spent nine months in Konigstein Castle, near Dresden, where he had witnessed Special Air Service sergeants captured in Yugoslavia 'subjected to constant interrogations'.

Yes, Farewell expresses Micky's thoughts, as he said, not just about how prisoners might get out of Colditz, but how they got into it. It evokes the tedium and depression of their confinement. As an account written in the castle at the time it captures much of the camp's physical conditions; the litter, graffiti, the fag ends and the squalor. It sketches relations between prisoners and recognisable Germans, such as the Security Officer, Lissow (based on Reinhold Eggers) and the distant Commandant, Freiherr von Grednitz. It is frank about aspects that Pat Reid ignored or minimised: tensions between prisoners, selfishness, depression, sexual longings and release, rackets, and even the temptation of collaboration. More importantly, though, it also describes with subtlety and sensitivity what went on in prisoners' minds during the long months of captivity. *Yes, Farewell* is really a gigantic argument that Micky held with himself, debating whether the politics with which he grew up could survive in a totalitarian world. As Clive had observed to John Westlake, with whom he enjoyed a bond as fathers, 'he is a determined creature with very firm views'. In the war's last winter Micky was to give all who would listen the benefit of those views.

'A THOUGHT TO OUR OWN BOYS': THE 1944 ANNIVERSARY

The effects of grief and the pressures of a fifth year of war (constraints weighing heavily upon what were then called 'housewives') were becoming apparent, and by this time some of the Burns' correspondents knew each other well enough to be able to share their feelings. Phyllis had sent Maud Harrison a copy of one of Micky's Colditz poems. She replied that she and Samuel liked it very much and they wanted to know when it and others would be published. Maud confessed that she felt as if she were 'growing into a hard, cynical woman, carrying on from day to day like a senseless machine'. The reason for her dismaying change was not just the gruelling effects of rationing and shortages and the many demands made upon women on the misplaced grounds that they had time to be exploited: it was of course also the continuing effects of Maurice's death, which remained only 'presumed'. 'There has been no further notification from the War Office', Maud complained in

February 1944, 'but I have no more hope'. She desperately wished 'if only we could talk to the men who were with the boy' at the time of his death, 'it would ease the pain a little, I think'. From Colditz Micky had sent a Christmas message (sent on 30 November, it arrived in London at the end of January). Maud gratefully wrote that 'he never forgot Maurice and therefore never forgot us': the responsibilities of friendship continued after parting.

In 1944 the BBC again broadcast a short tribute to St Nazaire on 28 March, twice, in the afternoon and evening. Samuel Harrison wrote to thank Clive for his kindness in alerting them to the broadcast, saying that it was 'high time the BBC gave a thought to our own boys' (he seems to have meant the dead of St Nazaire, and not British rather than American troops). This time instead of an American, Stuart Chant delivered a talk, once again carefully scripted to eliminate any potentially embarrassing spontaneity. While the families were glad that St Nazaire had been remembered, they naturally looked for a fuller account than the fifteen minutes allowed. Clive saw nothing new in the newspaper articles published after Chant's return 'but I am glad they did not forget', he told John Westlake. Dorothy Peyton—by this time doing voluntary work in a YMCA van—heard the evening broadcast. She thought that Chant's reserve—he delivered the scripted talk in the customary stilted manner—made the 'whole heroic and tragic event so very insignificant'. She was particularly unhappy that Chant concentrated on the story of HMS *Campbeltown* (where he had been) rather than on the launches 'where I suppose the men had a far worse time'. Time had not diminished Dorothy's grief, and she had since met many others bearing the same burden. Having held a quiet memorial service for Tommy, she had become more demonstrative. 'I could not help wishing that we were not so terribly reserved as a nation', she wrote to Clive on the raid's second anniversary.

As the available St Nazaire spokesman—the only officer, even though five other ranks had returned (after, it must be said, much more arduous ordeals in evading capture)—Chant became an obvious candidate for public attention. Chant's address was hardly a spontaneous account. The files of Combined Operations Headquarters show how closely scripted and vetted it had been. A staff officer described how

Chant had 'a very excellent story to tell'. However, not one to let a good story get in the way of a better one, he had arranged for 'a suitable version' to be cleared by PR and Security, and it would then not only undergo 'further vetting through the normal censorship channels' but would also be seen by Naval Intelligence and the Admiralty. Even then, Chant would need 'careful handling'. Goebbels had little to learn from his British counterparts about manipulating news, it seems.

Having assisted British wireless propaganda Chant soon, ironically, found himself facing a charge of abetting German propaganda. When later in 1942 staff at Combined Operations Headquarters in Richmond Terrace had learned that a commando officer especially had 'gone to a Hun mike', they felt 'considerable anger and dismay'. In due course—not for nearly a year after his repatriation—Chant was called to account. He affirmed stoutly that he had not participated knowingly in a broadcast intended to assist the enemy. After a tense wait—had he been deemed to have co-operated in the recording he would have faced court-martial—his explanation was accepted. Chant described how the wounded and captured commandos saw a stream of visitors, including civilians with Red Cross brassards on their arms. They encouraged men to give their names and addresses and a message for their families, promising that the messages would be sent via neutral intermediaries. As more experienced prisoners of war they later met officials from the International Red Cross and realised that the men they had seen had been bogus. Chant claimed that the microphones had been hidden and that they had been recorded clandestinely. What appears in the transcript as Chant's shock and confusion—'My name or my father's name?'—might also be read as his suspicion that all was not above board. Chant made no mention of this recording in his memoir *St Nazaire Commando*, his shame at how close he came to being charged with collaboration masking his memory. In the end, however, it is the memory of Chant's heroism in the raid that should prevail over his error in having talked into a German microphone.

Violet Hudson, who by this time had learned that her brother George had indeed been killed, wrote to thank Clive for alerting the families about the anniversary broadcast. Speaking for all the bereaved families, she wrote that 'it is good to know that they are still remembered, not only by us, but by everyone'. Few had as profound a reason to remember St Nazaire in particular, and what was an interesting broadcast for most remained a subject of tender recollection by others. Violet was again writing for her mother, who remained 'not at all well': how much illness arose not from germs or injury but from the corrosive effects of grief on the spirit?

Families at home continued to send letters and cards: a Christmas card, a letter passing on snippets of news from behind barbed wire: less commonly news of those in 2 Commando still overseas. 'I thought I would drop a note', wrote Alex Bell. 'I was thinking it is just two years this month since the St Nazaire Raid.' He voiced a note of concern for Clive and Phyllis: 'my wife was saying as late as last Sunday, "I wonder if the Burns are alright?"' Almost all the families repeatedly voiced their gratitude for the Burns' help. Mary Bushe wrote simply at Christmas 1943 that 'it was your dear husband gave me the first consolation I got' after Paddy was posted missing. With the passing months the burden of grief gradually changed from acute pain to chronic ache. Even the Tomsetts, as severely grieved as any, at last accepted that Reg lay in a grave at Escoublac and resolved to visit as soon as they could after the war.

On the second anniversary of the raid Lewis Roach again wrote to thank Clive Burn for advising the Six Troop families that the BBC had broadcast an anniversary feature on the raid. He had again enclosed an In Memoriam notice for Tom, including the verse beginning:

> He lies beneath a foreign sky,
> The lad we loved so well;
> He did his duty like a man,
> And like a hero fell.

Clive replied, conscious that 'we might have been so easily in the same position'. He reflected—probably not for the first time—how 'it is only a matter of a few inches when bullets are flying about'. Writing as one Great War survivor to another, Clive felt 'deeply conscious of the fortune we have had'. All the same, Micky remained a prisoner of war. 'I think he has made himself a thorough nuisance to the Germans', he wrote, 'and is now at the "bad boy's" camp at IV C'—Colditz.

In the 'bad boy's camp' a week before, the four St Nazaire men had gathered on the second anniversary of the raid to celebrate their success and remember their dead comrades. The four were Micky, Corran Purdon, Dick Morgan and Micky Wynn, the skipper of MTB 74, who had been captured after he stopped his vessel to rescue men clinging to a life-raft in the estuary. He lost an eye when his boat was sunk and managed to be repatriated later in 1944.

The wider world of war continued to break in on the closeted world of Colditz. In May 1944 Micky heard through his mother from his great friend Jean Butler at the Star Hotel in Moffat. The Butlers' son Oswald, a 24-year-old lieutenant, had died in fighting north of Naples the previous January. ('They could not get the stretchers up ...') The news broke the Butlers, and they felt unable to stay in Moffat. The Six Troop families also suffered further blows. Maud, Samuel and Molly Harrison, still suffering from Maurice's death, heard in March 1945 that his childhood friend and fellow member of 2 Commando, Nelson Smallbone, had been killed in Italy. Smallbone's parents, Nelson and Lucie, had written to offer condolences to Phyllis Burn in 1942, and now it was her turn to console them: she noted on their letter 'Wrote to his parents 14-4-45'.

The Burns' papers suggest how vortices of grief must have whirled behind every operation. In due course came a letter from the mother of Jimmy Prescott (now a company sergeant major, still with 2 Commando in Italy). Alice Prescott reported that they had heard from Nelson Smallbone's father—'very brave letters'—and that Jimmy had written to them with 'particulars' of where and how Nelson had died.

'STUBBORN, PROUD AND UNCOMPROMISING': COLDITZ LATE 1944

By mid 1944 prisoners were receiving almost all their nourishment from Red Cross parcels. Each man received about half a Red Cross parcel each week, distributed from a stockpile created by the prisoners: deliveries had ceased in April 1944. By July 1944 the store held only enough for another nineteen weeks. Only seven weeks of tobacco remained. While 490,000 cigarettes remained as the basis of barter with the Germans, Colditz's guards remained less amenable to trading than most camp guards. On meagre German rations all prisoners were, according to a Red Cross inspection, 'insufficiently nourished'. Seventy per cent had lost weight compared not with their condition at capture, but at previous inspections. Ominously, the all-important postal deliveries faltered as the German railway system came under increasing Allied bombing. By the autumn of 1944 food became, as a new arrival told war crimes investigators, 'really appalling'. He had arrived in Colditz after a long journey from Serbia, through two concentration camps, but he was still shocked by the quantity and quality of rations in Colditz.

If parcels addressed to prisoners of war became a low priority for Germany then letters from them became even less important. A year before VE Day, Micky had warned his parents that letters were becoming rarer and later and that 'as the war comes to an end they are bound to get rarer still'. At the end of March 1945 Clive told John Westlake the Burns had not heard from Micky since December 1944. 'It is always an anxiety', he agreed. In the war's last six months, families again entered a period of ignorance and worry. Clive and Phyllis continued to write to prisoners' families, not only of Six Troop men, but also of men with whom Micky had shared huts or messes. In March 1945, by which time nothing had been heard for months, Clive wrote to the mother of Micky's fellow Colditz inmate, Giles Romilly. All he could tell her was that in December Micky had sent a message that Giles was well and had also sent her some verses that seem never to have arrived. As another mother to whom Clive wrote replied, 'one appreciates any scrap of news'.

Within the camp, morale remained buoyant, with few cases of mental disturbance, partly a result of the news supplied daily by Micky and the wireless teams. A Red Cross inspector in October 1944 found that most prisoners in Colditz remained of 'strong character, stubborn, proud and uncompromising'. Conditions deteriorated in the winter of 1944–45. After parcels ran out in December 1944 prisoners depended upon German rations: 14 ounces of potatoes or 21 ounces of turnips a day, with 11 ounces of ersatz bread, with ersatz coffee and jam. A morsel of fresh meat was served on Sundays, too little to halt the symptoms of malnourishment—chilblains and oedema, which left men puffy and swollen with fluid. Hygiene was 'primitive'—a kind euphemism. Everyone stank and scratched. Sheets went unchanged for up to six weeks and men queued for a shower bath every ten days: cold, of course—there was too little coal to heat the barrack rooms. As the war's final winter advanced medical officers detected a marked increase in nervous disorders like insomnia and dyspepsia, with over half of the inmates struck down by a 'flu easily transmitted in the crowded barrack rooms. The prisoners' five medical officers now had even fewer means with which to treat disease—the last medical parcel had arrived in May 1944, nearly a year before liberation.

All sport was impossible except savage and exhausting games of stool-ball in the tiny cobbled courtyard ('a very dangerous kind of rugger ... I've no skin on my knees or elbows', Micky told his parents). Exercise walks, often withdrawn as part of the continuing feuding between guards and prisoners, continued under such close restraint—a Red Cross report described prisoners exercising 'in a veritable crowd of sentries'—that many preferred not to bother. Some prisoners attempted to distil speakeasy alcohol known, from its starting constituent, as Jam-alc. Micky described it as 'fiendish stuff'. It produced a deceptive gaiety and then 'suddenly, without the least warning, knocked you straight out'. While it gave men an interval of oblivion, the inevitable hangover deterred many from trying it more than once. Colditz's favoured drug, nicotine, also became scarce. The prisoners' only consolation was that however difficult conditions became for them, their German guards and their families had it even tougher. One of the clearest signs of Germany's plight was, as Micky noticed, patrolling sentries stopped to pick up prisoners' dog-ends.

'ALL MEN ARE BROTHERS':
COMMUNISM IN COLDITZ

At the other end of Colditz's social scale to the Bullingdon mess were the camp's British orderlies. 'Other ranks' sent to Colditz worked as senior officers' servants and in the kitchens. Micky introduced them in the opening chapter of *Yes, Farewell*, standing in their shirt-sleeves at *Appel*, 'looking critically at the officers, now and then nudging each other'. They had been sent from camps like Lamsdorf, where they had laboured in mines and on farms. Micky's autobiographical character, Alan Maclaren, 'wondered what they thought of him and the rest' of the officers. Successive Senior British Officers had trouble with their orderlies, often conscripts or Territorials, who objected to having to work for officers who lived in idleness. Not until a batch of Welsh regulars arrived in 1944, happy to peel spuds and fetch wood for British officers rather than hew coal for the Germans, did the orderlies cease to irritate their superiors. In *Yes, Farewell* the orderlies became a reminder of the good sense and goodwill of the ordinary man. In the meantime, the orderlies quietly courted Polish or Ukrainian girls in the town, intimidated and traded with guards, unobtrusive but indispensable to the running of the camp.

'A curious thing happened to us,' Jim Rogers (Micky's fellow wireless scribe) recalled, 'a stirring of Communism'. He described how 'one of our more brilliant types, educated and very articulate', started a series of lectures on Russia. A total war fought between rival ideologies reached into Colditz in the war's last year. Micky became notorious as one of Colditz's 'two Communists'. The other was Giles Romilly, a fellow member of the Bullingdon mess. Romilly was even less conventional than Micky, a rebel since his schooldays. He and his brother Esmond wrote *Out of Bounds*, a frank joint memoir of their school, whose chapters trace his journey from 'Conforming' to 'Defying'. His 'personal hatred' of his school's Officers' Training Corps led him to declare his pacifism, and in sixth form he became a communist and an atheist ('without in the least considering what it meant to be either'). He had fought for the republic in Spain and as a correspondent for the *Daily Express* in Norway had been interned in early 1940. His family connections—Clementine Churchill was his mother's sister—ensured that the Germans saw him as a useful bargaining chip, and he was sent to Colditz as one of the *Prominente*. True to his principles, Romilly argued about the necessity and inevitability of communism. His fierce communism helped to inspire Micky to ponder the idea of joining the Red Army if its troops were to reach Colditz before the western allies.

Micky later recalled how he 'thought and talked and wrote about a dream of Britain after the war'. He introduced a small-scale version of Six Troop's 'E.P.'. Micky described in *Yes, Farewell* how two evenings a week a group of fifteen or so, including orderlies, met in one of the doctor's rooms. 'They talked about communism and socialism and the brave new world.' Micky's copyist, the orderly Sydney Smith, ('Cockney born and bred') attended what he called Romilly's 'secret Communist meetings' over the war's final winter. Micky later reflected that many in Colditz dwelt on the problem of how they were to get out, but that he thought more about how they had got in. Like many, he pondered, and spoke and argued about what it was in the international order of the 1930s that had caused the war. Colditz was, as Morshead argued to Alan in *Yes, Farewell*, 'only a replica of England before the war', perhaps even 'a forecast of England after the war as well'. Alan countered that 'even the German papers say that England is altering'. Clive Burn, whom Micky had warned to expect 'a pretty sharp surprise' on liberation saw that 'he will not put up with the old regime', though he hoped Micky would seek revolution 'without extreme violence'.

Despite the scepticism towards Stalin's regime Micky had expressed in *The Labyrinth of Europe*, by the war's final year he had become more sympathetic to the ideal of Soviet communism. A critical motif in Micky's turn towards communism was his dream of the Chinese boy. Micky dreamed of a vast medieval battle on the plains of Central Asia. Among the heaps of dead and dying he found a hideously wounded Chinese boy with a beautiful face who murmured 'All men are brothers' before dying. He returned to this dream repeatedly; in *Yes, Farewell*, his verse, a foreword to a new edition of the novel (capitalising on the 1974 television series *Colditz*) and in his memoir *Turned Towards the Sun*. Micky attached

great importance to dreams—they became a motif throughout
Yes, Farewell. The dream of the Chinese boy gave him a motto on
which to base his life.

In the meantime ideological schisms appeared in Colditz. Micky,
Gris Davies-Scourfield recalled, 'actually told me one day that I was
a typical barrier to all social progress and I would undoubtedly end
up one day, nice fellow though I might be, hanging from a lamp
post'. The two later became friends, but the barb hints not just
at the tensions inevitable in crowded messes but also at the real
ideological differences dividing British officers sharing captivity.
Boredom, the Red Army's victories and Giles and Micky's eloquence
and enthusiasm awakened an interest in their political creed in the
unlikeliest place.

Giles Romilly, seizing on the popularity of the Red Army's
successes in battle (and on the willingness of bored inmates to
listen to anything) now offered lectures on Soviet ideology. 'These
lectures', Jim Rogers remembered, 'became highly popular'. They
discussed the future. It was an impulse common to millions of
Britons, and others, at that time. Micky described how like 'tens
of thousands of other young Englishmen, in ships, in the desert, in
prisoner of war camps' he pondered the Britain they had fought for.
'Who would rule?' became the most pressing question, he later wrote.
The impact on his fellow prisoners was not to incite them to red
revolution. Colditz's inmates included the most resolute and tough
prisoners of the Reich, and they were unmoved by either admiration
for the Red Army or the workings of dialectical materialism. Many
attended out of boredom; others abstained out of anger. Micky,
even his father had to admit, displayed an 'insolent manner, derived
from his education in journalism'. This, he conceded, 'must mean
trouble'. It did; though not so much from his captors as from his
fellow prisoners.

Douglas Bader, the legless fighter ace, forbade members of the
RAF to attend; another officer wanted Micky charged with treason.
The Senior British Officer, Willie Tod ('a grand soldier and a fine
man', Corran Purdon remembered, to whom many prisoners rightly
thought they owed their survival) was also 'deeply perturbed' with

Micky and Giles's lectures. Jim Rogers, Micky's team-mate on the secret wireless, suggested that a Yugoslav officer who had served with the Russians should speak about his experience of Soviet rule to counter their proselytising. Tadeusz Bor-Komorowski, the commander of the survivors of the Polish Home Army imprisoned after the suppression of the Warsaw uprising, also lectured on the evils of the Soviet regime. He reminded his audience that Stalin had betrayed them, the Red Army watching from the far bank of the Vistula while the German army systematically suppressed the patriots in Warsaw. 'It ruined Giles and my campaign', Micky recalled.

Charlie Hopetoun, one of the *Prominente* in the Bullingdon mess, also gave a lecture challenging Micky and Giles's views. But Corran Purdon, bound by the ties of commando comradeship, described Micky as 'the nicest communist he'd ever met'. No one denounced them to the Germans. Micky and Giles had wrested 'a foothold of free speech in a bog of censorship ... outside the castle walls', he reminded readers of his novel, 'such lectures had been punishable by death for years'. In the heart of Nazi Germany, Micky and Giles spoke freely. It remains perhaps the greatest of Colditz's distinctions.

'FULL OF ANTICIPATION FOR AN EARLY LIBERATION': THE WAR'S FINAL WINTER

With the rapid advance of Allied armies across France and Belgium in the autumn of 1944, the war seemed as good as over. In the camps, men began to think seriously about post-war lives. They sorted through their possessions, discarding what they did not want to take home, and packed and repacked their belongings. Letters home conveyed their excitement: in November 1944 Mrs Penfold confided that Fred was optimistically 'looking forward to being home shortly'. Soon after Willie Bell's father passed on the news that at Lamsdorf 'they are all well and in good spirits. Full of anticipation for an early liberation.' (Curiously, Alex Bell came to form a greater rapport with Phyllis than with Clive; though he never signed himself other than 'A.G. Bell'.) So hopeful were they that they would see their men before the year's end that well-wishers began to consider how they would treat liberated prisoners of war.

Clive had kept in touch with serving commando officers and in October 1944 one wrote reminding him that 'when last I saw you we spoke of the need for very careful handling of our prisoners of war'. He warned of 'the danger of upsetting them by careless treatment'. They had agreed to help 'put their families on the right lines' to 'avoid unhappiness in the homes'. Clive endorsed the idea and took it up with the Next of Kin Assistance Committee. In passing, he revealed how after his own demobilisation in 1919 he 'got back my nervous system': a solid fortnight's roulette at Monte Carlo. 'However this treatment might not recommend itself to the "National Council of whatever it may be"', he conceded. *The Prisoner of War* magazine warned families of the hazards of overdoing welcome-home parties and counselled that returning prisoners needed 'a lot of care', advising families to be 'good receptive listeners'. Others realised that after enduring crowded barrack rooms for years, liberated men might want to be alone—in November 1944 Micky asked his parents to find him a flat 'for use immediately … I must be on my own'.

The German winter offensive in the Ardennes dashed any hope of victory in the west in 1944. In the east, the Red Army advanced into the Reich itself. Facing a Soviet invasion, one every bit as frightening as Nazi propagandists had feared, the Germans began evacuating the *Stalags* on the Reich's eastern frontier. By the late winter of 1944–45 over a quarter of a million prisoners of war of half a dozen nationalities were making their way across Germany, all moving westwards. Hundreds of thousands of refugees, rightly terrified of the mass rapes and brutality of an avenging Red Army, were all around them.

Located far to the east, Lamsdorf came under threat from the renewed Soviet winter offensive beginning in January 1945. Late in January its commandant ordered the entire camp to evacuate. Prisoners gathered up what they could carry, took bread and the contents of hoarded parcels and marched out of the gates in bitter winter weather.

They turned north-westwards into Swabia or westwards into Bohemia. Moving in vast, slow-moving columns, they trekked for eight or ten hours a day, sleeping in barns or factories when they could. Those who had worked in mines, factories or farms had greater strength, but all suffered from cold and hunger, and the snow and slush. Weakened by poor rations and often unused to exertion, men threw away the belongings they had accumulated and kept going for as long as they could. They traded clothing, chocolate or soap for bread or slops, some hearing artillery fire in the distance to the east but always driven on to the next resting place. They risked attack from Allied fighter-bombers and random violence from frightened or fed-up guards. After two weeks the leading column reached *Stalag* VIIIA at Gorlitz, where they rested for a week before setting off again westwards. The thousands of prisoners broke up into smaller columns, and parties became scattered for miles across the Silesian plain, the hills of Swabia and into Bavaria. Late in April the foremost American units advancing from the west found and liberated them.

During the war's final winter the comfortable life at Hohenfels had become markedly harsher. The bread ration became more meagre, the potatoes smaller, the soup thinner. Electricity, water and—some thought worst of all—tobacco were cut off. The guards' regime weakened, with roll calls held less often. The camp's Man of Confidence, David Mackenzie, did his best to try to arrange for Red Cross supplies to be delivered, telegraphing Geneva directly (obviously with the commandant's co-operation) until on 22 March a convoy of white-painted Red Cross lorries—'White Angels'— arrived (along with a party of prisoners marched from Lamsdorf). 'Feeling in the camp very intense', a diarist recorded on 7 April, 'we all expect something'. By the middle of April—fortunately with the worst of the winter over—an SS detachment arrived ('all youngsters and well armed', a diarist wrote, 'they would shoot you as soon as look at you'). Overruling the prisoners' protests, they forced the prisoners to leave the camp. Stan Rodd saw David Mackenzie lead the prisoners out of Hohenfels, forced to trek westwards. 'Later on the march', he wrote, 'he never slacked or rested. He told our hosts what he wanted and never gave in trying till he succeeded.' Eventually, after a week on the road, with the signs of Germany's disintegration all around and the prisoners' guards deserting, American troops reached the column and Stan Rodd and the Hohenfels kriegies were free.

Having seen optimistic projections for rapid victory dashed repeatedly, by the end of 1944 no one wanted to venture rash predictions. Among the Six Troop families, worry over their sons' fates tempered the elation of following on newspaper maps the Allied advance into Germany. John Westlake echoed Churchill's 'very proper caution' in November 1944, but hoped that 'maybe it will all be over in Europe within a few months'. The Westlakes, concerned at not hearing from Peter since September, were also worried for their other son Alan. On a flying training course of 30, he was one of two to have survived air operations.

No one knows where the six men of Six Troop who had been imprisoned in Lamsdorf went: perhaps they themselves had little idea at the time. Urged on westwards, Lamsdorf prisoners were scattered over south-eastern Germany when the leading units of George Patton's Third American Army picked them up in Bavaria in April. Other St Nazaire officers, in Spangenberg, were marched out late in March but, moving slowly in beautiful spring weather, were soon overtaken by the Allied advance. The Spangenberg prisoners disarmed their guards and waited for the Americans to arrive.

In Colditz the prisoners also waited, more hungry than ever, following the progress of the Allied advance as it crept slowly closer. At last, on Thursday 12 April, they heard the rumble of artillery fire in the distance to the west: the war had finally reached Colditz. Two days later the *Prominente's* purpose at last became clear. Having been held as hostages against the fate Germany was now suffering, they were spirited away from Colditz by their captors. However, unable in the confusion of defeat to actually use these supposedly valuable prisoners as bargaining chips, the Germans subsequently let them go, to make their way into Allied hands.

The next day Willie Tod refused to make the prisoners leave the castle on a pointless march. Approaching American artillery observers ranged guns on the castle, but their fire orders were cancelled within seconds of execution when a driver noticed a French flag hanging from the windows. The next morning, on 16 April, American soldiers entered the gates, to be greeted with jubilation. On Wednesday 18 April, the prisoners finally left the castle, loading their personal belongings (in Micky's case including the manuscript of *Yes, Farewell*) onto American lorries. Their drivers (blacks in America's segregated army) drove like the clappers westwards to an airstrip near Erfurt. The next morning they boarded American Dakota transports and flew to Westcott in Buckinghamshire. It was exactly a week since they had heard the first rumbles of artillery fire. The long-hoped-for liberation had come. The war would soon end and become a memory to live with.

CHARIOTEERS: REMEMBERING ST NAZAIRE

<hr/>

'INSPIRATION AND LEADERSHIP': GALLANTRY RECOGNISED

In the closing weeks of the European war the advancing Allied armies recovered huge numbers of prisoners of war—over 120,000 British alone. Getting them home swiftly became a preoccupation and a massive logistic operation: 'the great air repatriation of our prisoners', as a *Times* correspondent described it. Bomber Command, having bombed to rubble every German city of any size, no longer had worthwhile targets to destroy. Beginning on Easter Tuesday, its Lancasters flew eastwards again, along with Dakotas of Transport Command, pressed into service in Operation Exodus. Many of the liberated men, including the St Nazaire commandos, had become prisoners before Lancasters had entered service. They clustered around the bombers' steps, exclaiming repeatedly how they 'could not believe it'. Bombers and Dakotas carried them from airfields all over central Europe to airfields in Britain. One of the busiest days was 8 May, VE day itself. Hundreds of Lancasters landed, each carrying twenty or so former prisoners, and returned to collect more, their navigators winking 'VE, VE, VE' with their Aldis lamps as they flew off eastwards. 'There was no need to be in Trafalgar Square', *The Times* correspondent thought, to be conscious that a hateful but victorious war had ended with 'the particular feeling of pride and fellowship and thankfulness'. Among the prisoners, though no longer together, were eight members of Six Troop, who came home individually: Arthur Young, for example, liberated from *Stalag* XIIID near Nuremberg on 17 April and arriving by air on 28 April. The next day he wrote to

Clive, thanking the Burns for all they had done but disclosing that he had heard nothing from the others for six months.

On arriving home Micky the journalist immediately went into print. *The Times* published his despatch the next day, the very first to describe Colditz's liberation, written 'while the building was shaking with the reverberations of the bombardment'. On his arrival at Buckingham Gate Clive showed him 'Michael's file' of Clive and Phyllis's correspondence which, as Clive told his friend John Westlake, 'is becoming quite big'. Though Clive had expected that 'it will be interesting reading for him' Micky was unable to take a close interest in the letters at the time, but he kept the battered manila folders, and at length began to browse through the papers. He contacted Buckingham Palace to give the Princess Royal news of her son, though Allied troops did not find the *Prominente* for another fortnight. Giles Romilly had escaped, to hide with an SS sergeant's wife until the Americans occupied Munich; the others saved by German officers at last more fearful of Allied than Nazi retribution. A courtier told Clive that 'Their Majesties were *most* interested in his note'.

As Gordon Holman had predicted with a wink in his first anniversary story in the *Evening Standard*, some of the repatriated commandos did indeed receive decorations for bravery. Within days of his return Micky was writing to Bob Laycock, the general officer now commanding Combined Operations, describing Colonel Charles's conduct before, during and after the raid. His careful but highly descriptive account of Newman's leadership must surely have been decisive in persuading the War Office to recommend Newman for one of the two Victoria Crosses awarded to commandos for St Nazaire. Micky pointed out that Colonel Charles's 'personal calm and leadership' kept the commandos together 'as much as the lessons he had drummed into us on exercises'. He praised Newman's decision to lead from the forefront of the fight ('he seemed to be enjoying himself', Micky wrote, a hint of appalled incredulity apparent from the typed citation). As the Germans closed in on the surviving raiders, Newman rallied his men, 'calm, cheerful and amused', helping them to 'think that we were merely on another exercise'. Micky explained that 'I haven't put anything in about inspiration and leadership, because in such a unit it was taken for granted' but he was probably speaking for himself when he recalled that Newman was 'easy and natural and anyone with any nervousness had only to see Col. Newman's conduct to be quit of it'. At Micky's suggestion the War Office invited commando officers to comment on and support the recommendation: they did so willingly.

With Charles Newman's liberation, citations could at last go forward to recognise the bravery of the St Nazaire raiders. While in captivity he evidently discussed with other officers the commandos he would recommend for decorations and in May 1945 he submitted recommendations for two Victoria Crosses, twelve gallantry decorations for officers, twelve decorations for 'other ranks' and fifteen Mentions-in-Despatches. (This, he pointed out, totalled 41 awards—assuming that they were all accepted—for 264 commandos. He knew that the Royal Navy had already awarded 62 medals to its 355 participants.)

Although it declined to accept more than half of Newman's recommendations, the War Office processed them with uncharacteristic celerity and in the *London Gazette* in July 1945 nineteen citations for awards appeared. Despite the weighting towards the navy, Operation Chariot's 611 men became one of the most highly decorated forces in British military history. Many awards went to sailors who had not volunteered for the raid, many awarded posthumously. Micky received the Military Cross for his persistence in fulfilling his task in the raid despite the loss of his troop. His citation explained how 'after being nearly drowned and pulled ashore by one of his men' he 'showed his determination to carry out his task although his men were out of action'. The citation made clear that 'most of his Assault Group were killed or wounded'. 'His courage and initiative', it concluded, were 'an example deserving the highest praise'.

Did Micky act correctly in pressing on with his task rather than finding the remnants of his troop? He did. The commandos valued persistence in fulfilling orders over misplaced sentiment: finding and succouring his men might have been noble, but attempting to complete his job mattered more, and the War Office recognised it accordingly.

The only other award to a member of Six Troop went to Arthur Young, who had saved Micky's life. Stuart Chant had already recommended Young for a Mention-in-Despatches after his repatriation to Britain. Pleasingly, while in captivity Micky had given Chant everything he needed to submit a recommendation. Chant described how Young, although wounded, had swum towards the shore after his motor launch had exploded, and had got Micky ashore, 'instrumental in saving Capt. Burn's life'. Though in the end only two of Six Troop's 29 men received decorations, they at least recognised the two who apparently did perform extraordinary deeds during those hectic hours.

'WHEN THE BOYS ALL RETURN': COMING HOME

In Colditz in 1943 a Canadian had compiled a scrapbook of sketches and stories 'short and punchy, but true'. Other prisoners contributed their pieces and soon after the war they appeared as *Detour: the Story of Oflag IVC*. Several St Nazaire men offered contributions, like almost all the others short, descriptive pieces. Richard Morgan of 3 Commando wrote an impression of the raid on St Nazaire, ending ironically, 'The transport as usual has not arrived ... I'm in the drink'. Corran Purdon wrote a report on the raid, a model of impersonal military prose. His piece ended by describing how the raiders, 'after fighting in the streets, were rounded up in various houses'. Micky's was one of a handful of poems. Unlike most, it looked not backwards at how they had ended up in captivity, but imagined what it would be like 'After a War', the poem he had sent to Samuel and Maud Harrison a year before. It ended:

> *And ships come home, and parliaments prepare*
> *Rewards for all, and dancing in the street –*
> *... I had my son and he will not be there.*

As Tom Roach's family had realised, in one of the 'In Memoriam' notices they placed for him, 'the hardest blow is yet to come/when the boys all return'. The prisoners' return brought home the hard fact that while other families were reunited, theirs never would be. The survivors' arrivals at least allowed bereaved families to contact or even meet those who had last seen their sons in the darkness of the early hours of 28 March 1942. Maurice Harrison's father, Samuel, who remained seemingly impassive through the long months of uncertainty, at last showed his feelings on VE Day. His daughter Molly remembers how he did not break down, but was 'greatly affected' as people around them rejoiced at the war's end, a jubilation the Harrisons could not wholeheartedly share. They cannot have been alone in reflecting on what they had given for victory.

Micky especially was in demand. Lewis Roach had already expressed a desire 'if ever he did return to you and [if] I keep alive' to meet Micky and 'grip his gallant hand only for my poor son Tom's sake'. The families of the dead wanted him to write to them or even see him, perhaps to say what he could not in postcards written from captivity. They wanted to put to him the questions they had been asking themselves for three years. How did our boy die? Did he say anything? Did he suffer? Where is his body? Micky could answer those questions in person no better than he could in writing, and he seems to have wanted to evade the families' demands. 'I am beginning to wonder if my letter reached you', Maurice Tomsett gently reproached him. But he visited Cécilie Birney. 'It was lovely seeing you', she told him, after Micky had travelled to Hampshire to talk to her about David and meet the daughter David never knew. (Ann, then three, is now a stalwart of the Committee of the St Nazaire Society.) Peter Westlake also complained that he had written twice wanting to talk over old times but that Micky had seemed evasive. 'I put it down to your complete subjugation to the Communistic Doctrine', he told his troop leader in the democratic style Micky had encouraged. A later letter discloses that the breach was temporary.

The war's end brought more direct questions and challenges to answers that families had been mulling over the several years. In January 1946 Reg Tomsett's younger brother, Alan, returned from Egypt, where he had been since 1941 as a corporal in the Royal Air Force. Alan recalled that he had learned of the raid on St Nazaire while at Helwan, and soon afterwards heard that Reg had been posted missing. He had made inquiries of the Red Cross, 'but the answer was always the same': that only the Red Cross in Britain could help find word of Reg's fate. Having stewed on this lack of news for so long, Alan now arrived home and had become 'acquainted with many facts'. Reg was dead—he accepted that—but 'the events immediately preceding are somewhat obscure'. Alan wanted answers. 'Personally Mr Burn,' he began belligerently, 'I am not at all satisfied in my own mind of the War Office report'. Then he became conciliatory: 'it would be of great comfort to me if you could find time to write to me ...' What could Micky tell Alan Tomsett? 'I saw so many people', he remembered in *Turned Towards the Sun*, 'it got rather exhausting'. He later described how he fell into 'black fits', explaining 'nearly all of those I loved were killed and ... seeing their girls and mothers I have a sense of emptiness'.

Another mother and girl Micky heard from was Ella van Heemstra and her daughter. Ella wrote in October 1945, from Amsterdam. 'Nazi terror has been terrible in Holland', she wrote, evidently completely over her infatuation with fascism. She offered Micky a copy of the photograph she had cut from the newsreel in April 1942. She and her daughter had survived being caught up in the battle of Arnhem, which had literally descended on them the previous September. Fighting had forced them out of their home as refugees and they had suffered privation and real hunger during the war's final winter. The baroness's sixteen-year-old daughter had narrowly evaded being rounded up and sent to Germany as a forced labourer. Now, though reunited with stepbrothers and living in Amsterdam, the privation of the war had finally caught up with them. Her daughter, emaciated and suffering from anaemia and jaundice, lay desperately ill. Ella wrote to Micky asking for his help. Dutch doctors had told her that if only she could procure some of the new wonder drug, penicillin, her daughter might recover.

In the months following VE Day cigarettes could buy almost anything on the European mainland. Could Micky send cigarettes that Ella could use as currency? Micky did, sending 'hundreds and hundreds, thousands of cigarettes'. Ella soon converted one drug into another and her daughter recovered. Years later, opening a newspaper one day, Micky was surprised to recognise Ella van Heemstra. She had, it seemed, become the mother of one of the rising stars of Hollywood and Broadway. Ella's daughter, whose life Micky had saved, turned out to be none other than Audrey Hepburn. She later remarked that liberation had had 'the smell of English cigarettes'. It has usually been taken to mean the smell of cigarettes on the streets of newly free Amsterdam, but perhaps Audrey meant the aroma of the cigarettes that Ella sold or traded to obtain the drug that saved her daughter's life. Ella wrote inviting Micky to 'come up and see me some time', but by now deeply in love with another, Micky did not visit Amsterdam, though he kept in touch with Ella until her death in 1984.

Dorothy Peyton, while welcoming the return of her eldest son John, who had endured five years as a prisoner, still wanted to know the truth about how her younger son had died. She had had 'a very few minutes' with Micky: perhaps he quailed before the prospect of having to describe how his last sight of Tommy had been a glimpse of him floating face down in the Loire. Micky wrote to her, promising also to put her in touch with Arthur Young, another witness, 'but I expect he has been very busy and he has forgotten', she concluded charitably. She finally obtained Arthur's address through the Next of Kin Committee, one of its last services before it wound up at war's end. At last, in January 1946 Mrs Peyton was able to write to Arthur Young. She was anxious to speak to a man who had been with Tommy 'when he was wounded and when he died'. She invited him to Ascot, pressing him with train times and promises of lunch. Did he meet her, or did he too evade the prospect of facing a bereaved mother, to whom he could offer little but an impression glimpsed in the glare of tracer and the flames of a burning motor launch?

'CIVVY STREET': THE SURVIVORS DE-MOBBED

Between mid 1945 and early 1947 all of the Six Troop survivors walked out of the gates of the various demobilisation centres, wearing the utility pin-striped 'de-mob' suit and pork-pie hat offered by a grateful nation. Some men left the army within months—Paddy Bushe first in August 1945, his papers endorsed 'no army employment suitable to his age and category'. Most had to wait months for de-mob. In the meantime they were posted not even to the units they had left in 1940 but to other regiments. Willie Bell went to the Duke of Wellington's Regiment, the Essex Regiment and finally to a holding battalion of his own regiment, the Royal Fusiliers, 'browned off before I even got here', he wrote restlessly. John Cudby went to the Lancashire Fusiliers, Fred Penfold to the South Staffords. This enforced wait frustrated men who had postponed life for war and captivity enough. Willie Bell went absent without leave several times, as he had in the frustrating months before the raid. He took a course in English (expression rather than literature) in anticipation of resuming his career as a Civil Service clerk. According to a report completed in his Holding Battalion, Peter Westlake was 'considering "staying on" as a regular soldier', but he thought the better of it and took his de-mob in March 1946, returning to a career in newspapers.

All over Britain 1945 saw a rash of weddings. Marriages put off until the war's end or until men returned filled churches or register offices. By the time they had been discharged at least four of the St Nazaire survivors were married. Willie Bell returned to Moffat to marry Andrea Henderson in the Manse at St Andrew's and Paddy Bushe married Marjorie Moore in Silkstone, Yorkshire. Peter Westlake married Catherine (Kay) Bamborough at York the following month (they had met while the troop had been mountaineering at Keswick in 1941) and Fred Penfold married Joan Woolton in June 1946.

Survivors pondered on how the war had changed them. Peter Westlake reflected on how 'I have grown from a boy into a man', and how he had acquired 'a physical toughness and a mental resilience', with far more 'energy and Push' than he had in 'Civvy Street'. Their discharge papers support this judgment, all containing resounding endorsements of their characters. Peter Westlake's officers found him an 'intelligent chap, fairly good scholar'. Willie Bell's commanding officer described him—despite his spells of absence—as 'smart, honest and hardworking. Suitable for responsible civil employment.' Willie met Micky by chance in Moffat in May. He had escaped from London to the peace of the Lowlands. They had 'a long talk together', and Willie said he had considered staying on in the army. He decided against it, and left the army almost exactly seven years to the day since he had joined the Territorials. The final glimpse of his army file is of him and Andrea setting up house in Nursery Cottage at Moffat, the Scottish town where Micky's commandos had been so welcomed.

Army bureaucracy had made life difficult for the families of the commandos' dead, and at the war's end it intruded again into their lives. Having failed to return men's personal effects in 1942 promptly or at all, army records offices sent letters advising families that parcels of belongings had at last turned up. Maurice Harrison's father, Samuel, heard from the Rifle Record Office at Winchester in July 1946. A few days later a parcel arrived containing ten odd socks, a towel, six wallets, a fountain pen, a civilian cap, a brush, a pair of gloves, a New Testament and two pious books (*On the Imitation of Christ* and *In Need of Christianity*) and, most importantly, 'sundry letters and cards'. Someone in the Effects Branch must have launched a determined push to clear up outstanding files because in the same week Reg Tomsett's father Maurice also received a letter. Maurice had been sent an identity disc and a leather belt in 1944. He replied that he had been hoping to receive Reg's wristwatch, Ronson cigarette lighter and especially a gold signet ring. Reg probably had the lighter on him and it was swept into the Loire when ML 268 exploded, but Mr Tomsett knew that Reg had left the watch behind when embarking on the raid. He was very glad to receive the ring: where it had been between 1942 and 1946 was never revealed. The Rifle Record Office 'feared that after such a long lapse of time ... further articles are not forthcoming' and assured him that if anything turned up he would be advised. Needless to say, the mystery was never solved.

In due course (as the Effects Branch's clerks were wont to say) army records offices contacted families to distribute the medals to which they were entitled. Having served mainly in Britain and (briefly) in the raid, most of 2 Commando's men became entitled only to two campaign medals, the 1939–45 Star and the War Medal 1939–1945. Those who had served also in Norway received nothing: traditionally campaign medals were rarely awarded for a losing campaign. In 1948 families were able to claim the medals awarded to a dead son or husband: many understandably chose not to. Some failed to claim their medals at all: John Cudby not until 1983.

'ALL THE LIFE I HAVE EVER KNOWN': MICKY AND MARY

Micky's demobilisation went smoothly. It was not until he left the de-mob depot that he realised that he had been wearing two ties, one khaki, the other red, a neat symbol of the state of his mind. *The Times* had kept in regular contact throughout the war, generously paying various bonuses, and he swiftly returned to a job with it. In the meantime, he threw himself into the task of electioneering for a Communist Party candidate standing for the constituency of Westminster in the 1945 general election. In Micky's 'highly excited imagination Communism took the place of … the Commandos'. He spoke on street corners, a losing fight in a winning cause. While addressing the electors of Westminster on one of these street corners Micky saw Arthur Young for the first time since the early hours of 28 March 1942 and they enjoyed a long talk.

Inevitably, the Communist candidate in Westminster lost but the Labour Party won the election. Characteristically, Micky spent election night at a Tory party at Grosvenor House, watching Conservatives cheer, ironically, as they heard of the defeat of candidates they personally disliked. Contrary to popular myth, the services vote was not in itself decisive in turning out Winston Churchill in favour of Clement Attlee. Still, the sort of vision Micky had championed while at Moffat in 1941 through his 'E.P.' seems to have been part of the sea change that moved the electorate leftwards as victory approached.

He later acknowledged, in *Turned Towards the Sun*, that at the time he had been 'hard and heartless ... consumed by theory'. He revised its principal expression, the manuscript of *Yes, Farewell*, which appeared in March 1946, on the fourth anniversary of the raid. The novel aroused good reviews in the *Times Literary Supplement* and in the *Daily Worker*, which praised it as the 'War's Greatest Novel', a reflection of its doctrinaire presentation of communist ideology. He later adapted the novel as a play. It premiered in Redditch, near Birmingham, in 1947 and later played in Vienna, where its pro-Soviet tone attracted warm praise from the occupying Red Army. Praising its dialogue ('now supple and amusing, now taut and expressive'), *The Times*'s drama critic thought that it 'fails to make good its allegorical intentions'. At the same time, bound by profound ties of affection and comradeship, Micky helped to organise the inaugural anniversary dinner of the St Nazaire Society.

Neither the high water mark of Micky's devotion to communism nor his obligations to former comrades prevented him from pursuing a memory from the weeks before the raid. Early in 1942, a few weeks prior to the raid, Morgan Jenkins and Micky's leave coincided and Morgan had asked to go to the Dorchester to see what he thought of as the 'posh London world'. Micky took Dinah: Morgan did not take his wife, Edna. While Dinah talked with Morgan, Micky glanced at the dancers. There, in a grey dress, was 'the most beautiful woman I had ever set eyes on'. Entranced but resigned to never seeing her again, he was astonished when he called at Charles Haydon's flat the following evening to her opening the door. She was Haydon's cousin, Mary Booker. Micky chatted with her awkwardly. Although by this time he thought of himself as homosexual, when he returned from Colditz he sought her out. He met her within a month of his return and they embarked on a swift and intense courtship. Within weeks he was affirming that she was 'all the life I have ever known' and in June they travelled to North Wales to spend the first days of many happy years at Minffordd, in what was then Merioneth.

Mary and Micky were married on 27 March 1947—on the fifth anniversary of the eve of the raid. After a spell with *The Times* in Hungary (in which his faith in communism crumbled in the face of

Stalinist show trials) they lived together in North Wales, where Micky still lives. He wrote a dozen more books, besides scraping a living for a time as a mussel-farmer. Mary's love sustained him for nearly three decades and beyond her early death in 1974. Increasingly secure as a writer and poet, he remained disturbed by his sexual ambivalence, though buoyed by their love for each other. Micky lived eccentrically to the common taste but firmly grounded in the principles he had formed, of justice, honesty, decency and generosity. His unconventional life was to see complications, coincidences and contrasts to fuel several novels (and indeed, he wrote two based on his life). There was to be much more to Micky's life than commandos and Colditz; but he has told the story in his novels, his *Poems as an Accompaniment to a Life*, and

Micky Burn, in his mid nineties, living in Wales. A portrait of Mary lies on the table.

above all his autobiography, *Turned Towards the Sun*, and no one would attempt to better them.

Clive, knighted in 1948, retired in 1954 and died the following year after a sudden decline. Micky never really knew what his parents felt about his growing reputation as a playwright and author: 'I never learned what my parents thought of my book about George Lyward's community', he wrote (his *Mr Lyward's Answer* dealt with an unorthodox champion of troubled adolescents). It was likely, he thought, 'they had had enough of troubled children in real life'. Phyllis commissioned a memorial window in Canon Andrews's church at Stoke Climsland in the Duchy he loved. Clive's death devastated Phyllis. Uncertain how to continue without him, nervous disturbance blighted her life and the resulting tension made Micky and Mary's life difficult. Phyllis lived for three further years. A few days before she died Micky on impulse kissed her, and Phyllis responded by putting her arms around his neck. 'I don't ever remember her putting her arms around my neck', he wrote, sadly. A family that in wartime had shown so much love, for each other and for so many others, seemed unable to find or sustain that love in peacetime.

'OPERATION UNFORGETTING': CEMETERIES AND MEMORIALS

When French workers dug the common plot into which the dead commandos and sailors were laid on the morning of 1 April 1942 the cemetery at Escoublac-La Baule already existed. A few of the more than 3000 dead of the *Lancastria*, whose wreck the raiders had passed as they approached the port, had already been interred in what had been a hillside field. The Chariot raiders had joined them in 1942, and many airmen shot down in raids on St Nazaire. Throughout the long occupation a French woman, Madame Louise Jaouen, the wife of a local pharmacist, cared for the graves. Collecting money secretly from generous neighbours, she erected a cross over every grave, built a small monument, had a hedge planted and employed a gardener. When the Allies returned in 1945 (the Germans held St Nazaire as an isolated bastion almost to the last) the cemetery was taken over by the Imperial (later Commonwealth) War Graves Commission. German prisoners of war removed the German graves to a nearby cemetery and the commission's gardeners began to turn La Baule into a cemetery reminiscent of the hundreds of commission cemeteries from Scapa Flow to Imphal.

Although the hostilities-only commandos had mostly been de-mobbed, their former officers established the Commando Benevolent Fund. Its first advertisements appeared in late 1946, sponsored by the makers of Genatosan Nerve Tonic—fittingly in the light of the anxiety the commandos' parents had endured. They featured a grainy photograph of the rows of graves at Escoublac, each white cross decorated with flowers, perhaps placed by Madame Jaouen the previous March. The fund's drive was christened 'Operation Unforgetting'.

In the decade after 1945 several memorials commemorated the commandos, in England, Scotland and France. The army saw commandos as 'Special Service' troops and at the war's end disbanded them. Returning to his work as a journalist in eastern Europe, Micky wrote to *The Times* praising Charles Haydon's achievement in forming and training the earliest commando troops, reminding its readers

Escoublac cemetery, during one of the St Nazaire Society's annual pilgrimages.

that he had shaped the force that had carried out the early raids on Vaagso and St Nazaire. Micky's reminder reflected the concern that the disbandment of army commandos would lead to neglect of their memory. It was 1957 before the army came to choose its battle honours for the Second World War—over a thousand of them—including St Nazaire. Because 2 Commando existed only during the war 'St Nazaire' has never appeared as an army battle honour (on a regimental colour, say) though there is a new HMS *Campbeltown* in the Royal Navy, and its complement have forged a strong bond with the St Nazaire Society.

With the passing of the army's commandos, thoughts turned to commemorating the force. Over one thousand seven hundred men had died serving in commando units all over the world, in Norway and North-West Europe, in Italy and the Mediterranean, in Burma and South-East Asia. Winston Churchill had unveiled a memorial in Westminster Abbey in 1948 and a Roll of Honour book was later dedicated in the cathedral's St George's Chapel. Families were told of this: indeed, so many wanted tickets to the ceremony that a ballot had to be held. Isabel Wyles wrote to Micky, now in Vienna for *The Times*, hoping to see him and thinking that the unveiling of the memorial would be a good time to meet. 'I'm keeping my fingers crossed waiting for a ticket', she wrote. Micky did not attend, preoccupied with the injustice of Soviet show trials in the opening years of the Cold War.

One of the Commando Association's first acts was to commission a memorial in Scotland, where so many had trained. (Though it would be near the training centre near Achnacarry, in Invernesshire, not where 2 Commando had mainly trained, on Scotland's west coast.) Within two years of the war's end the association had raised funds to enable it to invite designs from the Scottish School of Sculptors. It chose a design by Scott Sutherland, a Dundee art teacher, of three gigantic figures, over 10 feet high. Since 1952 they have stood on a plinth overlooking the Great Glen and the broad valley of the River Spean, with Ben Nevis beyond.

'IN PROUD MEMORY': THE MEMORIALS

One of the St Nazaire Society's first tasks was to erect a memorial. Encouraged by the mayor and corporation of the city, the society began to consider the project in mid 1946. St Nazaire, still recovering from the desolation of the war, both the bombing and the protracted German occupation into 1945, evidently had not forgotten its most intense and costly night of the war. Surprisingly soon after the war, and long before the Normandie Dock was repaired a memorial was erected at St Nazaire. It was to be a 15 feet high block of granite, roughly shaped as a menhir, a Breton megalith. The mayor explained the choice 'in view of the close relationship that exists between the British and the French, in particular the Bretons, whose Celtic origin is often common'. Besides donating 400,000 francs and the granite block, the French municipal authorities wanted to recognise that the raid was more than a British triumph. They wanted to commemorate the Nazaireans who had died in the raid (though dozens more foreign workers or Frenchmen conscripted to work at the base remained unknown and not formally commemorated). The corporation supplied eighteen names, from the five-year-old Bernard Pelven to the 75-year-old Marie Allaine. French organisation ran ahead of British. The corporation was eager to dedicate a memorial on 28 March 1947, the raid's fifth anniversary. By February the St Nazaire Society had to admit that it would not have a plaque ready and the ceremony had to be deferred until August.

Charles Newman, the society's president, turned to the still-extant Combined Operations Headquarters and early in 1947 asked for official support. Combined Operations, now working closely with the navy, turned to the Admiralty for help. By the summer the practical and the political arrangements coincided. The St Nazaire Society had a bronze panel cast, which their office-bearers were to bring with them to be fixed to the menhir just before the ceremony. The British Embassy in Paris had also weighed in. Its political counsellors had decided that Anglo–French relations in socialist St Nazaire in particular ('not normally particularly pro-British') would be enhanced by a suitable ceremony, and its officials lent a hand to 'put on a good show'. As Duff Cooper, the British

Ambassador, explained in his memoirs, relations between Britain and France remained delicate. The Treaty of Dunkirk early in 1947 had re-established British and French relations and the presentation to Churchill of the French Military Medal by the new Prime Minister Paul Ramadier in the courtyard of Les Invalides in May confirmed the rapprochement. The unveiling occurred during the negotiations surrounding the acceptance of the Marshall Plan: gestures of Anglo–French solidarity were particularly welcome. Not only did Duff Cooper and his wife, Diana, attend, but the embassy lubricated Anglo–French conviviality, supplying four cases of gin and three of vermouth from a mysterious 'Government Hospitality Fund'. While bringing 'ample liquid refreshments' the *Sirius*'s supply officer also indented for quantities of pate de fois gras, smoked salmon, stuffed olives, prawns and shrimps, small white pickled onions, and 200 cocktail sticks.

Meanwhile the St Nazaire Society urged its members to attend. Though generous with small white pickled onions, British official support otherwise turned out to be niggardly. Members of the St Nazaire Society were able to travel to France in the cruiser HMS *Sirius* (matching French naval presence in the minesweeper *Kleber*). In the event 150 members of the St Nazaire Society travelled aboard the *Sirius*, steaming from Weymouth on 1 August. Admiralty officers agreed that women could not share the austere accommodation of a cruiser and several mothers and sisters who attended went under their own steam. Jo Goss, still a teenager, went with her sister and mother to the unveiling of the memorial. She remembered how, when she at last saw Lenny's grave, her mother fainted. Molly Harrison also travelled with her mother, Maud. They had arranged tickets through the Commando Association and made their own way by ferry to St Malo, train across Brittany and bus to Escoublac. They lodged with Madame Jaouen, with whom they communicated through Molly's schoolgirl French. On a hot August day Maud and Molly walked to Maurice's grave, the day before the main ceremony. They had the cemetery to themselves. Like many bereaved, reluctant to reveal their distress in public, Maud and Molly grieved at Maurice's graveside away from the crowds who arrived the next day.

Early on 2 August, an overcast summer's morning, HMS *Sirius* steamed into the Loire, 'dressed overall', exchanging salutes gun-for-gun with the *Kleber*. From its deck the raiders saw St Nazaire in daylight for the first time. Richard Collinson, who had survived the loss of ML 192 and had become a trainee dentist at Guy's Hospital, at last saw the docks. He spoke for many survivors, 'amazed ... that we had ever got in without being sunk'. Among the group were Arthur Young, who saw the Old Mole where he had saved Micky's life, and Jack Heery, one of the seven men of Six Troop who had made it back home. An enthusiastic crowd greeted the *Sirius*, British officers remarking upon its goodwill and the 'complete absence of resentment' though the port still lay in ruins.

Admiral Sir Geoffrey Layton, the Senior British Officer present, reported that he did not think that he had ever sat through so many long speeches in one day before, though 'everyone seemed to enjoy it, especially the French officials who delivered most of them'. Despite his sarcasm, one of those speeches set the tone for the day.

The Old Mole, St Nazaire, today. ML 192 blew up in the foreground after scraping along the Mole.

Dedicating the memorial, Prime Minister Paul Ramadier described the raid's significance for France. 'You', he said to the raiders, 'were the first to bring hope'.* The memorial, inscribed (in English and in French) 'in proud memory of those who gave their lives', was dedicated as a thoroughly Anglo–French gesture of remembrance.

After lunch, Nazaireans, survivors and dignitaries held 'an intimate and impressive service' at the cemetery, though Duff Cooper recorded his restlessness at the interminable sermon delivered by a French Protestant minister. Royal Marine buglers sounded the 'Last Post' and for two minutes all stood in silence in the hot sun. Then French trumpeters, standing out of sight, sounded the 'Reveille'. Commander Ryder and Colonel Newman moved forward to thank Madame Jaouen 'for the tender care with which she had looked after the graves' of their men.

That evening, while the ships' companies and many of the returning raiders enjoyed an open-air ball aboard the *Sirius*, the dignitaries and office-bearers attended a more select dinner. Ryder spoke ('in French with great courage', Duff Cooper noted). He thanked the people of St Nazaire for the reception the visitors had received. With admirable sensitivity he made clear that they had come not only to honour their own dead, but to 'render homage to their French comrades in arms who had died also'. Sadly, while it commemorates the sailors as much as the soldiers, and names French victims of the attack, the menhir is today only known as the memorial to *Les Commandos Britanniques*. After the reception Duff Cooper won 35,000 francs at St Nazaire's casino—'a good end', he thought.

Cooper's naval attaché, Rear Admiral Richard Shelley, did not quite come out as well financially. He had regarded the ceremony as 'a valuable contribution towards cementing the friendship and developing cooperation between our two nations'. But after the speeches were over he found himself stuck with an accounting problem. The costs of the small white pickled onions and the rest became a source of contention within the Royal Navy's bureaucracy. The Admiralty, which had agreed to pay for the 'bag lunch' on the beach at La Baule, baulked at paying for the sit-down spread that arrived. The St Nazaire Society,

*All previous books quote Ramadier as saying 'You were the first to bring us hope', but none of them drew upon the archival sources. Contemporary records (and *The Times*, 4 August 1947, p. 4) make it clear that he said ' … the first to bring hope'.

many of whose members had travelled a long way to get to Weymouth and back, refused to impose on them further. Admiral Shelley faced the prospect of having to make up the shortfall—£80—from his own pocket and only after three months of correspondence was the impasse resolved after he worked on contacts within the Admiralty.

There would be many other pilgrimages to St Nazaire, both privately and as part of St Nazaire Society visits, with Six Troop represented in many official visits. But many were drawn back to St Nazaire individually, perhaps to reflect without the accompanying social events. In August 1949 Jack Heery characteristically hitchhiked across Brittany to report to the society that the memorial and cemetery were well cared for, that the Old Mole was under repair and a former German liner (part of France's reparations) was occupying the Normandie Dock. The most notable of the society's visits was in the fortieth anniversary year, when the St Nazaire Society prevailed on the Duke of Edinburgh to intercede with Queen Elizabeth, who invited members to travel to or from St Nazaire aboard the Royal Yacht *Britannia*. Six of Six Troop's survivors—Micky Burn, John Cudby, Jack Heery, Taff Lloyd, Stan Rodd and Peter Westlake—were among the 145 veterans and 160 family and supporters to attend a late commemoration on 24 April 1982. *Britannia*, being refitted, was available only late in April, allowing the society to attend a ceremony at the commando memorial in Westminster Abbey on the anniversary in March.

'THE GREATEST RAID OF ALL': BOOKS ON ST NAZAIRE

The Admiralty had produced a restricted 'Battle Summary', *The Attack on St. Nazaire 28th March 1942*, in 1942, a fine piece of analytical history. It then ordered it be destroyed after preparing a revised version, drawing on the new evidence of former prisoners of war, in 1948. In 1947 Robert Ryder published the first unofficial account of the raid, curiously under the same title. Ryder, the naval commander of Chariot, sought Admiralty approval to consult the official records. At first forbidden, because the distinguished man of letters Arthur Bryant was supposed to be writing a 'preliminary Official History', Ryder's 'very special claims' persuaded their Lordships to consent, 'provided that no mention is made ... of the fact that this facility has been given'. Ryder produced a short, dry chronicle, but it is invaluable in describing the commanders' decisions. Bryant, perhaps daunted by the difficulty of writing an authoritative but popular account of such a long and complex war, never produced his book.

Soon after the war, though, the British official history series got underway, though if the First World War series was any guide its volumes would take years to appear. As well as fuelling a growing popular market for unofficial 'war books', the need to meet the widespread desire to know what had happened impelled His Majesty's Stationery Office to publish short popular books. In 1951 the former war correspondent Christopher Buckley provided the first public post-war official account in a detailed chapter in *Norway ; The Commandos ; Dieppe*, a book intended to meet the popular demand. Buckley's short history (covering the Norwegian campaign of 1940 and commando operations including the Dieppe raid) devoted 22 pages to St Nazaire and gave a scrupulously accurate account. (Perhaps Buckley tried to make up for the exaggerations of wartime reportage?) The full formal official history, by the distinguished naval historian, Captain Stephen Roskill, appeared in 1956, as part of the history of *The War at Sea*. But Roskill would devote only three pages to St Nazaire. In the restrained style of an official history, he gave an austere account, accurate and measured but without warmth or colour.

Neither Buckley's summary, nor even Roskill's official history would be seen as the definitive account. That distinction would go to a popular book written by a retired brigadier, Cecil Lucas Phillips, in *The Greatest Raid of All*, published in 1958. Lucas Phillips, a gunner officer in both world wars, funded his retirement in Surbiton by writing books on gardening. He also published several best-selling military historical books, most dealing with events of 1942, including

The Cockleshell Heroes (about a daring canoe-borne raid on Bordeaux) and on the battle of El Alamein. A rose, heather and delphinium expert, he was 'much happier', his obituary admitted, writing about gardens. His *The Small Garden* became the best-selling gardening book to that time.

Lucas Phillips wrote to many of the commando and naval officers and some of the other ranks. He told them that he had 'official approval' to write the book—not that he needed it. But he based *The Greatest Raid of All* more on accounts from informants he found congenial than on a comprehensive scrutiny of the sources. He did not consult official records and barely mentioned Six Troop's task or fate. This is partly due to Micky's modest preoccupation—his reply to Lucas Phillips's approach was 'I am afraid I have been quite useless to you, but could anyhow have contributed so little, having done so little'. But Lucas Phillips also called on Micky and it is clear that the two did not hit it off. (A man remembered as a 'strict disciplinarian', albeit with a 'Victorian charm', probably found little common ground with a poet living a Bohemian idyll on a Welsh estuary.) Micky felt that Lucas Phillips had perpetrated a great untruth in describing the officers' briefing before the raid. Seeking to affirm their desire to get on with the raid, Lucas Phillips described their reaction to the revelation of their objective—'Gurtch!'—on whose testimony is unknown. Micky remained indignant at this, as he saw it, uncouth sound, and he denied that it had been uttered. *The Greatest Raid of All*, though regarded as the classic account, is in fact misleadingly partial. It tells the story of those whom Lucas Phillips liked or listened to, hardly justifying its reputation.

The raid on St Nazaire remained one of the more memorable incidents in what we used to call 'the last war'. As a child, in 1964 Father Christmas brought me the *Victor* boys' annual featuring on its cover the story of the raid, the spectacular fate of *Campbeltown* providing inspiration for the comic's artists. The annual is now a rare item in the esoteric world of comic nostalgia, one selling on eBay in 2006 for £155. At about the same time an inmate of HM Prison Wandsworth entered a painting of the raid in a Home Office exhibition of prisoners' art. Perhaps he had read the same comic as me.

Besides memoirs such as Corran Purdon's *List the Bugle* and Stuart Chant's *St Nazaire Commando* (which omits the embarrassing disclosure to the German wireless reporters) each decade since a book has appeared. All drew heavily on Ryder and Lucas Phillips. David Mason's *Raid on St Nazaire*, part of the popular Pan-Ballantine illustrated series on the Second World War, kept the raid's significance alive. Ken Ford's *St Nazaire 1942* reprised Robert Ryder's 1947 account, though superbly illustrated. Finally, *Storming St Nazaire*, by James Dorrian, a graphic designer turned writer, began life as a novel and morphed into a detailed chronicle. Dorrian has lived with the raid for many years. He replicated Lucas Phillips's methods and wrote to almost every survivor he could find. While he drew on many primary documents, he too largely neglected the official records, by then freely available in what became the National Archives. *Storming St Nazaire* is a prodigious piece of research but it tends to leave nothing out. 'I can't read it', a survivor's relative told me quietly. I had expected her to say that it upset her, but she confided that all that detail confused her. But to his credit James Dorrian has become the premier authority on the raid and a strong supporter of the St Nazaire Society, instrumental in inducing a Hollywood producer to make a feature film based on Micky's autobiography and on his book.

(There have been other books. Duncan Harding's 1997 *Assault on St Nazaire* is a novel. The less said about it the better. Catherine Ross's novel *The War After Mine*, best described as sentimental feminist fiction, uses the raid as the fulcrum of the story of a hasty and somewhat improbable romance between a commando and a Geordie Romany woman working as a waitress in Falmouth, who produce a child and are then reunited years later.)

As well as drawing largely on published sources and survivors' memories, all the non-fiction books (except the one you're reading) end with the raiders' burials at La Baule. Not one of them follows the prisoners into captivity or asks what happened to those who survived, or what effect the deaths of the raiders had on their loved ones.

'SO MOVINGLY TOLD':
ST NAZAIRE ON FILM AND TELEVISION

Meanwhile, the St Nazaire story had inspired two feature films and several documentaries. Neither of the feature films is especially memorable. The 1952 film *Gift Horse* portrays the drama aboard the destroyer *Ballantrae* as it steams towards a raid on a French port. It seems to have missed its mark, badly. Trevor Howard played its captain with 'authority', but actors playing members of the crew, notably Richard Attenborough, were 'given parts taken from the stock of second-rate British film comedy'. *Monthly Film Bulletin* dismissed the film as 'a mixture of action, lower deck comedy and sentiment ... but without feeling or imagination'. The film came under the shadow of plagiarism but disappeared for artistic reasons. The St Nazaire Society's verdict was as lukewarm, but more polite. The film was 'tolerable'; at the premiere members were 'disappointed' (probably because the raid featured only in the film's final ten minutes), but they hoped that 'all members and next-of-kin' should see it. Did any of Six Troop's bereaved do so, and what did they feel?

The Mirisch Films 1967 production, *Attack on the Iron Coast*, is also deservedly forgotten. It starred the American Lloyd Bridges (naturally, playing a Canadian), a commando who leads an attack on dock gates not unlike St Nazaire's. Perhaps influenced by the growing distaste for war films, *Monthly Film Bulletin* condemned it as a 'curiously old-fashioned ... low-budget production', with a script that 'mistakes platitudes for original statements about war' presenting 'comic paper heroics'. The St Nazaire Society had nothing to say about it.

Television documentaries, on the other hand, have conveyed the St Nazaire story much more effectively. Though the BBC had played a further tribute to the attackers of St Nazaire in June 1945, it seems that it broadcast no further story for nearly thirty years. Not until the early 1970s did the St Nazaire story reach television, when Micky wrote and presented a documentary, *The Raid on St Nazaire*. Produced by Tony Broughton, one of a succession of writers impressed by Micky's story and his gift for telling it, the program went to air on Budget night 1974 and attracted an audience of over ten million viewers. The documentary prompted letters from distant friends, praising it as 'the best programme of its kind ... so movingly told'. Indeed, it is the presence of the veterans—by then mostly in their fifties or sixties—that distinguishes it. Invariably officers, they describe their experiences in clipped, generally public school voices, but modestly and vividly, all the more powerful for their understatement.

The program brought another poignant letter, unsigned, undated and without an address, from Janet Burns, Bobby Burns's mother. Mrs Burns was pleased to learn that Micky had returned safely after 'that great adventure'. 'He often mentioned you to us', she wrote, an echo of conversations on leave more than thirty years before. 'I went across to France a few years ago to see his grave and walked along the docks ... I have two letters from your father', she ended. An accompanying letter from Mrs Burns's daughter-in-law explained that Mrs Burns was living in Devon, aged 80 and that she had begun the letter but had been too ill to finish it. Fortunately Mrs Burns was well enough to read Micky's reply, and appreciated his 'kind words, and the fact that you remembered her son'. As Dorothy Peyton neared her own death a few years later, her surviving son John, by then a peer, told Micky how much she had appreciated Micky troubling to tell her of her son Tommy's death.

Further television programs appeared: *For Valour* for the BBC in 1995 and *Commando* for Channel 4 in 2004. In 2007 the motoring celebrity Jeremy Clarkson brought his considerable charm to present a documentary *The Greatest Raid*, using computer-generated special effects to tell the story of the raid. It was a strong, mostly accurate and memorable production that brought St Nazaire vividly to the consciousness of a new generation, attracting almost four million viewers, a higher proportion of a more competitive market than 33 years before. Whether the occasional documentary keeps memory alive is a moot point. Books have a greater longevity and arguably do a better job of informing. The one unforgettable thing that television programs can do is to show us the Charioteers on the dockside at St Nazaire at moments in time, thirty and fifty or even sixty years on, explaining in their own words what they remember. These images remain with poignancy.

'WE WILL REMEMBER THEM':
ESCOUBLAC AND BROOKWOOD

The British dead of St Nazaire lie in ones and twos in nine communal and churchyard plots around the region, but 56 of the raid's 169 British dead lie in the Commonwealth War Graves Commission cemetery at Escoublac-La Baule, where Stan Rodd and Corran Purdon helped to bury them on 1 April 1942. Escoublac is not one of the most impressive of the more than 23,000 cemeteries the Commonwealth War Graves Commission maintains in 150 countries. It does not occupy the grand setting of, say, Kranji, whose headstones look out to the Strait of Johore, which the Japanese crossed to take Singapore. It is not impressive by the sheer number of headstones, like Tyne Cot, or quietly beautiful like Labuan. It is not starkly dignified like Alamein or intimate like the smaller plots on Gallipoli, or a surprising haven of peace like Phalerion, Athens. In truth, Escoublac-La Baule is among the least prepossessing of the commission's cemeteries. It occupies a rather cramped patch of ground in what is now a suburban street of the straggling resort of Escoublac-La Baule, hard to find and disappointing in situation.

Like all such cemeteries, it includes a Cross of Sacrifice at one corner and at the other an alcove with its graves register and visitors' book. The headstones stand in neat rows. The first surprise for the unprepared visitor is that most headstones have nothing to do with the raid. Many commemorate airmen shot down in raids on the Atlantic U-boat bases. Most others are of men washed ashore after the sinking of the *Lancastria*. The Six Troop dead are among the 33 commandos buried there; a surprisingly small proportion of the 325 who lie there.

The Six Troop's nine members mainly lie in the rows nearest the Cross of Sacrifice, close together in Plot 2. Only Peter Harkness is across the broad grass aisle, sadly separated in death from his great friend Bill Gibson, whose body was not recovered. Four lie in one row. Presumably their bodies were collected from the same stretch of foreshore, carried to the cemetery and buried more or less together. Each has a standard Commonwealth War Graves Commission headstone, made of Portland stone bearing their regimental badges (though each is also identified as belonging to 2 Commando). As if they were facing interrogation, they give name, number and rank. Many visitors notice and remark on how inscriptions include a man's age, and the date of his death. The most poignant element on the stone is the epitaph, chosen by the family and consisting of up to 66 characters: the number determined by masons (and perhaps also accountants) after the Great War.

It is the epitaphs that give the headstones much of their power to prick the eyes. They continue to do so, no matter how many cemeteries one sees. The eight epitaphs on the headstones of Six Troop's graves (George Hudson's headstone has none) collectively summarise the impact of their deaths on their loved ones, and the broader significance of their loss for us. Some epitaphs speak of the profound grief that we have seen in families' letters and recollections. Bobby Burns's mother must have written his: 'At rest in God's garden'—a reflection of how strongly held is the idea that the dead in commission cemeteries should lie in beautiful surroundings. Deep love and personal grief animates Maurice Harrison's epitaph: 'Death cannot dim the radiance of a happy smile and a gentle heart. RIP'. Surely Maurice's loving sister Molly had a hand in its composition, and surely too the friend who loved him, his troop captain Micky, would also remember Maurice's smile and gentleness. Norman Fisher's headstone also bears a message from a heartbroken mother: 'In loving and precious memory. Mother. Until the day break'.

Epitaphs hint at powerful emotions, all the more expressive for their brevity: haikus of pain. They often bear the marks of having been composed by groups of relatives, in the years after the war, striving to express feelings in sometimes-unaccustomed formal diction. Some put their feelings into simple phrases: Peter Harkness's headstone reads 'So well remembered'. Tom Roach's family drew on words that they had heard at remembrance services for 30 years, and knew that they would again and again. They chose the familiar 'At the going down of the sun and in the morning we will remember them', and every time they would hear those words in future they would think of Tom. Albert Lucy lies in the grave closest to the Cross of Sacrifice. The Lucy family chose a statement of intent for Albert's headstone. They wrote 'Gone but not forgotten. Never shall thy memory fade'.

Isabel Wyles's choice relates not only to Christ the redeemer, but also to her son Bill Spaul and all those who gave their lives in freedom's cause: 'He died that we might live'. Read one way it is a conventional profession of Christian faith: read another, it powerfully unites Bill's death and the deaths of all those killed, at St Nazaire and on a thousand other battlefields, with the ultimate cause for which they fought. Truly, Bill's death did win life for his nation and its allies.

Escoublac cemetery is not visited very often, though its location in the resort of La Baule seems to draw occasional casual visitors. In 2004 only one visitor signed the book on 28 March. In 2005 some two hundred and fifty people signed the book through the year (who knows how many did not?) until the autumn (and the commission's gardeners reseeding the lawns) kept all but the most determined visitors out. Few arrived in winter, naturally enough, and the year got off to a start later in March, with three visitors, at least two veterans. Almost all arrive in the four summer months. Over two-thirds of visitors are from Britain, though most identify their nation as 'England'. Almost a fifth are French. As one often sees in France, many of these people write simply and sincerely of their gratitude that these men should have given their lives for France's liberty—'thank you, you have saved us'. Liberty is still a word with powerful associations in France. Visitors come from other European and Commonwealth nations in ones and twos. Two German visitors asked others to 'remember in hope for peace'. Comments made in 2008 follow similar lines.

Visitors' comments are illuminating. Ostensibly directed to the commission—what does it do with these comments?—invariably they address the dead who lie a few yards from the little stone porch. However oddly spelled and punctuated, they offer heartfelt and moving testimony that, here in this little cemetery at least, the dead of St Nazaire still have a presence in the lives of people born decades after the night of 28 March 1942. One young visitor from somewhere he thought of as 'Leed's, England', a child of the SMS generation, wrote 'thank you for the freedom u have given us'. Their comments in the visitors' book are often as moving as the inscriptions on the headstones. Now a very few visitors are survivors of the raid, and their comments reflect on the bonds that unite young men who faced death with old men now once again in the same boat. 'Remembering our people who fell', wrote one veteran: the bonds of comradeship strong still. Visitors still come as pilgrims, some year after year. Molly Harrison has often laid flowers on Maurice's grave. David Tait, Morgan Jenkins's nephew, who never knew him, is also a frequent visitor. But most visitors have no special reason to visit, though many are moved all the same. They write repeatedly of gratitude: 'Another year of my life paid for with yours'.

Those whose bodies were lost are commemorated on the great memorials that stand in some Commonwealth War Graves Commission cemeteries. A memorial at Brookwood in Surrey commemorates the commandos without a known grave, including five of Six Troop. Brookwood, the largest military cemetery in Britain, is the resting place of over 5000 British, Commonwealth and Allied dead, and the largest American cemetery in Britain. Encircled by military institutions at Sandhurst, Camberley and Bracknell, it adjoins a modest late-Victorian suburb, within earshot of the national shooting range at Bisley. On the wet February afternoon when I visited, the woods echoed to the muted sounds of rifle fire, a reminder of battle. A modest stone rotunda forms the memorial to nearly 3500 missing British servicemen and women who died in and on operations mounted from Britain itself. Green marble panels bear the names of commandos who died in raids on Vaagso and Dieppe as well as St Nazaire. Like all British memorials the names are inscribed in order first of rank and then by name. It is as if the class system that Tommy and Micky railed against and the bureaucracy that made their parents' anxiety all the sharper had the last word. Though united in death, the men of ML 192 and 268, soldiers and sailors are separated in memory.

Because men were only seconded to the commandos, 2 Commando's dead are not listed together, but in the order of their parent regiments. It is hard to find individual names, and the word St Nazaire appears nowhere. Sadly, it is impossible to discern that the missing of Six Troop served and died together. The sailors are even more scattered in death. Twenty-three of the Royal Navy's dead lie at Escoublac, but only one, Ordinary Signalman Angus Hale, was of ML 192. Most of his shipmates died in the estuary. The names of the Royal Navy dead of

St Nazaire—including nine men of MLs 192 and 268—are inscribed on the plinths on the great naval memorials at the naval bases at Chatham, Plymouth, Portsmouth, and at four other memorials.

The names of the dead of St Nazaire also appear on war memorials in communities all over Britain. In 1953 Morgan Jenkins became one of the 30 old boys of Brecon Grammar School listed on a memorial in Brecon High School, the comprehensive that replaced it. His name was also added to a headstone on the Jenkins family's plot in the cemetery at Penrhyn. Maurice Harrison's name was likewise listed on the roll of honour at the Strand School in Streatham. Surely others are on local memorials from Scotland to London.

The man most prominently commemorated is Tommy Peyton. Dorothy commissioned a memorial in the Lady Chapel of All Saints, Ascot, the scene of his memorial service in 1942. Windows, an altar and a reredos are dedicated to Tommy Peyton; but also to his comrades 'who gave their lives at St Nazaire', as a tablet in the chapel proclaims. This is the product of Dorothy Peyton's love for her youngest son. After the war the 'Waifs and Strays' who had shared Englemere Wood moved to another grand house at Ascot named in memory of Tommy. Sheila Stewart, who unusually for a Maurice Homes girl finished school and went to college (to become a schoolteacher and an author), attended the dedication ceremony. She recalled how a photograph of Tommy had been hung 'with sadness and respect' in its front hall, and how 'in the awed silence that followed the quiet voice of an important person' announced 'In memory of a gallant soldier, Thomas Grenville Pitt Peyton', and named it Grenville House. The house seems since to have closed.

Except for the names on the memorial to *Les Commandos Britanniques*, strangely perhaps, there is no memorial specifically to French civilians who died in and after the raid, or to those killed when British and American bombers returned to systematically destroy St Nazaire over the following two years. In the light of these losses it is striking to consider the warmth of the welcome that the Charioteers receive whenever they return to St Nazaire.

'WHO IN MY THOUGHTS ARE YOUNG':
TO THE FAR SIDE OF TEARS

In captivity St Nazaire survivors often talked about meeting again. Colonel Charles hosted a memorial dinner in Spangenberg in 1943. Arthur Young, in his only letter to the Burns from Lamsdorf, talked about how 'we shall all meet, together with Capt Burn, at our reunion in London after the war, and make up for lost time'. In Colditz Micky, Corran Purdon and Dick Morgan planned memorial dinners, and not just as gourmet fantasies for men living on turnip and ersatz fish-waste cheese.

As the first post-war anniversary of the raid approached many officers had suggested that a St Nazaire Society should be formed. A Preliminary Committee got the ball rolling. It included the three surviving VCs—Ryder, Beattie and Newman—as well as Micky, and (the sole 'other rank') Sergeant Ron Steele as acting honorary secretary. Its aim would of course be to perpetuate the memory of the raid, 'to keep all ranks ... in touch with each other' and to assist any member who might require help. Membership was 'Open to the Raiding Forces only'; that is, those who had 'proceeded up the River Loire into action'. The Preliminary Committee hosted a dinner at Chez Auguste in Frith Street, Soho on 28 March 1946, and the society has been in continuous existence ever since. Over sixty years on, it continues to thrive. While the numbers of survivors inevitably declines, the society has been reinvigorated by accepting the sons or daughters of Charioteers as committee members, including Ann Mitchell, David and Cécilie Birney's daughter. Impressively, the society supports well-digging projects in Africa as well as commemorating the dead of March 1942.

Not everyone eligible joined. Richard Collinson, who had got ashore from ML 192 before it broke up, did not consider himself 'reunion material'. In any case, as a sailor, his closest bonds were with those who shared three years of captivity in Westertimke rather than a few days or hours of one operation. Micky did not attend the first reunion dinner. As Phyllis explained to Maud Harrison, he was abroad (as *The Times*'s correspondent in Vienna) but, more importantly, 'I think he will really be rather thankful in a way as he would feel the absence of his friends so much'. As they all do. Every year the St Nazaire Society would place notices 'in proud memory' of their commando and Royal Naval comrades who had not returned. The words 'in proud memory' appear on the menhir at St Nazaire.

As the first return visit was planned Isabel Wyles, Bill Spaul's mother, had written to Micky hoping to see him at the unveiling of the memorial. By then he was in Hungary, reporting on the gradual strangulation of post-war optimism and witnessing the snuffing out of democracy by a ruthless Soviet regime, a process that cured him of the idealistic communism he had preached in Colditz. Mrs Wyles lamented that it seemed such a long time since she had seen him, and hoped to see him again. 'I'm hoping to go to St Nazaire this summer.' It was the beginning of a series of visits to her son's grave. Every year parties would travel to Escoublac, and later Falmouth, as well as gathering in London on the anniversary of the raid.

A memorial to those who died in Operation Chariot until recently stood in the car park at Fish Strand Quay, looking out across Carrick Roads to where the *Prinses Josephine Charlotte* had lain at anchor in the sunny days before the force steamed out of Falmouth harbour. In 2008 the Prince of Wales, like his father a supporter of the St Nazaire Society, re-dedicated the memorial in a more prominent position. Nearby was where Bill Gibson, Tommy Peyton, Maurice Harrison and all the other men of Six Troop had written their last letters to families whose lives were about to be changed forever.

Bill Gibson wrote in his last letter to his father that he could 'only hope that by laying down my life the generations to come might in some way remember us and also benefit from what we've done'. Allied victory in the Second World War was surely worth the sacrifice. It destroyed Nazi tyranny and Japanese oppression over millions of people in Europe and Asia. We who read this book have benefited from the actions of Bill Gibson, his comrades in Six Troop, and many thousands like him.

Gradually the Charioteers have passed away: Arthur Young in 1992, Peter Westlake in 2004, John Cudby in 2005. Micky, once again a survivor, became a senior office-bearer of the St Nazaire Society and often spoke at its ceremonies. Once, he quoted Bill Gibson's final letter as a reminder of the spirit of those he led into the raid. He found it too upsetting to do so again, but Bill's letter demands repetition. As Clive Burn wrote to Alex Gibson, 'I don't think anything that happens to him in life after the war will matter so much as the friendship that ... they had together before Saint Nazaire'. It was a measure of Clive Burn's growing emotional maturity through the responsibility of speaking for the dead of the raid that he was able to reach this insight of profound significance in his son's life. Clive was right. Despite a life filled with warm relationships with lovers, friends, and at a deep level with his wife Mary, the intensity of the bond between Micky and his men remained special.

In a long, rich life, he never ceased to grieve for the men of his troop, and especially for those who died in the first hours of 28 March 1942. In his autobiography, *Turned Towards the Sun*, Micky recalled part of a poem that gained him the Keats Prize for 1973. 'In Memory of Peter Small, Underwater Explorer, and His Wife Mary', expressed his powerful feelings of affectionate remembrance for two young dead friends and, soon after for the death of his own wife Mary, for whom always 'the sun-dust dances'. He had submitted the poem for the competition under the pseudonym 'Chariot'—the code name for the raid—and he came to think of it as also conveying his grief for friends killed at St Nazaire 'who in my thoughts are young'. It ends:

> *Then join her hands with his and close the tomb,*
> *And speaking to the absence, to the silence,*
> *From the far side of tears, remember them*
> *Where sun-dust dances, when the Eroica is played.*

Survivors grow older, reunions fewer; the St Nazaire Society's newsletter records obituaries. Feelings of loss transmute in time to acceptance and remembrance, in journeys to the 'far side of tears'. One day soon all the men of Six Troop will be together again, as they were on that dark evening in March 1942 when their little flotilla steamed up the Loire towards their destiny.

To all whose lives were touched by the raid on
St Nazaire, 28 March 1942, and especially to the men
of Six Troop, 2 Commando and their families

BURIED AT ESCOUBLAC-LA BAULE, FRANCE

Rifleman Ronald Edward David Burns, 6895664, Queen's Westminsters
Son of Edward and Janet Burns, Brockley, London, aged 22,
killed in action, 28 March 1942

Corporal Norman Lucas Fisher, 6896443, Queen's Westminsters
Son of Mabel Fisher, East Acton, London, aged 22, died of wounds,
25 April 1942

Lance Sergeant Peter Harkness, 2879689, Gordon Highlanders
Son of Peter and Catherine Harkness, aged 26, killed in action,
28 March 1942

Lance Sergeant Maurice Harrison, 6896247, Queen's Westminsters
Son of Samuel and Maud Harrison, Streatham, London, aged 21,
killed in action, 28 March 1942

Lance Corporal George Herbert Hudson, 6896827, Queen's Westminsters.
Son of Mrs J. Hudson, Guildford, aged 22, killed in action,
28 March 1942

Fusilier Albert James Lucy, 6461459, Royal Fusiliers
Son of Albert and Lily Lucy, Kentish Town, London, aged 22,
died of wounds, 28 March 1942

Rifleman Thomas Ypres Roach, 6849064, Queen's Westminsters
Son of Lewis and Winifred Roach, Caerau, Bridgend, Glamorgan, aged 25,
killed in action, 28 March 1942

Corporal William Albert Spaul, 6088619, Queen's Royal Regiment
(West Surrey) Son of Albert Spaul and Isabel Wyles, Guilford, aged 21,
killed in action, 28 March 1942

Corporal Reginald Morris Tomsett, 6896917, Queen's Westminsters
Son of Maurice and Edith Tomsett, Shirley, Croydon, aged 21,
killed in action, 28 March 1942

COMMEMORATED AT BROOKWOOD
CEMETERY, BRITAIN

Lance Sergeant William Gibson, 2879864, Gordon Highlanders
Son of Alexander and Margaret Gibson, stepson of Elizabeth Gibson,
Thornliebank, Glasgow, aged 22, killed in action, 28 March 1942

Fusilier Leonard George William Goss, 6459167, Royal Fusiliers
Son of Leonard and Lillian Goss, Brixton, London, aged 23, killed in action,
28 March 1942

Second Lieutenant Morgan Jenkins, Welsh Regiment
Husband of Doris Jenkins, Tottenham, London, aged 25, killed in action,
28 March 1942

Lieutenant Thomas Grenville Pitt Peyton, King's Royal Rifle Corps
Son of Ivor and Dorothy Peyton, Englemere Wood, Ascot, aged 20,
killed in action, 28 March 1942

Fusilier Robert Salonica Woodman, 6467448, Royal Fusiliers
Son of Agnes Woodman, Battersea, London, aged 24, killed in action,
28 March 1942

NOTES ON SOURCES

PROLOGUE: CARRICK ROADS, 24 MARCH 1942

Throughout this book, almost all the quotations from letters to or from Micky or his parents come from the Burn family papers, which include copies of letters and other documents by others associated with the story. I copied and arranged these papers as volumes of 'Burn Papers' (BP) in several series, as described in the Bibliography. (Bill Gibson's letter to his father, for example, is at BP 2/4.) These papers will, I hope and expect, be donated to a suitable repository. Much of Micky's retrospective reflections come from his autobiography, *Turned Towards the Sun* (*TTS*), from his autobiographical novels (mainly *Yes, Farewell—YF*) or from interviews with him. Sources of quotations are suggested in the text, which refers to sources listed fully in the Bibliography. The text often shows the sources of quotations—the words 'Maurice described' or 'recorded', for example, show that the source is his diary or letters preserved by his sister Molly. Abbreviations used are BFI (British Film Institute), IWM (Imperial War Museum), NAUK (British National Archives) and SNS (St Nazaire Society). Full notes can be found in my portion of the website of the National Museum of Australia's Centre for Historical Research: www.nma.gov.au/research

PART 1 COMMANDOS: MICKY BURN AND SIX TROOP

Martin Andrews's *Canon's Folly* provides additional insights into the Burns. 'Wire you when war breaks out' draws on *The Labyrinth of*

Europe and on Ella's letters in BP. In 'Terriers', Micky's men are documented in their various army personnel files, with the addition of an interview with Maurice Harrison's sister, Molly. 'Churchill's commandos' draws on David Niven's *The Moon's a Balloon*, Joan Bright's recollections of the commandos' formation in the IWM and Hermione Ranfurly's memoir *To War with Whitaker*. The landlady's rusty bayonet is taken from Hilary St George Saunders's *The Green Beret*. The vignette of commando selection comes from Donald Gilchrist's *Castle Commando*. Micky quoted Geoffrey Dawson's diary (in the Bodleian Library) in *TTS*. Tommy Peyton and Morgan Jenkins's 'Powers of leadership' are documented in their army personnel files, while additional details come from Sheila Stewart's *A Home From Home*. The details of commando training come from the DEFE files, while the American observer is the anonymous author of the US Army's *British Commandos* handbook of 1942. This section also quotes Maurice Harrison's diary and Jean Westlake's papers. Six Troop's men are documented in their army files, and in BP, which include letters from Edith Penfold, Alex Gibson, Lewis Roach, Alex Bell and Martin Andrews as well as from Clive and Phyllis. The context of commandos in the wider army is found in David French's *Raising Churchill's Army*, though he disagrees that commandos were 'contrary to the whole hierarchic and class system within the British army'. Micky's 'Educational Programme' is taken entirely from letters and papers in the BP, with the addition of some material from Molly Harrison's papers. The changes when Mountbatten took over are documented in Alanbrooke's published diary, and Charles Messenger's *The Commandos 1940–1946*. The staff officer who thought that the commandos had failed to deliver was J. Hughes-Hallett, who wrote to Cecil Lucas Phillips in 1957. His letter is among the Lucas Phillips papers (IWM). Signs of the commandos' disciplinary state can be found in Willie Bell, Tom Roach and Peter Westlake's army files. Micky's defence of Charles Haydon was published in *The Times* on 6 November 1946.

PART 2 'CHARIOT':
SIX TROOP IN THE RAID ON ST NAZAIRE

In 'Something in the wind', Bill Copland's memoir may be found in the Lucas Phillips papers in the IWM, David Paton's in his contribution to the BBC People's History website, while Micky's poetic remembrance appeared in his *Poems to Mary*. Reports on British morale appear in the Ministry of Information (INF) files (NAUK). The raid's 'High strategy' is documented in Winston Churchill's published *Memoirs* and in Admiralty, Cabinet, Combined Operations (that is, 'DEFE') files (NAUK). Six Troop's preparations are described in the BP. The propaganda plan is in INF files and security concerns (by Stuart Chant and other commandos) in DEFE files (all in NAUK). Micky's tongue-in-cheek response at the briefing is in *TTS*. His poem 'Just before the Briefing for St Nazaire' is in the BP at 6/50; his 'Order of landing' notes at 5/3. The sailor who described the rehearsal as a shambles was Ralph Batteson in *St Nazaire to Shepparton*. Six Troop's last letters and their families' responses are preserved in the BP. The raid itself is documented in a huge range of private and official records, and only direct quotes are noted here. Security briefings are preserved in WO 208/3264 (NAUK). Gordon Holman published many articles about the raid: this section quotes his 'We Raid St Nazaire' in the *Saturday Evening Post* of 11 July 1942. The anonymous commando officer's account is in the Lucas Phillips papers in the IWM. The RAF's part in the raid is recorded in AIR and DEFE files (NAUK). Hitler's orders appear in Hugh Trevor-Roper's edition of his War Directives. The revelation that the bombing was more important than hitherto believed can be found in John Campbell's *Dieppe Revisited*. Billie Stephens's account of the raid is in his memoir in the IWM. Sam Beattie's letter to Cecil Lucas Phillips can be found in his papers in the IWM. Gordon Holman's 'hell of a clout' appeared in *The Times* of 6 April 1942. The description of the massacre of the motor launches is based on several sources, including letters in the BP and Micky's memories, given in *TTS* and in interviews. His shout of 'follow me …' comes from James Dorrian's *Storming St Nazaire*. The Admiralty report can be found in DEFE 2/132 (NAUK); the fate of the launches in Arthur North's *Royal Naval Coastal Forces*. Micky described his lone mission in *TTS*. Bill Copland's IWM memoir and Corran Purdon's memoir *List the Bugle* complement his account. The commandos' surrender is described by Micky in *TTS*, George Davidson's memoir in the BP and Stuart Chant-Semphill's *St Nazaire Commando*. (After the war Chant changed his name to Chant-Semphill.) The French patriot was Leon Marchal in his *Vichy: Two Years of Deception* of 1943, while the figure of 60 per cent of commandos did not get ashore comes from the *Admiralty Battle Report* of 1948. Colin Gray's verdict on the raid appears in his *Explorations in Strategy*. The navy's admission of the folly of using vulnerable launches appears in the *Admiralty Battle Report*. German propaganda reports were analysed in the PREM files and British morale in INF files, both in NAUK.

⟫◦◦◦⟪

PART 3 CASUALTIES:
DEAD AND MISSING; WOUNDED AND CAPTURED

Peter Westlake's photograph is held by Jean Westlake. Ronnie Swayne and Philip Dark's memoirs are in the IWM, Swayne's in the Lucas Phillips papers. Stuart Chant's recollection comes from his memoir *St Nazaire Commando* and Corran Purdon's from *List the Bugle*. The German propaganda recordings are preserved in DEFE 2/133 (NAUK). Micky's 'moans and sudden cries' comes from *YF*, his recollection of the trauma of memory from *TTS* and his poem 'To the Commando' from BP 6/62. Arthur Young's letter is also in BP, while the survivor's explanation 'we wept for them' comes from James Dorrian's *Storming St Nazaire*. The officer depressed by stories of the raid later in 1942 was Joe Nicholl, whose account is in IWM. Parents' letters, and Mora Hope-Robertson's, are in BP. Accounts of interrogation are drawn from Six Troop survivors' accounts in WO 344 (NAUK), Paul Schmidt's *Hitler's Interpreter* and *TTS*. Reports of the raid appear in INF and DEFE files (NAUK), and clippings in the Thorold Dickinson collection in the BFI. As always, letters in the BP (such as Mora Hope-Robertson's) supplement the official reports.

The section 'Six Troop's dead men' largely draws on letters in the BP, supplemented by an interview with Molly Harrison. The sad story of the Casualty Branch is told in WO 162/205 and WO 32/4674 (NAUK). These NAUK files, with the addition of ADM 1/13983 and of course the BP, also document the tragic story of 'bereavement and bureaucracy'. Naturally the main source for 'Morgan's file' is his army personnel file.

PART 4 CONDOLENCES: THE SIX TROOP FAMILIES

The story of Micky's fate is told by Clive's diary and letters in the BP, and virtually all quotations in this Part are from them. The BBC's wireless bulletins are documented in the BBC Written Archives. The soldier who commented on German newspapers was Donald Edgar in his memoir *The Stalag Men*. Details of the propensity to listen to German Propaganda come from Peter Martland's biography of Lord Haw Haw and Paul Schmidt's *Hitler's Interpreter*. The terrible story of Dorothy Peyton's loss is told mainly from the BP, but also Charles Haydon's papers in the IWM and Tommy's brother John's memoir, *Without Benefit of Laundry*. Phyllis's daughter-in-law, Mrs Carol Adams, provided insights into the war's effects on her. Micky's reflections on his father's helping the bereaved families appears in *TTS*. The story of *The Next of Kin* is told in Thorold Dickinson's files in the BFI, which includes many reviews as well as Dickinson's own (somewhat exaggerated) account. The families' responses to 'This cruel blow' are told entirely through letters in the BP. The file DEFE 2/127 (NAUK) documents the first anniversary broadcast and articles, notably Gordon Holman's piece in the *Evening Standard* on 28 March 1943. *The Times*'s incorrect report was published on 18 May 1943.

PART 5 KRIEGIES: SIX TROOP'S PRISONERS OF WAR

The anonymous commando officer's memoir is part of the Lucas Phillips papers in the IWM. The shocking statistics of French colonial prisoners of war is found in David Killingray's article 'Africans and African Americans in enemy hands'. Sam Beattie's diary is reproduced in Noel Barber's *Prisoner of War*. The Sandbostel and Westertimke camps are documented in Red Cross reports in WO 208/3270 (NAUK). The MI9 reports on the celebrations for Beattie's VC are from DEFE 2/699 (NAUK). The anecdote about 'Goosey' comes from Philip Dark's memoir in the IWM. Padre Platt's diary is available in Margaret Duggan's *Padre in Colditz*. The saga of Clive's fight against 'an enemy we shall fight forever' is told by the file WO 32/10798 (NAUK). In 'The Parcels Roundabout' (the phrase is Noel Barber's in *Prisoner of War*) the prisoner explaining the camp economy was Reginald Evans, in his memoir (IWM). James Badcock praised Sid Sherriff in his 'Life in Stalag VIIIB' (IWM). Grismond Davies-Scourfield described Lamsdorf's tunnels in his 'A Load of Rubbish', in Reinhold Eggers and John Watton, *Colditz Recaptured*. Donald Edgar mentions 'Table-enders' in *The Stalag Men*. The October 1943 repatriation is documented in INF 1/282 (NAUK). *Time*, in the National Army Museum, documents the artistic endeavours of Hohenfels, as does Albert Field's appendix to Barton Maughan's *Tobruk and El Alamein*. Stan Rodd praised David Mackenzie in his 1945 interrogation report in WO 344 (NAUK). Reports of abuses at Lamsdorf appear on TS 26/643 (NAUK).

PART 6 COLDITZ: MICKY IN CAPTIVITY

Micky's vision for the opening shots of a film come from *YF*. Noel Barber quoted a prisoner describing Spangenberg as 'a special sort of camp' in *Prisoner of War*. Jim Rogers commented on the dichotomy between Territorials and regulars in *Tunnelling into Colditz*, as did Padre Platt in *Padre in Colditz*. The major who commented on 'young blood' and 'the St Nazaire crowd' was Alexis Casdagli in his diary (IWM). Abuses at Spangenberg are documented in TS 26/250

(NAUK). The story of MI9's work in camps is told by TS 26/643 (NAUK). Micky recalled the comment that Micky was 'slightly to the Left of Major Attlee' in an interview with the author. Victor Fortune's regard for Clive is from *TTS*. Hitler's 'extermination order' appears in Hugh Trevor-Roper's *Hitler's War Directives*. Anecdotes about manacling come from Donald Edgar's *The Stalag Men* and Denholm Elliott's memoir (IWM). The Swiss inspector at Spangenberg is quoted in Albert Field's appendix to Barton Maughan's *Tobruk and El Alamein*. *The Times* reported the possibility of Germany abrogating the Geneva Convention on 23 October 1942. Dinah's death and the responses of her family and friends are documented in BP. Charles Newman's letter to Charles Haydon is in Haydon's papers (IWM). E.H. Baxter's 'Oflag occasions' (IWM) describes Rotenburg camp and its 'cliques and coteries'. Micky's view on Katyn is from *TTS*. Stuart Chant's correspondence with the historian Cecil Lucas Phillips is in Lucas Phillips's papers (IWM). The Red Cross's reports on Colditz are found in WO 32/11111 (NAUK). Jon Chrisp's views on 'the castle poet' can be found in his book *Escape*. Micky's description of Colditz resembling 'a bad hotel' comes from his interview with Windfall Films (IWM). Miles Reid's letters to his wife are in the IWM. Giles Romilly's recollections can be found in Giles Romilly and Michael Alexander's *Hostages at Colditz*. The story of the secret radio is told in 'History of Oflag IVC Colditz', WO 208/3288 (NAUK), Miles Reid's *Into Colditz*, Pat Reid's *The Latter Days at Colditz* and Jim Rogers's *Tunnelling into Colditz*. The official response to Stuart Chant's having spoken into a 'Hun mike' is told in DEFE 2/125 (NAUK). The officer shocked by Colditz late in 1944 was Captain Vic Vercoe, whose testimony appears in TS 26/344 (NAUK). Micky's 'dream of Britain' comes from his *Mary and Richard*. Sydney Smith's recollections were published in Reinhold Eggers and John Watton's *Colditz Recaptured*. Micky's strictures against Gris Davies-Scourfield are recorded in Davies-Scourfield's *In Presence of My Foes*. The diarist at Lamsdorf in the war's last winter was Charles Baggs, whose diary is in the IWM. Stan Rodd's record of the final months is in his 1945 interrogation, in WO 344 (NAUK).

PART 7 CHARIOTEERS: REMEMBERING ST NAZAIRE

Micky's recommendation to Bob Laycock can be found in DEFE 2/125 (NAUK). The citations are in this file and in the *London Gazette*, 5 July 1945. Audrey's recollection of liberation comes from Alexander Walker's *Audrey: Her Real Story*. The records of the survivors' de-mob and of the despatch of the effects of their dead comrades can be found on their army files. Micky's defence of Charles Haydon appeared in *The Times*, 6 November 1946. Details of the 1948 commemoration come from DEFE 2/1544 and ADM 1/20718 (NAUK). Richard Collinson's recollections were part of a letter to the author, 29 November 2005. I am grateful to John Julius Norwich Esq. for allowing me to quote from an unpublished portion of the diary of his father, Duff Cooper. The report of Jack Heery's trip comes from the St Nazaire Society newsletter, 1949. The record of the 1982 visit is John Allen May's *The St Nazaire Society: Return to St Nazaire 1982*. Robert Ryder's special access to the records is documented in ADM 1/18251 (NAUK). Cecil Lucas Phillips's obituary appeared in *The Times* on 23 February 1984. Micky's letter to Lucas Phillips is in Lucas Phillips's papers (IWM). The report of the Wandsworth prison artist appeared in *The Times* on 7 April 1964. The critique of *Gift Horse* appeared in *The Times* on 21 July 1952. Micky's poem 'In Memory of Peter Small ...' appeared in his *Poems as an Accompaniment to a Life*.

A NOTE ON MEASUREMENTS

The people whose stories this book tells used measurements that will be unfamiliar to some readers. They can be converted thus:

  yard—about a metre
  mile—about 1.6 kilometres
  pound (weight)—about 0.45 kilograms
  inch—about 2.5 centimetres
  foot—about 30 centimetres

ACKNOWLEDGMENTS

This book would not have become possible without the trust and co-operation of Micky Burn, who welcomed a complete stranger into his life and his home, entrusting him with precious family documents and personal memories in the hope that he would do justice to his life story. How an historian from Canberra came to tell the story of a poet from North Wales bears explaining.

In the northern summer of 2004, during a trip to Britain to complete research for *Quinn's Post: Anzac, Gallipoli*, I stayed again with my brother-in-law, Gordon Cruickshank in Wimbledon. Gordon, a motoring writer specialising in racing history, was researching an article on the racing driver Sir Tim Birkin. He had located Michael Burn who had ghostwritten Birkin's autobiography as a student in the early 1930s. Burn had recently published his autobiography, *Turned Towards the Sun*, and Gordon had a copy. Each morning, I devoured it with my cornflakes before leaving for the National Archives. Day by day I found his account of his life compelling.

As a military historian, I was interested in his account of his part in the raid on St Nazaire. But the part that brought tears to my eyes was a short, six-page chapter, called 'Remember!'. It described how after Burn's troop had been virtually destroyed in the raid his parents had, as he had asked, made contact with his men's families. This story moved me to write to Michael—whom I soon learned to call Micky—to suggest that it deserved more than a few pages. He replied positively to a letter from a stranger arriving out of the blue from the other side of the world and in December 2004 I was able to travel to Minffordd to meet him. In mid 2005 he allowed me to copy the first batch of his family papers, and generously hosted several further visits to Wales.

Thanks are therefore due to Micky, but also to Gordon Cruickshank, to whom I dedicate this book in appreciation of his friendship and support.

Producing this book has been a joy, and I would like to thank Ms Diana Hill and Mr Paul O'Beirne at Murdoch Books for their confidence and support, Ms Karen Ward for her sympathetic editing, Mr Ian Faulkner for his beautifully clear maps, and the designer Mr Hugh Ford.

I am particularly grateful to those who knew characters in this story—Ms Carol Adams, Miss Molly Harrison (who allowed me to borrow and consult her brother's papers), John Julius Norwich Esq. (who kindly allowed me to consult copies of the diary of his father, Duff Cooper), the late the Rt Hon. Lord Peyton of Yeovil, Mr Maurice Roe, Elizabeth and John Ungly and Mrs Janet Westlake (who provided papers relating to her late husband).

The support of members and associates of the St Nazaire Society has been vital, and I gratefully acknowledge the aid of Ms Siobhan Blake, Mr Richard Collinson, Mr Eric de la Torre and Clare de la Torre, Mr James Dorrian, Mrs Ann Mitchell (née Birney), Mr Bob Montgomery and the Taits, David, Jennifer and Stuart, who shared with me their memories, knowledge and respect for those associated with Operation Chariot. I am also grateful for the interest and encouragement of many individuals, including Mrs A. Bell, Mr Phil Cudby, Mr Alan Doward, Mr Simon Dowsell, Mr Billy Duncan, Mr John Sinnott, Mr Sam Small (of the Star Hotel, Moffat) and Mr Arthur Williamson.

I am grateful to relatives of several individuals from whose papers I have also quoted. They include Ms Lynda Harvey for allowing me to quote from the papers of her father, James Badcock. Mr Stephen Reid for permission to quote from the letters of Miles Reid. Mr Sebastian Stephens, executor of the estate of W.L. Stephens, and the Trustees of the Imperial War Museum for permission to quote from the papers of E.H. Baxter. Every effort has been made to trace copyright holders and the author and the Imperial War Museum would be grateful for any information which might help trace those whose identities or addresses are not currently known.

Historians depend upon the advice and assistance of archivists, librarians and curators. Ms Beverly Hutchinson and Mr Roddy Hay, Army Personnel Centre, Glasgow, enabled me to consult and copy crucial personnel records. I thank Miss Pamela Clark, Registrar of the Royal Archives, Windsor and Miss Elisabeth Stuart, the Archivist at the Duchy of Cornwall, who kindly allowed me to examine Duchy records to gain an idea of Clive Burn's personality and work. I thank Ms Natalie Adams at the Churchill Archives Centre (who helped to establish that Thorold Dickinson's account of *The Next of Kin* was exaggerated), Dr David Stevens and Mr John Perryman of the Royal Australian Navy's Sea Power Centre, Canberra, Ms Louise Watt at the BBC Written Archives Centre, Mr Andrew Lucas of the Stockport Local Heritage Library, Mr Ian Hook of the Essex Regiment collection and Mrs Margaret Biskup at the Commonwealth War Graves Commission. I am grateful to archivists and librarians at the British Film Institute, the British Library, the British Library Newspaper repository (Colindale), the Imperial War Museum, the National Archives (UK), the National Archives of Australia (Canberra and Melbourne), the National Army Museum, London, the Australian Defence Force Academy Library, the Research Centre at the Australian War Memorial and the National Library of Australia.

Colleagues and friends who have been particularly helpful include Dr Peter Liddle of the Second World War Experience Centre, Leeds, Prof. Bob Moore of Sheffield University (who kindly located and copied British prisoner-of-war records), Prof. Paul Mackenzie of the University of North Carolina, Dr Michael McKernan, Dr Robert Nichols, Dr Bruce Scates and Dr Mark Johnston.

Finally, as ever, I acknowledge that this book would not have been possible without Claire's love and support.

BIBLIOGRAPHY

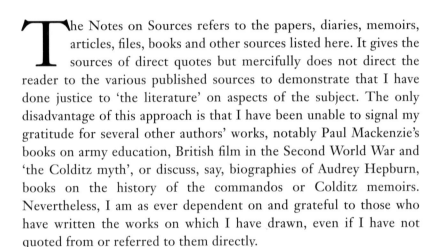

The Notes on Sources refers to the papers, diaries, memoirs, articles, files, books and other sources listed here. It gives the sources of direct quotes but mercifully does not direct the reader to the various published sources to demonstrate that I have done justice to 'the literature' on aspects of the subject. The only disadvantage of this approach is that I have been unable to signal my gratitude for several other authors' works, notably Paul Mackenzie's books on army education, British film in the Second World War and 'the Colditz myth', or discuss, say, biographies of Audrey Hepburn, books on the history of the commandos or Colditz memoirs. Nevertheless, I am as ever dependent on and grateful to those who have written the works on which I have drawn, even if I have not quoted from or referred to them directly.

ARCHIVAL SOURCES

Mr Michael Burn, private papers

Series 1/ Documents concerning the fate of Micky Burn
Series 2/ Documents concerning the fate of Six Troop
Series 3/ Letters, 1940–42
Series 4/ Miscellaneous documents 2005
Series 5/ Miscellaneous documents 2006
Series 6/ Miscellaneous documents 2008

Interviews and meetings, December 2004, 1 October 2005, 11–12 February 2006, 2 July 2008, 22–25 November 2008

Miss Molly Harrison
  Papers of Sergeant Maurice Harrison
  Interview, 10 February 2006

John Julius Norwich, Esq.
  Diary of Duff Cooper, 1947

Mr David Tait
  Papers of Lieutenant Morgan Jenkins

Mrs Jean Westlake
  Papers of Rifleman Peter Westlake

BRITISH ARMY RECORDS CENTRE, GLASGOW
Personnel records of members of Six Troop:
Reginald Bell, 6461342
Michael Burn, 74087
Ronald Burns, 6895664
Patrick Bushe, 7014446
John Cudby, 6468006
John Dawson, 6465567
Norman Fisher, 6896443
Reginald Fursse, 6896474
William Gibson, 2879864
George Goss, 6459167
Peter Harkness, 2879689
Maurice Harrison, 6896247
George Hudson, 6896827
Morgan Jenkins, P/156336/1
Albert Lucy, 6461459
Frederick Penfold, 6460208
Thomas Peyton, 6091899
John Prescott, 2878579
Thomas Roach, 6849064
William Spaul, 6088619
Reginald Tomsett, 6896917

William Watt, 6460971
Peter Westlake, 7016551
Robert Woodman, 6467448

BBC WRITTEN ARCHIVE CENTRE, READING
Home News Bulletins, 1942–44

BRITISH FILM INSTITUTE, LONDON
Thorold Dickinson collection, Box 7

DUCHY OF CORNWALL ARCHIVES, LONDON
Secretary's Letter Book, Jan–Jun 1941
Secretary's Letter Book, Jan–Jun 1942

IMPERIAL WAR MUSEUM, LONDON
Department of Documents
66/213/1, Brigadier C. Lucas Phillips
67/284/1, Joan Bright, 'Research Notes for *The Green Beret*'
76/131/1, Captain J.H. Sewell
78/43/1, Captain J.E.C. Nicholl
83/37/1, Lt Col M. Reid
85/8/1, Lt Col P. Brush
86/7/1, Lt Cdr W.L. Stephens
90/4/1, Sgt W. Margerison
90/18/1, Reginald Evans
93/28/4, Maj Gen J.C. Haydon
94/7/1, P. Dark
94/26/1, J.H. Brooker
94/49/1, Charles Baggs
95/6/1, S/Sgt E.G. Evans
98/7/1, D. Elliott
99/47/1, J. Badcock
99/82/1, R. Holme
Con Shelf, W.K. Laing
P129, 2Lt E.H. Baxter
P463, Maj Alexis Casdagli

Department of Sound Records
21744/1-5 Interview with Michael Burn, 1999

NATIONAL ARCHIVES, LONDON
ADM 1/13983 St Nazaire Operation, Presumption of death of
    missing personnel
ADM 1/18251 Request for Admiralty approval to write an
    account of St Nazaire raid
ADM 1/20718 Naval participation in Anglo–French ceremonies
    of commemoration
ADM 1/11970 Operation 'Chariot'—Combined Operation against
    St Nazaire 28/3/42—preparations for

AIR 8/870 Operation 'Chariot'
AIR 14/694 Operation 'Chariot'

CAB 79/18/30 Chiefs of Staff Committee 25 February 1942
CAB 79/56/13 Chiefs of Staff Committee

DEFE 2/125 Operation Chariot, Part 1
DEFE 2/126 Operation Chariot, Part 2
DEFE 2/127 Operation Chariot, Part 3
DEFE 2/130 Operation Chariot, Vol. 1
DEFE 2/131 Operation Chariot, Vol. 2
DEFE 2/132 Operation Chariot, Vol. 3
DEFE 2/697 History of Combined Operations
DEFE 2/698 History of Combined Operations
DEFE 2/699 History of Combined Operations
DEFE 2/843 Commando casualties 1940–1945
DEFE 2/851 Honours and awards
DEFE 2/881 Reports on exercises
DEFE 2/879 Drugs for fatigue
DEFE 2/956 Honours and awards
DEFE 2/960 Special Service Brigade 1942–44
DEFE 2/1373 Index of names in files DEFE 2/781–1377
DEFE 2/1544 Proposed memorial at St Nazaire

INF 6/1043 'The Next of Kin'
INF 1/917 Publicity regarding Combined Operations
INF 1/284 Public morale: monthly reports to the cabinet
INF 1/282 Home intelligence reports, Part 1 [1941–44]

PREM 3/376 Reports on St Nazaire

TS 26/344 At or near Belgrade, Vienna, Kaiseresteinbruch or Colditz
TS 26/650 Spangenberg—assault on Captain Stoker
TS 26/643 Alleged war crime at Lamsdorf

WO 32/11111, Reports on *Oflag* IVC (Colditz)
WO 32/4674 Notification of casualties to next-of-kin and royal
    message of sympathy
WO 32/10798 Disposal of effects of personnel reported missing
    or prisoner of war

WO 162/205 History of Casualty Branch

WO 208/3264 St Nazaire MI9
WO 208/3288 Camp history of *Oflag* IC Colditz
WO 208/3293 Secret camp histories *Oflag* A/H Upper and Lower
    Haina Kloster
WO 208/4681 *Stalags* 8A Gorlitz, 8B Sagan, 8C Teschen and
    344 Lamsdorf, Germany: ill treatment of POWs

WO 218/33 War diary, 2 Commando

WO 309/1083 *Stalag* VIIIB

WO 311/186 Lamsdorf—ill-treatment of prisoners of war
WO 311/733, Shooting of a British PW at *Stalag* 344,
    November 1944

WO 344/ 24/2 Interrogations of liberated prisoners of war: (Bell),
    50/1 (Bushe), 271/1 (Rodd), 340/1 (Westlake)

NATIONAL ARCHIVES OF AUSTRALIA, MELBOURNE
MP508/1 255/711/252 Reports from British legation at Berne on
    POW camps
MP508/1 255/736/81 International Red Cross, Visit *Stalag*
    VIII Report
MP508/1 255/711/117 Reports on camps … *Oflag*
    IX A/11 [sic]
MP508/1 255/711/196 Inspection reports on German
    POW camps *Oflag* IX

NATIONAL ARMY MUSEUM, LONDON
6005/276 Bulletins from *Stalag* 383
6112-609 Records relating to *Stalag* 383

PETER LIDDLE COLLECTION, UNIVERSITY OF LEEDS
2781, Interview with Mr Edward Tucker

ST NAZAIRE SOCIETY PAPERS
Newsletter of the St Nazaire Society

ON-LINE SOURCES
James Laurie, 'Where next?: a Record of my Journeyings',
    <http://www.stnazairesociety.org/Pages/index.html>
T.J. Lees, 'Through the barbed wire',
    <http://www.bakerlite.co.uk/TBW>
David Paton, 'St Nazaire – Operation Chariot – The Doctor's
    Perspective – Finale', BBC People's History,
    <http://www.bbc.co.uk/dna/ww2/A3723383>

PUBLISHED WORKS
Admiralty Battle Report 1736 (34) (48), *The Attack on St Nazaire
    28th March 1942*, Admiralty, London, 1948
After the Battle, vol. 15
Martin Andrews, *Canon's Folly*, Michael Joseph, London, 1974
Anon, *Combined Operations: the Official Story of the Commandos*,
    Macmillan, New York, 1943

Anon, *The Commando Memorial Spean Bridge and a Short History of the Commandos 1940–1945*, Commando Association, np, 1965

Richard Arnold, *The True Book about the Commandos*, Frederick Muller, London, 1954

Michael Balfour, *Propaganda in War 1939–1945: Organisations, Policies and Publics in Britain and Germany*, Routledge & Kegan Paul, London, 1979

Noel Barber, *Prisoner of War: the Story of British Prisoners held by the Enemy*, George G. Harrap, London, 1944

Correlli Barnett, *Engage the Enemy More Closely: the Royal Navy in the Second World War*, Hodder & Stoughton, London, 1991

Ralph Batteson, *St Nazaire to Shepparton: a Sailor's Odyssey*, High Edge Historical Society, 1996

Christopher Buckley, *Norway ; The Commandos ; Dieppe*, HMSO, London, 1951

Michael Burn, *The Labyrinth of Europe*, Methuen, London, 1939
Yes, Farewell, The Reprint Society, London, 1947
The Modern Everyman, Rupert Hart-Davis, London, 1948
Poems to Mary, Rupert Hart-Davis, London, 1953
The Flying Castle, Rupert Hart-Davis, London, 1959
Farewell to Colditz, White Loom, London, 1974
Mary and Richard: The Story of Richard Hillary and Mary Booker, Mandarin, London, 1988
Turned Towards the Sun, Michael Russell, Norwich, 2003
Childhood at Oriol, Turtle Point Press, New York, 2005
Poems as an Accompaniment to a Life, Michael Russell, Norwich, 2006

Rupert Butler, *Hand of Steel: the Story of the Commandos*, Hamlyn, London, 1980

Geraldine Calca Cash, (ed.), *Keats Prize Poems: an Anthology of Poetry*, London Literary Editions, London, 1973

Alan Campbell, *Colditz Cameo*, Ditching, Ditching Press, nd

John Campbell, *Dieppe Revisited: a Documentary Investigation*, Routledge, London, 1993

Alan Carswell, *For Your Freedom and Ours: Poland, Scotland and the Second World War*, National War Museum of Scotland, Edinburgh, 1993

Henry Chancellor, *Colditz: the Definitive History*, Hodder & Stoughton, London, 2001

Stuart Chant-Semphill, *St Nazaire Commando*, John Murray, London, 1985

John Chrisp, *Escape*, Panther Books, London, 1960

Winston Churchill, *The Second World War*, Vol. IV, *The Hinge of Fate*, The Reprint Society, London, 1951
   Memoirs of the Second World War, Houghton Mifflin, Boston, 1987

Dudley Clarke, *Seven Assignments*, Jonathan Cape, London, 1948

Mary Cleare and Nicholas Cranfield, *All Saints' Church Ascot Heath*, All Saints' Church, Ascot, 2008

Commonwealth War Graves Commission, *Escoublac-La Baule War Cemetery*

Duff Cooper, *Old Men Forget: the Autobiography of Duff Cooper*, Rupert Hart-Davis, London, 1954

Charles Cruickshank, *The Fourth Arm: Psychological Warfare 1938–1945*, Davis-Poynter, London, 1977

Alex Danchev and Daniel Todman (eds), *War Diaries 1939–1945 Field Marshal Lord Alanbrooke*, Wiedenfeld & Nicolson, London, 2001

Gris Davies-Scourfield, *In Presence of My Foes*, Wilton 65, Bishop Wilton, 1991

Peter Dennis, *The Territorial Army 1907–1940*, Royal Historical Society, London, 1987

James Dorrian, *Storming St Nazaire*, Sword & Pen, Barnsley, 2001

Margaret Duggan (ed.), *Padre in Colditz: the Diary of J. Ellison Platt M.B.E.*, Hodder & Stoughton, London, 1978

Donald Edgar, *The Stalag Men*, J. Clare Books, London, 1982

Reinhold Eggers, *Colditz: the German Story*, New English Library, London, 1975
   and John Watton, (eds), *Colditz Recaptured*, Hale, London, 1973

Sean Hepburn Ferrer, *Audrey Hepburn: an Elegant Spirit*, Sidgwick & Jackson, London, 2003

M.R.D. Foote & J.M. Langley, *MI9*, Bodley Head, London, 1979

Ken Ford, *St Nazaire 1942: the Great Commando Raid*, Osprey, Oxford, 2001

David French, *Raising Churchill's Army: the British Army and the War against Germany 1919–1945*, Oxford University Press, Oxford, 2000

Donald Gilchrist, *Castle Commando*, Oliver and Boyd, Edinburgh, 1960

R.D. Grange-Bennett, *1st Centenary History of the Church of All Saints Ascot*, Church Publishers, Ramsgate, 1964

Colin Gray, *Explorations in Strategy*, Westport, Greenwood, 1996

Warren Harris, *Audrey Hepburn: a Biography*, Simon & Schuster, New York, 1994

F.H. Hinsley, *British Intelligence in the Second World War: its Influence on Strategy and Operations*, Vol. II, HMSO, London, 1981

Gordon Holman, *Commando Attack*, Hodder & Stoughton, London, 1942

Andrew Jeffrey, *This Time of Crisis: Glasgow, the West of Scotland and the North Western Approaches in the Second World War*, Mainstream Publishing, Edinburgh, 1993

Kelly's Directory of Devonshire and Cornwall, 1939

David Killingray, 'Africans and African Americans in enemy hands', in Bob Moore and Kent Fedorowich, (eds), *Prisoners of War and their Captors in World War II*, Berg, Oxford, 1996

Arieh Kochavi, *Confronting Captivity: Britain and the United States and their Prisoners of War in Nazi Germany*, University of North Carolina Press, Chapel Hill, 2005

James Ladd, *Commandos and Rangers of World War II*, New York, 1978

E.H. Larvie, *The Man who came in from Colditz*, R. Hale, London, 1975

S.P. Mackenzie, *Politics and Military Morale: Current-Affairs Education and Citizenship Education in the British Army, 1914–1950*, Clarendon Press, Oxford, 1992

British War Films 1939–1945: The Cinema and the Services, Hambledon and London, London, 2001

The Colditz Myth: British and Commonwealth Prisoners of War in Nazi Germany, OUP, Oxford, 2004

Leon Marchal, *Vichy: Two Years of Deception*, Macmillan, New York, 1943

Princess Marie Louise, *My Memories of Six Reigns*, Penguin, London, 1956

Peter Martland, *Lord Haw Haw: the English Voice of Nazi Germany*, Scarecrow Press in association with the National Archives, Lanham (MD), London, 2003

David Mason, *Raid on St Nazaire*, Pan Ballantine Books, London, 1970

Barton Maughan, *Tobruk and El Alamein*, Australian War Memorial, Canberra

John Allen May (ed.), *The St Nazaire Society: Return to St Nazaire 1982*, St Nazaire Society, Dorking, 1982

Charles Messenger, *The Commandos 1940–1946*, William Kimber, London, 1985

G.H. Mills and R.F. Nixon, *The Annals of the King's Royal Rifle Corps*, Vol. VI, *1921–1943*, Leo Cooper, London, 1971

Eric Morris, *Churchill's Private Armies: British Special Forces in Europe 1939–1942*, Hutchinson, London, 1986

Robin Neillands, *The Raiders: the Army Commandos 1940–1946*, Fontana, London, 1989

David Niven, *The Moon's a Balloon*, Coronet, London, 1971

Arthur North, *Royal Naval Coastal Forces*, Almark, New Maldon, 1972

John Peyton, *Without Benefit of Laundry*, Bloomsbury, London, 1997

C.E. Lucas Phillips, *The Greatest Raid of All*, [1958], Pan Macmillan, London, 2000

Joseph Platt, *Padre in Colditz*, Hodder & Stoughton, London, 1978

Jack Pringle, *Colditz Last Stop*, Temple House Books, Lewes, 1995

Corran Purdon, *List the Bugle: Reminiscences of an Irish Soldier*, Greystone Books, Antrim, 1993

Hermione Ranfurly, *To War with Whitaker: the Wartime Diaries of the Countess of Ranfurly 1939–1945*, Mandarin, London, 1995

Miles Reid, *Into Colditz*, Michael Russell, Wilton, 1983

Patrick Reid, *The Colditz Story*, Hodder & Stoughton, London, 1952
The Latter Days at Colditz, Hodder & Stoughton, London, 1953

Jeffrey Richards, *Thorold Dickinson: the Man and His Films*, Croom Helm, London, 1986

Jim Rogers, *Tunnelling into Colditz: a Mining Engineer in Captivity*, Chivers Press, Bath, 1986

David Rolf, ' "Blind Bureaucracy": the British Government and POWs in German Captivity, 1939–45', in Bob Moore and Kent Fedorowich, (eds), *Prisoners of War and their Captors in World War II*, Berg, Oxford, 1996

Giles Romilly and Michael Alexander, *Hostages at Colditz*, Sphere Books, London, 1973

Giles and Esmond Romilly, *Out of Bounds*, Hamish Hamilton, London, 1935

S.W. Roskill, *The War at Sea 1939–1945*, Vol. II *The Period of Balance*, HMSO, London, 1956

Robert Ryder, *The Attack on St. Nazaire 28th March 1942*, John Murray, London, 1947

Harold Satow and M.J. Sée, *The Work of the Prisoners of War Department during the Second World War*, Foreign Office, London, 1950

Hilary St George Saunders, *The Green Beret: the Story of the Commandos 1940–1945*, Michael Joseph, London, 1949

Peter Scott, *The Battle of the Narrow Seas: a History of the Light Coastal Forces in the Channel and North Sea, 1939–1945*, Country Life, London, 1945

William Seymour, *British Special Forces*, Sidgwick & Jackson, London, 1985

Paul Schmidt, (ed. R.C.H. Steed), *Hitler's Interpreter*, Heinemann, London, 1951

Daniel Siccard, *St Nazaire 1939–1945 La Guerre L'Occupation La Liberation*, Editions Ouest-France, Rennes, 1994

Sheila Stewart, *A Home From Home*, Longmans, London, 1967

Hugh Trevor-Roper, *Hitler's War Directives, 1939–1945*, Pan Books, London, 1966

United States Army, *British Commandos*, Washington, 1942

Vasiliis Vourkoutiotis, *Prisoners of War and the German High Command: the British and American Experience*, Palgrave, London, 2003

Alexander Walker, *Audrey: Her Real Story*, Weidenfeld & Nicolson, London, 1994

War Office, *Prisoners of War British Army 1939–1945* [1945], J.B. Hayward & Son, Polstead, 1990

J.E.R. Wood, (ed.), *Detour: the Story of Oflag IVC*, The Falcon Press, London, 1946

Peter Young, *Commando*, Ballantine Books, New York, 1969

Phillip Ziegler, *Mountbatten*, Harper & Row, New York, 1985

Bulletin (Glasgow), 1942

Evening News (London), 1942
Evening Standard, 1942
London Gazette, 1945, 1947
Monthly Film Bulletin, 1942, 1952, 1968
Sunday Express, 20 February 1944
The Bulletin and Scots Pictorial (Glasgow), 1942
The Camp, 1944–45
The Prisoner of War (London), 1942–45
The Times (London), 1933–85

Newsletter of the St Nazaire Society

Visits to St Nazaire, Colditz, Brookwood, Ascot: September 2005, February 2006, July 2007, July 2008, November 2008

MAPS

Page 51: Britain, showing places associated with Six Troop.
Pages 66–67: Europe, showing St Nazaire and the prisoner-of-war camps in which Six Troop men were held.
Page 82: St Nazaire during the raid.

ILLUSTRATIONS

INDEX

Published in 2009 by Pier 9, an imprint of Murdoch Books Pty Limited

Murdoch Books Australia
Pier 8/9
23 Hickson Road
Millers Point NSW 2000
Phone: +61 (0) 2 8220 2000
Fax: +61 (0) 2 8220 2558
www.murdochbooks.com.au

Murdoch Books UK Limited
Erico House, 6th Floor
93–99 Upper Richmond Road
Putney, London SW15 2TG
Phone: +44 (0) 20 8785 5995
Fax: +44 (0) 20 8785 5985
www.murdochbooks.co.uk

Publisher: Diana Hill
Project Editor: Paul O'Beirne
Designer: Hugh Ford

National Library of Australia Cataloguing-in-Publication Data

Author: Stanley, Peter, 1956–
Title: Commando to Colditz / Peter Stanley.
ISBN: 9781741963847 (pbk.)
Notes: Includes index.
             Bibliography.
Subjects: Burn, Michael.
             Prisoners of war—Germany—Colditz.
             World War, 1939–1945—Prisoners and prisons, German.
             Prisoners of war—England.
             Prisoners of war—Family relationships.
             World War, 1939–1945—Commando operations—France—St Nazaire.
Dewey Number: 940.547243212

A catalogue record for this book is available from the British Library.

PRINTED IN CHINA.